Visits
from
Heaven

Visits
from
Heaven

By Josie Varga

4th Dimension Press ■ Virginia Beach ■ Virginia

This book would not have been possible had it not been for the many wonderful contributors who agreed to share their experiences. Therefore, this book is dedicated to all of them with heart-felt thanks.

Gary E. Schwartz, PhD
Natalie Smith-Blakeslee
Suzane Northrop
Raymond Moody, MD, PhD
Christina
The late Reverend Juliet Nightingale
Terry
Denise Lescano
Nancy Clark
Glenn Klausner
Karen Christopherson
Phyllis Hotchkiss
P.M.H. Atwater, LHD
Toni DiBernardo-Jones
Summersnow Wilson
Angela Denes
M.G. Raub
Phil Whitt
Carolyn B. Coleridge, LCSW
Mary Ellen "Angel Scribe"
R. Craig Hogan, PhD
Dianne Arcangel
Agnes J. Thomas, PhD
Dr. Claudio Pisani
John Edward
Mitch Carmody
Jen-Irishu

Janice E. Burpee
Lois Brunet
Reverend Rita S. Berkowitz
Barbara M. Veillette
Sheran Wickstrom
Mark E. Miller
Santina
Elly Vahey
Cindy Bigham
Joyce Keller
Guy Dusseault
Cherie, "D.J.'s" Mom
Cynthia D. Landrum
Carole Bellacera
Anthony Quinata
Ann Albers
Lynne Gawley-Hofstetter
T. Edgar
Judy Collier
Michelle Leech
Artie Hoffman
William
Maria Campanella
Donna A. Bowman
Patricia Federico
Sheila Upton
Christine Duminiak
Kathie Carrigan

Daniel M. Darrow
Anna O'Donoghue
Dr. Allan Botkin
Carol Rhodes
Adriana Martinez
Ruby Kennard
Helen Fisher
Herbert Hawkins
Antonietta LoGiudice
Marie
Christine Sherborne
Dr. Clark Schmidt
Larry Gibble
Mindy

Frankie H.
Patty Garris Layne
Glenn Dove
Judy C.
Karen Lasso
Annamaria Hemingway
Ellen Reid
Barbara Yule
Louis LaGrand, PhD
Melvin L. Morse, MD, FAAP
Marie D. Jones
George Anderson
Cheryl Booth

Contents

Acknowledgments .... *xiii*

Foreword by Dr. Gary Schwartz .... *xv*

Preface by Natalie Smith-Blakeslee .... *xix*

Introduction .... *xxiii*

A Ghost Named Andrea 1

Two for Two 5

A Reunion with Grandma 10

The Ring and My Father's Chair 14

Friends at the Factory 16

My Father's Energy Force 23

A Twin Brother's Wallet 25

Promise Me 29

The Chihuahua Named Tootsie 32

A Comforting Hug 35

A Kiss So Sweet 38

Margaret Matthews 41

My Brother Joey, the Angel 44

Misty Angel 47

Logan Gets Her Wings 51

A Visit from Denise 55

The Rose Petals 57

Healing Hands from Heaven 61

Lifelong Friends Keep Their Promise 66

The Greater Reality 69

Afterlife Encounters with Ghosts.. 75
    The Ghost of Fame Cleaners.. 76

An Afghan Hound Named Betty 79

Nicola's Story.. 81

The Purple Coat 84

A Message in the Garden 90

The Boy 95

A Greeting in a Candle Flame 98

A Kiss of Love 100

Get Rita to Say the Word Duck 102

The White Healing Doves 105

"Spookyman" 107

Timmy's Gift.. 110

I Can't Go 117

A Text Message from Heaven 119

I'm Here to Get Mama 126

Be Happy for Me 129

Signs from Our Son Billy 131

Angels Bowling in Heaven 138

Hi, Baby 141

I'm Happy Here 143

More Than Mere Curiosity 148

The Mess on the Floor 152

Tell Mom and Dad I'm OK 156

A Touch from Beyond 160

Pushed Out of Heaven 162

Quit Kissing My Ashes 164

Nanny and the Cockatoos 167

Tigger's Forewarning 169

Moo 172

Dad Makes His Presence Known 175

Flick the Lights 177

The Address on the Mailbox 180

Siena 183

Dad Came for Mom 186

Ricotta Cheese 189

Hey, I'm OK 192

An Officer's Regrets 195

Eliphalette Wrench, Mother of Francis 198

Induced After Death Communication 200

Tanya's Heavenly Bracelet 203

Two Hearts in the Snow 206

I'm in Peace 209

My Benji Boy 211

Our Special Butterfly . . . the Swallowtail 215

The Three Validations 221

A Shepherd Named Titan 225

Keep the Family Together 230

I Was Shaken Awake 233

An Auspicious Transition 235

The "Moving" Picture 239

One Lone Daisy 241

Joe Passed On 243

Grandma Was Just Here 244

Dad's Promise to Return 246

The Winding Staircase 249

The Money is in the Sock Drawer 252

White Tulips 256

They Will Find My Body 258

The Wild Bunny 261

Carol's Story 263

My Beloved Aunt Janet 267

A Phone Call from Michael 269

Music Was His Life 272

Asking for a Sign or Message 275
   Let Peace Be Your Guide 280

What Death Is 282

What It Feels Like to Die 284

What We Can Learn from Children who Have Almost Died.................. 287

Awakening to Our Inherent True Nature 299

Bridging the Gap between Science and Metaphysics 308

The World Hereafter—Life in the Garden of Souls 322
   The Road to the Hereafter 323
   The Portal 324
   The Garden of Souls 328
   Building the Garden of Life 331

Final Thoughts 337

Appendix: Forming a Physic Development Circle 341

About the Author 347

Acknowledgments

Whenever I am asked about the writing of "my" book, I repeatedly state that this is not "my" book but "our" book. This book belongs to all of those individuals who helped me in some way. They are not only the many contributors who are listed on the dedication page but are also the kindhearted individuals who helped to promote it or gave me their love and encouragement.

I would like to begin by making special mention of Juliet Nightingale. At the very beginning of my research, I came across her Web site (www.towardthelight.org) and contacted her. Juliet had multiple near-death experiences and was the host of a radio show called *Toward the Light*. For reasons that I cannot explain, I knew that I was meant to contact her. The day after receiving my e-mail, Juliet responded, "I am meant to help you so I am going to help you." I was amazed but not surprised.

Juliet gave two accounts to this book and put me in touch with many of the contributors; she even advertised my call for submissions on her Web site. I appeared as a guest on her popular Internet radio show, and whenever I began to get discouraged, she was always there with her love and support.

Sadly, Juliet was diagnosed with cancer and passed away on February 28, 2009. I will never forget the last conversation I had with her on this physical plane. I told her I was not ready to let her go yet. To this she immediately assured me with her sweet, calming voice, "Josie, it's OK. I will be there to help you from the Other Side." I can feel her presence as I write these words now. I know she is here with me, and I also know she played a big part in getting this book published. Thank you, Juliet. You will forever be in my heart.

As I continued to delve into my spiritual quest, I came to the Web site of John W. Sloat (www.beyondreligion.com). John, a former Presbyterian clergyman, retired following forty years in the ministry after having a spiritual experience in which he recalled a past death. His Web site includes various mystical accounts submitted by people around the world. John graciously allowed me to contact some of his contributors who then agreed to be part of this book.

I am very grateful for his support and encourage all of you to take a look at his wonderful Web site for more information. As John writes, "There is a vast ocean of spiritual truth waiting to be discovered. In the future, we will no longer be frightened by God's continuing revelation in our day."

My heartfelt thanks go out to Dr. Gary Schwartz for writing the foreword and for believing not only in me but also in the contents of this book. In addition, I send gratitude to Natalie Smith-Blakeslee for writing the preface and for helping me in so many ways including finding contributors for this book. Many contributors had an extra hand in helping me find afterlife accounts. They especially include Anthony Quinata, Christine Duminiak, R. Craig Hogan, and Ann Albers.

I would also like to thank Andrew Barone and Jane Heady for their kindness and support. To all the contributors who prayed for the release of this book, thank you from the bottom of my heart. So many of you believed in this book from the start including Cassie McQuagge, production manager with A.R.E. Press. Thank you, Cassie. You are a godsend.

It meant the world to me to have the support of so many experts in the field. I cannot thank them enough for agreeing to write a chapter for this book. They are Louis LaGrand, P.M.H. Atwater, Melvin Morse, Nancy Clark, Marie D. Jones, George Anderson, and Cheryl Booth.

Lastly, I would like to thank my loving family and all the wonderful friends who stood by me throughout the writing of this book. Special thanks go to Stan Paylago, a great lawyer and even better friend, for taking me on as his "pro-bono" client. I truly appreciate your help and guidance.

To my husband John, who is one heck of a proofreader, you mean the world to me. And to my two beautiful daughters, Erica and Lia, Mommy loves you very much.

Namaste!

Afterlife Science and Stories of "Visits" Where the "Whole is Greater than the Sum of its Parts"

Foreword by
Gary E. Schwartz, PhD
University of Arizona
www.drgaryschwartz.com

Is "life after death" real?
Do our departed loved ones continue to feel love
for us as we do for them?
Are "visits from heaven" true?

If you are a "professional" questioner and wonderer —in other words, if you happen to be employed as a full-time academic scientist—your answers will typically be qualified by tentative words such as "maybe" and "could be" and you would be cautious about drawing conclusions about the veracity of people's personal accounts of afterlife communication experiences.

So why would an academic agnostic like me agree to write a foreword for a book that presents generally unverified "anecdotes" and often seemingly "miraculous–sounding" if not unbelievable "stories"? And why would I consider it an honor and a privilege?

There are three important reasons:

First, as described in detail in my books, *The Afterlife Experiments* and *The Truth about Medium*, there are compelling scientific reasons to predict that "visits from the Other Side" can and do occur. In other words, the emerging science is generally consistent with these stories. In fact, I reveal in my books a number of unanticipated, evidential, and inspiring "anecdotes" that happened in the context of our laboratory experiments.

An illustrative and evidential "anecdote" that occurred in the context of our laboratory research is described in *Visits from Heaven* by Suzane Northrop, a distinguished and gifted medium. Her books include: *Everything Happens for a Reason: Love, Freewill, and the Lessons of the Soul* and *Second Chance: Healing Messages from the Afterlife*.

Second, for us to see the "big picture" and appreciate that the "whole is greater than the sum of its parts," it is extremely valuable to collect and present, in one place, meaningful and memorable accounts where people from all walks of life reveal their personal experiences with visits from beyond. *Visits from Heaven* provides a wealth of experiences that collectively point to the conclusion that life after death is real.

And third, I have had my own personal experiences that truly happened and cannot be denied. To reject them would be to reject the very foundation of science—which is our responsibility to follow the data where it takes us. I have witnessed remarkable spontaneous "spirit–initiated" visits that replicate the essence of the kinds of experiences shared in this book not only in my university laboratory but in my personal life as well.

As I confess in my latest book, *The Sacred Promise: An Urgent Call for Reuniting Science and Spirit*, I have experienced uncanny events associated with researching "sophisticated" deceased persons which have opened my eyes to seeing new ways of designing novel experiments that can establish not only (1) how the deceased are "consciousness and alive" but (2) how they continue to have "minds of their own."

A case in point, my adopted grandmother Susy Smith, the author of thirty books in the field of parapsychology and life after death, who used to say that she "couldn't wait to die" so that she "could prove that she was still here," appeared to do some truly remarkable things after she died. I share an account of how she "dropped in" unannounced to a medium in the Midwest who had previously read Susy for me on numerous occasions. What was unique was that this spontaneous visit occurred while the medium was driving her car, and furthermore, Susy had brought along a second deceased woman unknown to the medium. Susy apparently insisted that the medium do a reading on the mystery woman and e-mail the information to me. The medium wisely pulled over to the side of the road, took detailed notes summarizing her on-the-spot reading, and later sent me an e-mail detailing the information.

It turned out that the same day that this unplanned "double-deceased drop in" occurred, unbeknownst to the Midwest medium, I was visiting with a family on the East Coast who were grieving the loss of their daughter. I had, silently to myself, wished that the family could have had the same kind of experience I was having, made possible by the skills of the Midwest medium plus Susy's apparent persistence. In light of the uncanny timing of the medium's surprise e-mail with my visit with the family, I wondered whether the information provided in her e-mail applied to this family's daughter. I called the living sister; she scored the detailed information in the e-mail reading, and the overall accuracy of the off-the-road reading turned out to be more than 80 percent. After replicating Susy's ability to bring other unknown deceased people to mediums, my colleagues and I developed the "double-deceased" research paradigm for investigating life after death.

The editor of *Visits from Heaven*, Josie Varga, is an expert about real life happenings that point to the existence of life after death. Josie's remarkable personal experiences, coupled with her visionary and integrative chapters in this book, make this volume a veritable treasure of hope and inspiration.

We owe great thanks (1) to Josie, the editor and integrator of this book, (2) to authors like Suzane, who together in this book provide us with incredible instances of the power of love and caring, and (3) to those in Spirit like Susy, who remind us that life is like the light from distant stars, its energies and information —its essence—continue long after the stars have "died." A journey of wonder, opportunity, and comfort awaits you as you read this book.

Preface

By Natalie Smith–Blakeslee
Medium and Bereaved Mom
www.loveandlight.com

What happens to those who pass?

For thousands of years men and women have pondered the idea of life after death . . . we approach and retreat, we want to know, but yet in many ways we are afraid to find out. We obtain glimpses or glimmers, as I like to call them, from people who have had near–death experiences (NDEs).

IANDS, the International Association of Near–Death Studies, investigates and supports the men, women, and children who claim they have crossed over the veil to the Other Side. These people and many others, including me, can and do give verifiable PROOF that there is another side and that we continue from this lifetime to another.

During the 1970's, Elisabeth Kübler–Ross, Raymond Moody, Jr. and George Ritchie brought NDEs to public attention. This was an enormous breakthrough in our cultural predisposition to avoid death and dying until the inevitable happened to us. Since then, we, as a society, have become more accustomed to the idea of death as it relates "passing" from one existence to another. Both the general public and scientists alike are now realizing that we've had it all wrong. Perhaps, there is no death after all.

Requiring proof, or knowing something beyond any doubt, is human nature. For those of us who have been privileged to experience a "visit from heaven" or who have had an NDE, these events are usually enough to convince us of the reality of a life after death. For those of us who haven't, our search for evidence continues.

In *Visits from Heaven*, Josie has found the light and the truth; she has compiled incredible, verifiable proof that there is communication from the Other Side. As a medium, I have always known about the reality of an existence after this one. But aside from being a medium, I am also a bereaved mom. I sit on both sides of the fence knowing the pain I must endure without my daughter Carrie who passed from leukemia. At times, I wondered if I could ever get through the agony of losing my child. Even though I knew that she was still around me, I couldn't accept her death at first.

But the more signs I received from Carrie, the pain began to lessen bit by bit. Of course, the pain will always be there, but my daughter has given me the strength to go on with my life. She even communicates with me and my family through signs to reassure me that I am on the right path in relating her messages to others.

I know the joy I feel when I receive signs from my daughter as both a mother and a medium. I know the joy these "visits from heaven" bring to those who have lost loved ones. This book has touched me in very many ways, and I know it will touch you as well.

Josie Varga has put together a book that will soothe your soul and prove to you that, although there may be tears, there is no death. Life does not end. This reminds me of a poem by John Luckey McCreery (1835–1936), entitled, "There is no Death." The concluding verse reads:

And ever near us, though unseen,
The dear immortal spirits tread;
For all the boundless universe
Is Life—there is no dead!

I think by the time you finish reading this priceless book, you will agree with me. Someday, I will see Carrie once again. Someday, we will all unite with our beloved.

Introduction

The ancient Egyptians believed that it was important to keep a person's body preserved after death so that the soul or "ka" could continue to have a place to live. Death was seen not as the end but rather a temporary cessation. Therefore, a mummification process was used to protect the body.

There exist no records that document exactly how this process, which is said to have taken seventy days, was performed. However, it is known that the body's internal organs, with the exception of the brain and heart, were removed and placed in containers called canopic jars. The heart, believed to be the center of intelligence, was left in place while the brain was most likely discarded. The body was then covered with a type of salt called "natron" before being wrapped in linen strips and placed in a coffin.

Although everyone would eventually die, the "ka," it was thought, would continue to live on. However, for a short time immediately following death, the soul would be at rest while the physical body was mummified. The deceased could then join with his "ka" which, after being reconnected with the "ba" (his personality traits), would be resurrected as an "akh." This, the Egyptians held, was the soul's rebirth in the afterlife.

Today, many still believe in the existence of an afterlife. In a study released in 2008, the PEW Forum on Religion and Public Life reported that 92 percent of all Americans believe in God while 74 percent believe in life after death. If I had been conducting this survey, I would have added one more question which is: If you believe in life after death, do you then believe that it is possible for the deceased to continue to communicate with the living from beyond?

An after–death communication or ADC is a term coined by Bill and Judy Guggenheim, the original researchers of this phenomenon and authors of the groundbreaking book, *Hello From Heaven*, to mean " . . . a spiritual experience that occurs when someone is contacted directly and spontaneously by a deceased family member or friend." It is direct because it does not include any intermediary or third party such as a medium. It is also completely spontaneous because the deceased always initiates the contact.

Although I am among the 74 percent of Americans who believe in life after death, I never thought that I would ever write a book on the topic. Truthfully, you might say that the idea was actually given to me during a very special "visit from heaven."

The epilogue of my first book, *Footprints in the Sand: A Disabled Woman's Inspiring Journey to Happiness*, contains an inspirational e–mail written by my husband's friend and former boss, Rich, who died during the World Trade Center attacks on September 11. In it, Rich talks about the passing of his father but more so about the importance of living life to its fullest. About five months after the book's release, Rich came to me in a vivid or seemingly real dream that would not only forever change my view of the afterlife but would also strengthen my faith in God.

In the dream, I saw myself going through this long hallway. I had no idea where I was, yet there seemed to be a force pushing me forward as I eventually made my way through a doorway at the end. I walked into this room and looked around seeing a bunch of desks and windows. Although I say "walked," it was more like I glided as I do not remember my feet ever touching the ground. I should also mention here that I actually felt myself moving. It was as though my soul was out wandering while my body remained in a deep sleep. All of a sudden, Rich appeared before me. He was wearing glasses and smiled reassuringly at me as he telepathically communicated, "Josie, thank you for mentioning me in your book."

I had never met Rich in person when he was alive on this earth. I had only spoken to him on the phone and knew him through pictures, yet I had no doubt that this was my husband's friend standing before me. I looked up at him squinting because it was hard to look straight at him. The only reason I can give for this is there seemed to be a density or fog about us. To this day, I don't know why I did this, but I looked at him and said, "Rich, you have to give me proof that this is really you." He looked at me with a comforting glance and walked over to a desk picking up a cell phone. On the cell phone was a picture of him, his wife, and his son.

He then spoke to me again saying, "Boston is O.K." I had no idea what this meant, but the next thing I knew I was going through a window and found myself on the street looking up at a pickup truck. In the bed of this pickup truck was Rich standing behind his wife and son. He looked at me motioning for me to give his family the message. I don't remember anything much after that except for waking up, panting, and sweating in a sitting position feeling like something had just hit me in my chest.

I must admit I was scared and confused. Nothing like this had ever happened to me before. Though I could not understand what just happened, I was certain that I had to get this message to his wife. It was about 8:00 a.m., and my husband was already at work. I rushed quickly to call John and told him what had just happened. His response was nothing that I didn't expect. "You've got to be kidding me," he yelled. "You want me to call Rich's wife who just lost her husband and tell her that he said that 'Boston is O.K.'?" He was convinced that I had lost my senses.

I persisted telling him that I was certain the experience had been real and not a dream. It had been unlike anything that I had ever experienced. As I would later find out, I had just experienced a form of OBE (out-of-body experience) known as astral travel. When this occurs, the soul leaves the physical body to travel in its astral body to other dimensions or realms of reality. My husband listened reluctantly but finally agreed to forward to Rich's sister-in-law an e-mail written by me explaining what had occurred. He would ask her to forward the e-mail to Rich's wife only if she felt it was appropriate.

The following week we were on vacation when my husband received a response on his BlackBerry from Rich's sister-in-law. In short, she explained that her sister was considering moving to Boston where their brother lived. But, because they had purchased their home just before her husband's untimely death, she felt guilty about moving. My husband read this message to himself but did not grasp what the message meant until he read the e-mail aloud to me.

We both looked at each other in complete shock. I had never even met his wife let alone know that she had a brother in Boston. Now, it all made perfect sense to me. His words, "Boston is OK", were meant to let his wife know that she need not feel guilty about moving. He was telling her that it was alright with him.

At first, I honestly did not know what to think. A deceased friend had given me a message in my dreams that had actually been validated. What next? What did this mean? While I had no doubt that I had visited with Rich's spirit and that he was alive and well, my ego self had difficulty processing this information. Yet, while my unconditioned self or spirit believed what I had experienced was perhaps more real than anything I had witnessed on this earth, my ego self was afraid and doubtful. After all, I reasoned, if Rich were dead and if he did, in fact, communicate with me, then, not only was this confirmation of the existence of an afterlife, but it also pointed to the possibility of the dead being able to communicate with the living.

I did not realize it then, but this event would ultimately lead me on a spiritual quest which would later result in the book you now hold in your hands. I had been given a gift. Not only did Rich communicate with me, but he also gave me information that his family was able to validate. Surely, if this event had happened to me, then others must have had similar experiences.

Before I go further, I feel compelled to tell you a little about myself. I was born with a disability (cerebral palsy) and suffer from severe bilateral hearing loss. I was the youngest of three with one brother and one sister. My parents, hard-working Italian immigrants, did everything possible to provide us with the best life possible and raised us as devout Roman Catholics.

I strongly believe in God, Higher Power, or Supreme Presence and always will. I believe in the power of prayer. I am married to a wonderful man and have two beautiful daughters, Erica and Lia, who come first and foremost in my life. To me, the only thing that matters is love. I wish to make one thing clear and that is I would never do anything that I believed was evil or even remotely associated with the "occult," devil, or Satan. There are many who believe that Satan pretends to be the spirit of the deceased in an attempt to deceive the living. While I will not try to sway anyone who chooses to take that stance, I have to wonder why something so evil would want to bring joy to someone else. Why would the devil want to bring comfort to the living? Jesus himself made many "visits from heaven" appearing before many of his disciples after his death.

The beginning of my search led me to the story of Dr. Elisabeth Kübler-Ross, a psychiatrist who pioneered the study of death and dying and is credited with raising awareness about bereavement issues. Dr. Kübler-Ross frequently told a now famous story about a former patient of hers named Mrs. Schwartz who had appeared to her to ask that she not give up her work. As the story goes, Dr. Kübler-Ross was making her way over to an elevator after the conclusion of one her seminars on death and dying when she noticed a woman who looked very familiar. The woman approached her and asked if she could accompany the doctor to her office. At this point, Dr. Kübler-Ross recognized the woman as a patient who had passed away about ten months prior and began to second guess herself.

Dr. Kübler-Ross was sure that this was, in fact, Mrs. Schwartz, but how could this be? She even touched her skin to see if it were cold or warm or if it would disappear when touched. But Mrs. Schwartz was still there. When they arrived at Dr. Kübler-Ross' office, Mrs. Schwartz opened the door and told her that she had come to thank her for all the help she had given her and to ask her to promise not to give up her work on death and dying.

The doctor went to her desk and did a reality check, but Mrs. Schwartz was still there and again asked her to promise not to discontinue her work. She agreed but asked Mrs. Schwartz first to sign and write a note. Mrs. Schwartz did as she was requested, walked out, and disappeared.

The doctor kept the note and later told this story many times. Although Kübler-Ross considered having fingerprint and handwriting experts examine the note to determine if they matched up with those of Mrs. Schwartz, she never did. "Death is simply a shedding of the physical body like the butterfly shedding its cocoon," Dr. Kübler-Ross later wrote. "It is a transition to a higher state of consciousness where you continue to perceive, to understand, to laugh, and to be able to grow."

At the onset of my spiritual quest, I visited with a local medium from New Jersey named Artie Hoffman. This was my first visit with a medium, and I had no idea what to expect. To say that it was more than I could ever have imagined is an understatement. The reading which was scheduled to take thirty minutes took well over two hours. One by one my deceased relatives came through with validation after validation. I was just amazed by Artie's accuracy.

I bring him up, though, because of a message he gave me. Artie told me that I was working on a book that was meant to be written. "You are being guided by the Other Side and will be given many validations." This message confirmed what I had already known deep within and marked the beginning of my receiving several validations.

When the spirit of my father-in-law came through, for instance, he told my husband and me that we would receive a very special hello in the clouds. "I don't know what it's going to be, but I am being told that it will be well defined. As soon as you see it, you'll know what it is."

Five months later I was returning home from an evening at the mall with my family. As we made our way up the walkway to the front door, my eight-year-old daughter Erica exclaimed, "Mommy, look at that cloud!" My husband, six-year-old daughter Lia, and I immediately looked up at the night sky. What lay above me took my breath away . . . a beautiful cloud in the shape of an angel. Erica began yelling, "It's an angel! It's an angel!" All four of us witnessed the precise outline of its gown and big majestic wings.

It took me a few seconds to realize what was happening, but I yelled for my husband to run into the house to get the camera. Just as I said this, the cloud began to disperse. It was as though it was meant for our eyes only. Within seconds it was nowhere to be found. It simply disappeared the same way it had appeared.

It wasn't until much later that night when I remembered Artie's words. "I don't know what it's going to be, but I am being told that it will be well defined. As soon as you see it, you'll know what it is."

Is there life after death? If so, is it possible for those who have crossed over to communicate with us? In the pages that follow, I will attempt to answer these and many other questions. My intent is not to change minds but rather to open them. I have chosen to include third parties or intermediaries in this book. My reasoning is simple. I don't believe it matters how the communication from the Other Side occurs. Regardless of whether such communication is spontaneous or initiated by a medium, it does not change the fact that it occurred.

For the purposes of this book, therefore, the term after–death communication or ADC will not be used. Instead, I will use the term "visit from heaven" or "visit," for short, to refer to a metaphysical experience that takes place when a person is contacted either directly or indirectly through the use of a third party by someone who is deceased. Also, this book includes only evidential accounts, which means that every story is backed up by some sort of proof.

Do you believe in an afterlife? The answer must come from within. My hope is that this book will, in some way, help you discover what your soul has always known.

A Ghost Named Andrea

As I mentioned earlier, this book marked the beginning of many validations for me. Perhaps the most startling experience occurred when I received a visit in my own home from an unwelcomed ghost named Andrea.

When my six-year-old daughter Lia kept complaining about seeing a ghost in her room, I didn't think much of it. I suspected that it was just her imagination. But, after her complaints to both her father and me persisted for more than a month, I began to wonder if there was something more going on.

One day while I was on the phone with my friend, a medium named Anthony Quinata, he nonchalantly asked me why I had not told him that I had a ghost in my house. I was stunned beyond words as he continued to tell me that he sensed Lia had been complaining about seeing a woman in her room. He, then, told me to hang on and about a minute later came back on the phone and said, "Do you want to know her name?" I was totally speechless and wondered nervously, "What does he mean by her name?"

Anthony quickly interrupted my thoughts and told me that I, indeed, had a ghost in my home and that her name was Amanda or a name that sounded like Amanda. I stood there in my living room with the phone pressed to my ear. I couldn't believe what I was hearing and wasn't sure I wanted to hear more. But Anthony continued, "She lived in your house a long time ago. She used to sleep in Erica's (my oldest daughter's) room. She says that she is very fond of Lia and often visits her in her room just to watch over her."

I wanted to let out a scream, but my mind was too busy scanning the house for any signs of Amanda. "Who has the pink room?" he asked. Lia's room was pink. "Who has the purple room?" He went on. Erica's room was purple. "Is there a linen closet in hallway outside of Lia's room?" Yes, there is. "Do you have a big yard with a white fence around it?" Yes.

At this point, I couldn't hold it in any longer and yelled, "Anthony, STOP! How do you know that?" Anthony lives in Colorado, and I live in New Jersey. He had never been to my house before nor had I ever described it to him. Yet he was providing accurate descriptions of my house.

I can't say that I was relieved when Anthony replied, "She is showing me your house. Do you have a clock stuck between 8:45–10:45?" I was almost frantic at this point. "No, I don't know what you're talking about. I don't have a clock stuck on that time!" Anthony insisted that I did; Amanda was telling him so.

"Does Lia cough a lot at night?" Again, I couldn't believe what I was hearing. My daughter suffers from frequent sinus infections and often coughs at night. "Yes," I replied almost telepathically. "Why do you want to know?"

"Amanda is telling me that she watches over Lia. She said she is not ready to let her go. She does not mean to scare Lia."

"What? What does she mean she's not ready to let her go?" At this point, my motherly instincts set in. Maybe Amanda did not mean to scare my daughter, but she was. I yelled into the phone demanding that Anthony tell Amanda to leave Lia alone. To which he replied, "You just did. She's standing right next to you."

I felt like I was going to faint. "Anthony, you're scaring me!" I shouted. His feelings were somewhat hurt, but I didn't mean it the way it sounded. After all, I am a believer and have no doubt whatsoever in the afterlife.

Anthony tried to calm me by assuring me that this spirit was earth-bound and that he would guide her to the Light. Knowing that I was Roman Catholic, he then asked me if I happened to have holy water in the house which I did. At this point I was instructed to get the holy water and sprinkle it throughout Lia's and Erica's rooms as we both prayed. He told me to picture Amanda in a bell jar in my backyard. This suggestion made no sense to me, but I wasn't about to argue; I wanted this spirit out of my home.

My heart was racing the entire time, but, after about ten minutes, Anthony said, "Josie, she is no longer in your house. She's in your back-yard. I will now help to guide her to the Light."

This was all very hard for me to believe. So there was a ghost in my house named Amanda who was very fond of my daughter. And my friend, an amazing medium, was able to ask her to leave and to guide her to the Light, all while speaking over the phone?

Of course, the true test would come later when my daughter went to bed. Would she complain about things moving in her room as she had done for over a month? Would she continue to refuse to sleep claiming that a ghost was in her room?

Astonishingly, Lia stopped complaining completely from that day forward. She has not complained about sleeping in her room since. She has stopped running into my room crying and asking to sleep with my husband and me. She stopped just like that. Was this outcome just a coincidence? No, I don't believe it was.

Remember the clock that Anthony said was stuck between 8:45–10:45? Initially, my husband and I could not find this now infamous clock. Truthfully, I did not want to find it.

But one week later, I was reaching for something in the back of a cabinet in my living room. In its back corner my eyes caught sight of an old clock that belonged to my parents. My heart began to race once again. I stared in utter disbelief. There, before my eyes, was the clock that Anthony (through Amanda) had told me about, and it was indeed stuck between 8:45–10:45.

Shortly afterwards, I ran into my neighbor and asked her if she knew

whether a woman named Amanda had ever lived in my house. This lady has lived in my neighborhood her entire life, so if anyone would know the answer, she would be the one. No, there had been no Amanda at my house, but she said, "There had been an Andrea, though, who lived in your house back when it was first built."

So her name was really Andrea, a kind spirit who had watched over my daughter Lia and was now home in the Light. This unwelcomed and unknown guest in my own home helped give me one of the most incredible validations that I have ever received.

Two for Two

Suzane Northrop
New York
www.theseance.com

I have had the honor of working as a trans-medium for over thirty years and have experienced countless connections with dead people (DPs) along the way. In turn, these connections create some great stories for people to share. But here is a story I would like to share of my own special happening. It involves what transpired during the testing done by Dr. Gary Schwartz for the 2000 HBO documentary "Life Afterlife," which later formed the basis for his book *The Afterlife Experiments*.

There were a number of mediums involved in the testing, including John Edward, George Anderson, Anne Gehman, Laurie Campbell, and me. The tests were to be conducted at the campus of the University of Arizona in Tucson.

We landed in Tucson and went directly to the lab for the taping of the documentary. It was there that for the first time I met Dr. Schwartz and his team. Although we weren't fully familiar with the ground rules, we did know generally that each medium would be asked to do what he or she does so well.

We weren't told specifically what would happen until the next day. We would each meet with the same "sitter" (that is the person being read by the medium) whom we had never met. Each of us would be wired up to monitors as was the sitter (whose name I learned later was Patricia Price), and all information collected would go into the computer as data. From that data Dr. Schwartz would be able to ascertain percentages of "hits" or accurate information. The electrical impulses would be analyzed to see if any of the mediums were reading the sitter's mind. Yeah, I know it sounds crazy but hey . . . I was just the guinea pig! You can read all about this as it's been documented in Dr. Schwartz's book *The Afterlife Experiments*. However, here I would like to talk about a back-story that didn't make it into the book.

On the day of taping we all arrived at the lab which was appropriately named "The Living Energy Center." I remember noticing a large man in the waiting room. I assumed he was one of the grips or guys who work with all of the film equipment and crew. I honestly didn't really think much of it until later that night when all the filming was finished, at least as far as the testing of the mediums was concerned.

As it turned out, the sitter had lost her son who, along with his dog, had dominated the information coming through to each medium. After sixteen hours of taping, we would finally meet with Dr. Schwartz to discuss what had transpired. It was then that I learned the guy I had taken special notice of—Michael whom I thought was a grip—was actually the husband of the sitter whose son (also named Michael) had dominated the readings.

Michael (the father), who was not into all this medium stuff, had stood outside the testing room listening to all the information coming through from his son. Included was validating information that Michael had never told his wife of almost thirty years. The information was so strong that Michael went from being a total nonbeliever to feeling, for the first time since his son's death, a sense of connection, a sense of his son wanting his parents to know that he was alright.

Later I would learn that Michael actually went to his local biker bar in the mountains and shared with everyone all the information from his dead son. This was very out of character for Michael, and he was running the risk of having all his biker friends think he surely must have gone off the deep end. But he just told it as it was.

After performing the initial afterlife experiment, one of Dr. Schwartz's main concerns was that people would say this study wasn't perfect. He asked if we would come back to Arizona to do additional studies in a more demanding environment. This time we would have more than one sitter, and we would not be able to see or hear the sitters, so we didn't know if they were male or female, young or old, etc.

So, six months later, we were again coming back to Tucson, Arizona at Miraval, a luxury resort, where this time the testing would be even more intensive. The night before this second round of experiments, John Edward and I were sitting around talking and came up with the idea of doing our own little study. We decided to ask for his mother and my father to show up from the Other Side. We left it at that and returned to our own rooms until the next day.

Right before leaving to go to Miraval where all the testing was taking place, Laurie Campbell came into the room where John and I were getting ready to leave. Out of the blue she asked John, "Did you by chance sit on your mother's curler box or something like that?" John turned several shades of red. It seems that when he was very young in order to see out the car window, his mother had him sit on her curler box. We looked at each other not saying anything but knew, "Hmmmmmmm. That's one out of two!"

We left for Miraval where at this time there were only four mediums left from original five—John, Laurie, Anne, and me. We were scattered all over the facility away from each other. When the sitters arrived, as noted, we couldn't see or hear them.

This was a two-day affair. After seeing at least seven or eight people that day, it was towards the very end of the testing session when the next-to-last sitter walked in. I started giving the information I was getting. I sensed something familiar about this particular sitter and continued to read getting a wealth of clear information from her deceased husband such as how he died, his name, etc. When I was all done and the session was over, I was allowed to turn around and see who the sitter was—it was none other than Patricia Price, the original sitter from the original experiment! But here was the kicker: her husband Michael had died about a week before the testing. It was so odd, even for me, knowing that he had been there physically in January and now, six months later, he had joined his son.

Right after the first testing when Michael went to his biker bar and shared with everyone about what had happened, he started doing things that were totally unlike him—which is often a tip-off that the person's soul knows that the transition to the afterlife is near. For instance, Michael had never used a computer in his life, but Patricia was to find a number of love poems and letters from him on the computer after his death. And two weeks before their thirtieth wedding anniversary, Michael had started saying things like, "If I don't make it to our anniversary, know how much I love you." This was very out of character for Michael. It was revealed that Michael was now with his son Michael, Jr.

Needless to say, when I turned around after the session to see it was Patricia, I was in shock knowing her husband Michael had just joined their son.

After our session, she left to be read by John. I was finishing up with one more sitter when the next thing I knew John with Patricia and one of the facilitators came running over to me. John said to Patricia, "Tell Suzane what you just told me." Patricia turned to me and said that when she was around John, she kept hearing the name Paul. Paul is my father's name, and he did the same thing as her husband Mike: worked on cars and was a car salesman as well.

John and I looked at each other knowing, "That's two!" He had the validation of his deceased mother coming through Laurie, and now I had the validation of my father coming through Patricia and Michael. Both John's mom and my dad were playing their own tricks of the day from the Other Side and giving us two mediums our own personal validations pretty much on demand.

And so our secret experiment within the afterlife experiments had been an unforgettable success. All of the experiences were evidence of the fact that love truly never dies. And not even death can stop us from connecting to the ones we love.

About Suzane Northrop

Suzane is a nationally recognized trance medium and an expert in physic phenomena. She can be seen on TV in the *Afterlife with Suzane Northrop* on OUT TV in Canada and HERE TV in the United States.

She also hosts *The Suzane Northrop Show* on BlogTalk Radio.com. The author of *A Medium's Cookbook: Recipes for the Soul*; *Second Chance: Healing Messages from the Afterlife*; *Everything Happens for a Reason* and *The Séance: Healing Messages from Beyond*, Suzane is a faculty member of The Omega Institute for Holistic Studies. She has lectured extensively in the United States, Canada, and Great Britain and has appeared on several radio and television programs including an HBO documentary, "Life Afterlife," *Extra*, *Entertainment Tonight*, *MSNBC*, *Fox TV*, *The Bill O'Reilly Show*, and the Discovery and History channels. For more information, visit her Web site at
www.theseance.com.

A Reunion with Grandma

Raymond Moody, MD, PhD
www.lifeafterlife.com
Reprinted with permission from *Reunions: Visionary Encounters with Departed Loved Ones*
Ivy Books, Division of Random House

I was sitting in a room alone when a woman simply walked in. As soon as I saw her, I had a certain sense that she was familiar, but the event happened so quickly that it took me a few moments to gather myself together and greet her politely. Within what must have been less than a minute, I realized this person was my *paternal* grandmother, who died some years before. I remember throwing my hands up toward my face and exclaiming, "Grandma!"

At this point I was looking directly into her eyes, awestruck at what I was seeing. In a very kind and loving way she acknowledged who she was and addressed me with the nickname that only she had used for me when I was a child. As soon as I realized who this woman was, a flood of memories rushed into my mind. Not all of these were good memories. In fact many were distinctly unpleasant. Although my reminiscences of my maternal grandmother are positive, those with my father's mother were a different matter.

One of the memories that rushed into my mind was the annoying habit she had of declaring, "This is my last Christmas!" She did that every holiday season for the last two decades of her life.

She also constantly warned me when I was young that I could go to Hell if I violated any of God's many strictures—as she interpreted them of course. She once washed my mouth out with soap for having uttered a word of which she disapproved. Another time when I was a child, she told me in all seriousness that it was a sin to fly in airplanes. She was habitually cranky and negative.

Yet, as I gazed into the eyes of this apparition, I quickly sensed that the woman who stood before me had been transformed in a very positive way. I felt warmth and love from her as she stood there and an empathy and compassion that surpassed my understanding. She was confidently humorous, with an air of quiet calm and joyfulness about her.

The reason I had not recognized her at first was that she appeared much younger than she was when she died, in fact even younger than she had been when I was born. I don't remember having seen any photographs of her at the age she seemed to be during this encounter, but that is irrelevant here since it was not totally through her physical appearance that I recognized her. Rather, I knew this woman through her unmistakable presence and through the many memories we reviewed and discussed. In short this woman was my deceased grandmother. I would have known her anywhere.

I want to emphasize how completely natural this meeting was. As with the other subjects who had experienced an apparitional facilitation, my meeting was in no way eerie or bizarre. In fact this was the most normal and satisfying interaction I have ever had with her.

Our meeting was focused entirely on our relationship. Throughout the experience I was amazed that I seemed to be in the presence of someone who had already passed on, but in no way did this interfere with our interaction. She was there in front of me, and as startling as that fact was, I just accepted it and continued to talk with her.

We discussed old times, specific incidents from my childhood. Throughout, she reminded me of several events that I had forgotten. Also she revealed something very personal about my family situation that came as a great surprise but in retrospect makes a great deal of sense. Due to the fact that the principals are still living, I have chosen to keep this information to myself. But I will say that her revelation has made a great deal of difference in my life, and I feel much better for having heard this from her.

I say "heard" in an almost literal sense. I did hear her voice clearly, the only difference being that there was a crisp, electric quality to it that seemed clearer and louder than her voice before she died. Others who'd had this experience before me described it as telepathic or "mind-to-mind communication." Mine was similar. Although most of my conversation was through the spoken word, from time to time I was immediately aware of what she was thinking, and I could tell that the same was true for her.

In no way did she appear "ghostly" or transparent during our reunion. She seemed completely solid in every respect. She appeared no different from any other person except that she was surrounded by what appeared to be a light or an indentation in space, as if she were somehow set off or recessed from the rest of her physical surroundings.

For some reason, though, she would not let me touch her. Two or three times I reached to give her a hug, and each time she put her hands up and motioned me back. She was so insistent about not being touched that I didn't pursue it.

I have no idea how long this meeting lasted in clock time. It certainly seemed like a long time, but I was so engrossed in the experience that I didn't bother to look at the clock. In terms of thoughts and feelings that passed between us, it seemed like a couple of hours, but I have a feeling that it was probably less than that in what we consider to be "real" time.

And how did our meeting end? I was so overwhelmed that I just said, "Goodbye." We acknowledged that we would be seeing each other again, and I simply walked out of the room. When I returned, she was nowhere to be seen. The apparition of my grandmother was gone.

What took place that day resulted in a healing of our relationship. For the first time in my life I now appreciate her humor and have a sense of some of the struggles she went through during her lifetime. Now I love her in a way that I didn't before the experience.

It also left me with an abiding certainty that what we call death is not the end of life.

I realize how people can assume that these apparitional facilitations are hallucinations. As a veteran of altered states of consciousness, I can say that my visionary reunion with my grandmother was completely coherent with the ordinary waking reality that I have experienced all my life. If I were to discount this encounter as hallucinatory, I would be almost obliged to discount the rest of my life as hallucinatory too.

About Raymond Moody, MD, PhD

Raymond Moody is a world-renowned scholar and researcher and a leading authority on the "near-death experience"—a phrase he coined in the late seventies. The best-selling author of eleven books including *Life After Life*—which has sold over thirteen million copies worldwide—he continues to capture enormous public interest and generate controversy with his ground-breaking work on the near-death experience and what happens when we die.

He has appeared on Oprah as well as hundreds of other local and nationally syndicated programs such as *MSNBC, Grief Recovery, NBC Today*, ABC's *Turning Point, Geraldo,* and others. For more information, please visit www.lifeafterlife.com.

The Ring and My Father's Chair

---◦◦◦◦◦---

Christina
New Jersey

At this time in my life I had two toddlers, ages two and four, running around and a newborn. While I could count on Gabriella to sleep peacefully, Anthony and Gianna were constantly getting into some kind of mischief and especially loved playing with my husband John's wedding ring. Although I warned him several times, John would always leave it on his nightstand which, of course, was an easy target for the kids.

Soon the ring was lost, and I turned the house upside down in search of it. But it was nowhere to be found. I had no idea what my little angels had done with the ring and was anxious to find it. My husband, a police officer, was about to be promoted to sergeant, and I wanted him to have his wedding ring. I had no idea where else to look. In my room is a "Lazy Boy" recliner which belonged to my father before he passed. My father loved that chair. I thought that perhaps the kids might have dropped the ring in the chair and literally turned it upside down in search of the ring. But there was nothing.

Days dragged into weeks. I thought many times of going out and buying John a new ring, but something held me back. Of course, the ring was very sentimental to me. But it was also as if my intuition was telling me to wait. Two days before my husband's promotion ceremony, I thought of making a last minute trip to a local jeweler and buying him a ring. But that night I had a dream. My father came to me and said, "Chris, look in the chair. The ring is in the chair." It all seemed so real.

When I woke up the next morning, I didn't go and look in the chair right away. In my mind I had already looked there. I had turned it upside down so I thought I'd be wasting my time. But later that day I thought of my dream and my father's chair once again. I grabbed a flashlight and decided to give it another try. I had nothing to lose. Without knowing why, I pulled back the fabric on the back of the chair and there sitting peacefully on the wood frame shining up at me was my husband's ring. I couldn't believe my eyes. I would never have looked in my father's chair again had it not been for my dream.

The following day my husband was promoted. On his finger was a well–missed wedding ring—a special gift and a heavenly hello from my father.

Friends at the Factory

Reverend Juliet Nightingale
www.towardthelight.org

I've been a natural medium all of my life, so it's never been "odd" or uncommon for me to see discarnate entities at any given moment. Often I could see one individual or many, and it would occur quite spontaneously.

A very good example of this occurred while I was in the quaint old town of Franklin, Tennessee. I had a loft in the Factory at Franklin—a lovely artisans mall that used to be the Dortch Stove Works and Magic Chef Factory in bygone years. To say that this place was teaming with discarnate entities would be an understatement! My loft was located in Building 8. I'd walk through the breezeway to enter into Building 12 and take the long trek up through Building 11 where the main entrance was located. As I entered Building 12, I could see a whole group of former factory workers just standing round nattering back and forth (as they must have done when they were alive and working there), and they would actually greet me.

Then I saw a short white man in his factory clothes, but what was odd about him was the fact that he was a hunchback! However, he was so clear—with every little detail—and very present, so I was sure that this was a valid sighting. Thus, I went to the front desk and asked Alex about this character—asking him specifically about whether there had been a hunchbacked factory worker. "Come here, Juliet!" Alex called out as he motioned me to follow him. He took me to the column of letter boxes that were located just behind the front desk where a bunch of old black-and-white factory photos crowned them from above. "Look there," he exclaimed as he pointed to a large photo. (I must interject here that I am very visually impaired, so I cannot see something that's far away and especially black-and-white photos that lack color and contrast.) I got my monocular and looked up at the photo. Lo and behold, there was the hunchbacked factory worker but viewed from the back. I gasped! "That's him!" I exclaimed with delight, and he looked exactly as I had seen him—even his clothing—although I'd seen him from the front. So if you go to the Factory at Franklin and head back round the right of the front desk and look up at the photos above the letter boxes, you'll see the hunchbacked man in clear view.

Another interesting thing occurred one evening as I was sitting in

my loft in Building 8 and speaking with a good friend back in England. What's interesting is that we were talking about her mother, who'd recently crossed over, and I just happened to turn and look up to the right. As I did so, I beheld a tall and stocky black man just standing there facing me. He had a very gentle demeanor and also seemed rather melancholy.

Suddenly, I was having two conversations at once—one with my friend Paula in the UK and one with the tall stranger in my midst. With sadness I said, "You died here on the job, didn't you?" and he replied, "Yes, Ma'am," with his strong southern drawl and a gentle nod. I felt such sweetness about this man, and I could tell that he'd been a very hard and dedicated worker and one who loved his family deeply. Bear in mind that a lot of these workers' whole lives revolved round working in the factory and that's all they knew. So I was left with the distinct impression that this man felt disappointed in himself for having died "before his time" leaving his family and the factory behind.

I also kept getting the name "Stewart," but I don't know how it was spelled: Stewart or Stuart, or if it was his first name or surname. I saw him a few times, and then I was even able to tap in to his family. He had an older daughter and a younger son—both in their teens when he crossed—and his wife whom he dearly loved. I was moved to tears, but I was also extremely curious about this man—since he was already impacting me so deeply.

This time, since I was just too curious about this story and Alex wasn't at work yet, I went to the office that was situated upstairs. I spoke with Becky and asked her about "Stewart." "Do you know if there was a large,

gentle black man who died on the job here?" I asked pointedly. Becky told me straight away that indeed a black man had died on the job by falling into a vat of molten steel! I shuddered when she told me this. "Where did that take place?" I continued.

"You know when you're just coming into Building 12 from Building 8 . . . where that door is to the right where you see the spiral staircase through the window?"

"Yes, in fact, I see entities all round there all the time," I replied.

"There inside that door was where the vats were and where he died."

Again, I shuddered! Then I asked her if there was a way to verify his name, but she had no clue. Still, this was the validation that I needed for this episode, because his presence was so strong and so fitting . . . for what had happened to him.

I will add that these discarnate people really do appreciate it when someone can "see" them and acknowledge them. They aren't really "stuck" there; they just had had such a pronounced and strong connection to that factory, that they'd simply "toggle" between dimensions and spend time there . . . as if spending time at their favorite pub and so on. Also, I was known as the "local medium" throughout the Factory, so it wasn't unusual for me to approach someone and ask questions about someone/thing I'd seen, and likewise people would ask me for input.

Back in my loft, I was once again on the phone with a friend MaAnna, who lived in Nashville. All of a sudden, one by one, people were coming into view, and I started describing these individuals whom I was seeing—five in all. As it turns out, I was describing five of her relatives—most of whom she'd never met, because they had passed away before she was born or when she was too young to remember. However, one of the individuals that I described was her niece whom she did know well. But what was interesting about this is that I saw her when she was five; yet she'd died in her late teens. Well, what happened is that the child had had an NDE (near-death experience) at age five, and she couldn't wait to describe "Heaven" to her parents. That's also when she was at her happiest in life. This was huge for my friend, as she'd wanted input about these relatives for ages, and she told me that I described them perfectly—according to photographs that she'd seen of them. She had even asked her mum about them and everything that I described was absolutely correct.

Here's what she said: *Many of my mother's family members had crossed over either before I was born or while I was still an infant. As Juliet and I were chatting about my family, she declared that her room was suddenly filling up with folks who were connected to me. I took note as she described each one and was able to recognize a few of them from pictures that I had seen or stories I had been told. I shared the remainder of the information with my mother, who was able to verify the rest. It's an amazing thing to have Juliet describe so many details of a person who has crossed, considering that she cannot usually see that much detail on the physical plane. Her sight is quite clear with respect to the Other Side.*

(**Note:** When experiencing a visitation, we will often see people when they were in their "prime" in life or at their happiest and not as how they were when we last saw them on this plane, and so forth. This is very common.)

When it finally came time that I had to leave the Factory at Franklin, I was truly and deeply saddened. Not only did I have friends that were visible on this plane, I also had friends who'd lived and worked there before I'd ever even arrived in America. I actually cried as I bade farewell to the gathered group of workers by the entrance to Building 12 from the breezeway. Even now, my eyes fill with tears in thinking about this departure.

I wish to make two points here: First, the fact that I'm visually impaired may contribute to me being such a natural medium, because I've always been able to see into other dimensions or realms. Since my view of this plane is so restricted, as it were, I naturally tune into other frequencies and see into these realms, because I'm not so distracted by or focused on what is on the physical plane. Second, I'm also a multiple NDEr (near-death experiencer), which means that I'm already familiar with the Other Side. It is most common for NDErs to have pronounced psychic and mediumistic abilities as part of the aftereffects of the NDE.

When we reside on this plane, we're operating on a certain dimension or frequency. However, when we cross over, we move into a different and higher frequency—much like moving up on the radio band. So, as a medium—and anyone who experiences "visits from heaven"—we're simply seeing individuals who are very real and very much alive, but merely operating at a different frequency that we are able to tune in to. It's all quite simple and straightforward.

In fact, my take on all this phenomena is that if more people were willing to acknowledge "visits" and the fact that we can all experience them, there'd be far less grief in the world and that people can share in meaningful dialogue with those they love and care about who have crossed over. There's nothing "woo-woo" about this; it's simply mind-to-mind communication (telepathy) that's already been scientifically proven to be valid. It would also help us feel less "cut off" from those we love, because we can actually communicate with them freely.

After all, we do live forever . . . and we need to acknowledge the fact that people simply change frequencies and planes of existence, but they never die. And it is up to us to keep the lines of communications open by allowing ourselves to tune into these different frequencies and to share in communion with those we love.

About Reverend Juliet Nightingale

The late British mystic Reverend Juliet Nightingale was the founder of Toward the Light (www.towardthelight.org) and the creator of www.lightonthewater.ning.com, a near-death experience (NDE) support and interest group. She was a minister of metaphysics, a clairvoyant spiritual advisor/counselor and medium, a practitioner of Reiki and remote healing. She had had multiple NDEs before her death in February 2009.

A gifted musician and loyal friend, she was the host of the ground-breaking radio show, *Toward the Light,* on BBSRadio.com. The show focused on the nature of consciousness and life continuum as revealed through near-death, out-of-body, and other spiritually transformative experiences and related topics.

My Father's Energy Force

Terry
Canada

My father died in August 2006. On August 1, he had told me he loved me for the first time. Three weeks later, he was gone.

On the first anniversary of his death, I was awakened by the most powerful energy force I have ever experienced. The predominant adjective to describe this force was "invasive." It literally woke me up, and the force was so powerful that I did not know immediately if it were going to be a good or bad thing.

I soon realized, however, that this was the energy of my late father. The only way I can describe it, as it entered my chest, is to say that it was better than anything I have ever experienced in my lifetime—better than any pleasure, better than any relationship, better than anything exotic or beautiful in this world!

When people say, "I sensed a presence" in describing a "visit from heaven," that would not be an adequate way to describe what happened to me. It was like being hit by a force more powerful than anything one could ever imagine here on this earth. There was nothing subtle about it. It felt like a bolt of lightning had entered my chest. It was powerful, immediate, and enveloping.

I could see a light in the room and in it was the outline of my father's form. He was a big man, and his aura was in one of his familiar stances. His energy said, "I am here, and I am your father." I don't know how I knew this information, but I realized that it was he. There was nothing earthly about this magnificent form before me which was now my father. But I recognized his posture and his penetrating eyes.

So this was not a "ghost" as we would usually think of it, but more accurately it was the strong presence of my father. No words were actually spoken, but no words were needed. I knew instantly that he was there to let me know that everything would be OK.

Interestingly, my father was a 5:30 a.m. riser, and this had happened at exactly 5:30 a.m. I must admit I was a bit shaken by this experience. But, by its timing and strength, my father was sending me a clear message. He is still around, there is life after death, and there are many levels to our existence.

A day later I told my husband what had happened. Neither one of us is spiritual or religious. I was stunned and told him, "I don't imagine I will tell another living soul this story for fear of being deemed unstable or crazy." I am a professional insurance agent who had never before thought about afterlife communication.

But everything happens for a reason, and I know that I am meant to share my experience. Life goes on, but there is so much more to wonder about than we realize.

A Twin Brother's Wallet

Denise Lescano
Florida
www.deniselescano.com

As a professional medium, I am constantly receiving "visits from heaven." Every reading that I give offers a brief glimpse into the heavens, and I am as amazed as my clients are by the messages that spirits bring through for them. I have been very fortunate to have the honor of working with some very well-known and respected non-profit organizations that provide support services and counseling for those who have lost loved ones suddenly and tragically.

One such organization offered grief support for families who had lost loved ones to homicide, suicide, overdose, or accidental death scenarios. It also took referrals directly from local law enforcement agencies and the DA's office. I volunteered my time for this non-profit for two years. During that time I would sit with the different support groups with the grief counselor present and read for the family members offering them a last communication with their loved ones on the spirit side of life. Incidentally, the grief counselor that I worked with was also the "victim's advocate" for the local state attorney's office here in Naples, Florida. Due to the strict confidentiality rules of this organization, I was never told beforehand or even afterwards anyone's name. I was also not told the circumstances of death or even which support group I would be reading for each evening.

I have read for very many people, but every now and then one particular reading will really stand out in my memory. This is one of them, and it provides in no uncertain terms complete validation for the concept of life after physical death and that our loved ones in spirit are always with us. That night at the support group for an accidental death I was as amazed by this very special reading as was everyone in attendance.

A very attractive middle–aged women came in and took a seat with a very handsome young man whom I later learned in the reading was her son. Before I even started the reading, I knew immediately that she and her son were very skeptical. I found out after the reading that the mother had been attending the support group and that she had told her son about a medium coming to the group. Out of concern for her, he came along to make sure she was not being taken for a ride. He was certain that I was a fraud and that this reading was not possible so he came to protect his mom. They were both astounded by what came through that evening with the victim's advocate present.

The son had had an identical twin brother who had been killed in a car accident. His brother came through to me crystal clear, and with his wonderfully funny sense of humor, he kept us all laughing and the mood uplifted. There are so many things about this reading that I would love to share, but I will narrow it down to two specific very "evidential" messages.

The mother, on the way over in the car that evening, prayed in her head to her deceased son. She asked him to prove that I was real and that he was really coming through by telling a specific story about his brother and him. She almost fell off her chair as her son came through talking to his brother about a particular evening when, in order to fool their dates, the boys had decided to pretend they were the other one so that they could switch dates. It was the exact story that his mom had asked him to tell. Needless to say, the brother, sitting with his mom, was amazed at hearing the story, and I had really gotten his attention at this point. The next thing that happened was even more amazing.

The living brother had brought with him in his back pocket his deceased brother's wallet still containing all of his brother's personal effects. On the way over in the car, he had asked his deceased brother to prove to him that this reading was real and that he was really there by telling me about the wallet. As you can imagine, his jaw dropped to the floor when I told him that the deceased brother was telling me that his brother had his wallet in his pocket with all of his things still in it. He even went on to describe, in detail, a few of the items that were in the wallet.

The reading continued on with plenty more jaw–dropping information about their lives and a family business that the sons had run with their father. The mother and son may have walked in as skeptics, but they were walking out as believers. In that moment, I knew that their lives had been changed forever by the steadfast commitment of this young man on the spirit side of life to prove to his family, without a doubt, that he was alive and well and still with them. It was a very memorable evening for all of us and one that I will never forget. It was truly a miraculous "visit from heaven" for all the people who were present and fortunate enough to witness it.

Jane Heady, the victim's advocate and grief counselor who witnessed the above "visit from heaven," notes, "Denise did not know anything about the people who were there that night. I told her only how many people would be attending. As the first reading began, I could not believe what I was witnessing.

"The spirits were coming through her with facts that I knew to be true from my individual sessions with the clients. I was blown away! There was no way on this earth that she could have known these facts, not knowing the people or their circumstances. Later, in some of my private sessions with these clients, they would ask me how much I told her. I could truthfully tell them, 'Not a thing.' From that day forward, I was a true believer."

About Denise Lescano

Denise is a professional medium and is famous for her ability to deliver specific, detailed, and "evidential" information to her clients seeking to connect with the Other Side. She has been the guest on numerous radio programs and television shows over the years and is currently working on a book and TV series.

She specializes in working with families who have lost loved ones tragically as a result of sudden unnatural or accidental circumstances. Denise has worked with several non-profit organizations, reuniting people with their loved ones for over twenty years. For more information, visit www.deniselescano.com.

Promise Me

Nancy Clark, CT
Ohio
healeygarden@msn.com
www.freewebs.com/nancy-clark

Reprinted with permission from *Hear His Voice: The True Story of a Modern Day Mystical Encounter with God*, PublishAmerica

In this particular dream, I was in a German concentration camp walking alongside another woman. We were herded into a building and just before the door was locked, she pushed me out and said, "Tell Jake that I'm very happy, and above all, tell him it's all right for him to find happiness again. Do you promise to do that for me?" With my eyes tenderly looking into hers, I said, "I promise." At that same moment someone slammed the door shut and locked it, leaving her inside as I stood outside the building. The dream ended.

Two days later my husband came home from work and announced that Jake's wife died. I didn't know her and only casually knew Jake as a co-worker of Dean's. We went to the funeral service, and while the minister was delivering the eulogy, he mentioned she was Italian and proceeded to describe the life she had led while in Italy and then later when she married Jake.

Listening politely to the minister's words, I heard him say something that would rattle the bones inside of me. He recalled a time during her life she spent in a German concentration camp. Shocked by what I had just heard, I immediately thought of my dream and my promise to Jake's wife. *How would I tell him and when?* I wondered. Would he think I was crazy if I talked about my dream with him? It is not easy to step out in faith and assume everyone will believe what I tell him or her, especially when it deals with the unobservable reality. I was very reluctant to tell him the day of her funeral, so I didn't.

Several months later, my husband and I attended his company's Christmas party. Coincidentally, seated at our table directly across from me were Jake and his female guest. Both of them, in their late sixties, held hands and talked intimately like sweet lovebirds to one another. It was apparent they were very much in love. I knew it was now or never. I had to tell Jake about my dream. Excusing myself from the table, I told Dean I was going to talk with Jake for a little while. Nervously, I knelt down beside Jake and took his hand in mine and said, "Jake, I'm going to tell you something, and you may dismiss what I'm going to say as being fanatical, lunacy or whatever, but I have to tell you."

I proceeded to tell him that his wife appeared to me in a dream and made me promise to tell him she is very happy and, above all, she wants him to find happiness again. When he heard that, Jake spontaneously burst into tears. I looked at Dean sitting across from us and he had a wrinkled brow that said, *"What did you do to Jake to make him cry?"* With his eyes, Dean motioned me to come back to my chair, but I knew I had to stay with Jake a few moments longer.

Jake pressed his hands over mine and cried, "Oh God, this is a miracle happening! You did the right thing by telling me. I can't thank you enough." He proceeded to tell me during the summer shortly after his wife died, he went back to his high school reunion in Iowa. At that time, he met the woman who was seated beside him at the Christmas party. Apparently, they had been high school lovers and hadn't seen one another since then. She never married because Jake had been her only true love. She and Jake married shortly afterward.

Looking into my eyes, his eyes soaked with tears, Jake told me, "You had no idea I was dealing with a lot of guilt because I remarried so quickly after my wife's death. I felt guilty about finding happiness with another woman and it was tearing me up inside." He went on to say that he now believed that his wife was bringing him a message from the beyond to let him know that it's okay to be happy. Jake was elated and his tear-filled eyes expressed such gratitude to me for sharing this message with him. That evening his guilt was replaced with genuine freedom to love again and to be loved. A healing had indeed taken place that evening, and I felt privileged to have witnessed and honored it. If I had not listened to God's Voice within, I would have passed up the opportunity to express my Divine gift, that of bringing Light and comfort to others.

Dear friend, God's Voice encourages us to care for others, and when we do, greater gifts are given to us to be used for the well being of humanity. When we fine-tune our heart to listen to His Voice, we will be uplifted to truly recognize God's wondrous Love for us. There is no limit to the power of God's gifts; there is no limit to the service we may give and we cannot be happy until we give it.

The Chihuahua
Named Tootsie

Glenn Klausner
New York
www.glennklausner.com

During the past fifteen years, I have been conducting readings for people who have loved ones on the Other Side. My clients and I have personally experienced many validations from spirits that are inconceivable to the human mind. As a psychic medium, I know that life after death, in fact, continues from the evidential proof that in no shape or form I could possibly have had prior knowledge of.

On January 5, 2008, I had conducted an in-person reading with my clients Steve and Beth who were anxious to talk with their loved ones. During their reading, I had connected to both sides of their families. Throughout the reading, I had this familiar feeling that I knew Beth personally as well as her mother who was communicating with me. What was about to come next left me speechless and amazed at just how the spirit world works.

I make a tape recording of every reading for my clients. In this sixty-minute taped session, Beth's mother planned out the perfect timing to tell me her identity. The minute the tape was finished, Beth's mother told me that she knew me when I was a child growing up in Brooklyn. She went on to mention the exact street I lived on and that she knew my mother who, since 2005, has been in the spirit world.

Beth's mother Barbara also brought in Beth's father Joe. It was right then and there that I realized who these people were. I proceeded to mention it to Beth by telling her what her mom had just told me, and I said, "Your father is Joe, and he had the Chihuahua named Tootsie." The gasp along with look of shock on her face was priceless. I myself could not believe this person I was reading for was someone whom I knew and haven't had contact with in twenty-five years. This had to be one of the most unbelievable experiences I have had as a professional psychic medium.

I then asked Beth's parents if they have seen my mother, and they said that my mother was the one who directed them to have Steve, their son in-law, find me on the Internet. He told me he kept getting led back to me prior to scheduling the appointment and had a feeling himself that there was a reason why, even though he logically could not explain it.

By this point, I was very curious as to why Beth's parents did not tell me in the beginning of the reading who they were and why they waited until the tape ended at sixty minutes.

They told me that had they mentioned it earlier on in the reading, it would have not played out with the messages that were needed to be said and heard. The reason for this was because had they mentioned it, Beth and I would have ended up talking about our days growing up in Brooklyn. Her parents picked the perfect moment to reveal their identities so that there were no distractions or interference. When I finished my other readings that day with other clients, I reflected back on what occurred with Beth, Steve, Barbara, and Joe. I can't thank them enough for this experience.

Since my childhood days I have never doubted that my communication with the Spirit World was not real. I have always known and trusted that it, in fact, exists. This reading proved to me that life does continue on after physical death and that the bonds of love never die.

. . . .
About Glenn Klausner

Glenn is a nationally and internationally renowned psychic medium who has been reuniting thousands of people from all walks
of life with their loved ones who have crossed over. He has been
a popular guest on many radio and television shows and appeared
in a film documentary entitled, "After-Death Communication: Fact
or Fiction?"

Featured in many magazine and newspaper articles, he hosted
his own radio show, The *Glenn Klausner Hour* and co-hosted, *The
Spirit Side of Life*, both on Contact Talk Radio. Glenn conducts
lectures and seminars and is working on his first book. For more
information, please visit www.glennklausner.com.

A Comforting Hug

Karen Christopherson
Michigan
www.trilliumconsultants.com
TrilliumConsult@aol.com

My father-in-law Leonard had his first open-heart surgery when he was fifty-years-old. After ten years, the heart problems had recurred, and his cardiologist was strongly recommending repeat surgery.

Because his level of investment in his work was his primary source of stress at the time, he had decided on an early retirement. It was to be his sole year of retirement, because he died the following spring.

Leonard was a minister who had dedicated his life to spirituality and thus was completely unafraid of death. In retrospect, it became apparent to his family that he had "known" he would have only one winter in Florida and that he had made the most of every day there. Although he had always had close relationships with his sons, he had not previously taken the time to get to know his grandchildren well. This winter was an exception as he spent quality time with all of his grandchildren—

taking each of them on special excursions and then developing individual photo albums of their time with Grandpa. He spent money on
things he previously would have considered frivolous and unnecessary.

On the way home from Florida for spring break that year, all three of
our sons remarked how they had never felt closer to Grandpa than they
did at that time. One even expressed fear that his grandfather would die
soon because he had really gotten to know him in a special way for the
first time.

The following April, on his return to Michigan, Leonard stopped over
for a few days' visit in Atlanta with his step–grandchildren. While there,
he suffered further complications and had to undergo emergency open-
heart surgery. Although the surgery itself was successful, he did not
make it.

My husband Jim did not arrive at the hospital in time to see his
father before he died. He phoned me around 9:00 p.m. to tell me of his
father's death and of all the details he needed to take care of the following day.

At five minutes before midnight that evening, I was sitting on the
edge of my bed reflecting on the day's events when I felt the presence of
Jim's father with me. It did not surprise me since he and I had con-
versed many times regarding life after death and the differences between his traditional Christian views and my metaphysical ones. It
seemed natural that he had chosen me as his venue to let us know that
he was safe and secure on the Other Side.

I was aware of feeling slightly frightened at having Leonard present
himself to me in spirit when I was alone in the house. Since I knew my
husband would be open to and in need of his father's farewell visit, I
spoke out loud, "Leonard, I know you want to let us know you're at
peace and no longer in pain, but I would prefer that you go to Jim in
Atlanta and in some way communicate this to him." Instantly, I no longer
felt his presence in the room.

I neglected to mention this event to my husband until he returned
from his trip a few days later. As he was reporting the sequence of
events over the last few days, I recalled Leonard's visit and asked Jim if
anything had happened after 11:30 that evening. He hesitated and then
said that at midnight he had had a profound spiritual experience. He

related that he had gone to bed with his mind still flooded with concern for all the details he was responsible for taking care of the following day. As his mind was racing with concern for how he was going to accomplish everything, a general feeling of calm overtook him. He then physically experienced receiving a hug from his father along with the strong sense that he was not to worry and that everything would work out well.

Jim has no doubt that his father came to him in spirit as he so often had in life to comfort and reassure him and to tell him not to worry.

. . . .

About Karen Christopherson, MSW, LMSW, CAAC

Karen is a relationship therapist and executive and personal life coach with extensive experience in corporate environments and private practice. For more information, visit her Web site at www.trilliumconsultants.com.

A Kiss So Sweet

Phyllis Hotchkiss
Florida
AngelPM7@aol.com
http://duane-hotchkiss.memory-of.com/About.aspx
http://www.geocities.com/Heartland/park/4746/brian.html

In October of 2005, my husband Duane, who was my friend, lover, and life, was diagnosed with Stage 3 lung cancer. We were all very devastated when we heard the news. Duane was always so full of life, and to see him having to go through all of this was terrible. He remained positive, however, and was bound and determined to beat this. (He had already beaten both prostate and colon cancer.)

After various tests we found out that surgery was out of the question as the tumor was too close to the heart and bronchial tube, so the only option was to go through chemotherapy. He went through rounds of chemo; his last round was in January of 2006. He had a PET (Positron Emission Tomography) Scan which showed that the cancer had spread to his bones and to his brain. I took him to Muffett Cancer Center to see

if there were anything else that they could do, but there was nothing. His only choice was to go through another three rounds of chemo. After one round he ended up in the hospital. The cancer was spreading rapidly.

I promised him that he would not die in the hospital so he came home and hospice came in. He passed away in my arms with his family at his bedside. He was always skeptical but knew that I believed in "visits from heaven." Soon after our son Brian was murdered, my children and I began receiving many messages from him. So Duane promised that, if it were possible, he would come to us.

After Duane passed away, I started seeing butterflies, always two together. One day I was out in the golf cart getting ready to go to the pool. Two of the most beautiful butterflies were flying around the front yard together. I said out loud to myself, "Brian and Duane, if that's you, please give me a sign." All of a sudden they both flew over to the golf cart and flew three times around it and then flew off. I knew that it was Brian and Duane.

One afternoon I was lying back in my lounge chair watching a movie on TV. I shut my eyes to rest them. All of a sudden I could feel a presence over to the side of the chair. I knew someone was there, but I was not afraid at all. I tried to open my eyes because I knew it was my husband, but I could not get them to open. I wasn't sleeping as I could hear the television and people mowing their lawns. All of a sudden I felt Duane take my hand in his; I squeezed his hand, and it was so real. He picked my hand up, brought it to his lips, and kissed my fingers. I felt his kiss and wanted so badly to open my eyes to see him, but they wouldn't open. All of a sudden I felt myself rising from the chair going towards a light. That's when my eyes flew open, and I looked around for Duane.

It was the most wonderful "visit" as I knew my husband had been there even if it were only for a few minutes. Another time I was half awake and half asleep, and I felt him lying in bed with me holding my hand. I put my arm around him and fell into a deep sleep. When I woke up, of course, he wasn't there.

One night I was in a dead sleep and woke up sensing that someone was in the bedroom with me. It was very dark, but I could feel that someone was standing at the foot of my bed. I had no fear, though; as I knew it was a good presence. Then I heard someone saying in my ear, "Check the doors." I got up in the dark and checked the garage door which I had left up; the sliding screen doors were not locked, and the door leading from the garage to the inside laundry room was unlocked also. I forgot to check them before I went to bed. I locked them all and went back to bed. I knew that it was Duane telling me to check the doors.

I still feel his presence; no matter where I am, I know he wants me to be happy so I live my life to the fullest and am the happiest person I can be every day. I miss him so much, but I know that someday, when God calls me home, I will once again be in his arms.

Margaret Matthews

—••⟨∞⟩••—
P.M.H. Atwater, LHD
www.pmhatwater.com
Reprinted with permission from *We Live Forever: The Truth About Death*, A.R.E. Press

During the time I lived in Boise, Idaho, Margaret Matthews, a dear friend of mine, was killed in a horrible accident. Margaret, her husband Frank, and their grandson were traveling by car to Yellowstone Park for a vacation. He was driving; she was on the passenger side, and their grandson was wedged in between them. Just as they crossed a bridge, a pickup truck, driven by a drunken teen showing off for his girlfriend, slammed head–on into them. Margaret was decapitated. Frank was crushed, yet he stubbornly clung to life as he and his grandson were rushed to the nearest hospital. When the attending physician determined that only the boy's pelvis had been broken and that he would recover, Frank drew a sign of relief and promptly died. Even when mangled beyond belief, he was protective of his grandson and would not leave until he knew for certain that the boy would live.

The death of Margaret and Frank Matthews was a triple tragedy. Once their grown children were notified, they in turn broke the news to Frank's elderly mother, their grandmother. She was so shocked, she died instantly. As it happened, at Margaret's request, my former husband and I were in the Matthews's home early that evening holding a Search for God Study Group meeting (spiritual studies taken from the readings of the late Edgar Cayce). Their son telephoned, surprised that anyone was there, and we talked at length. The meeting became a prayer circle where each person in attendance served as a guide to assist the three souls in making their transition into God's great light and to help the grandson.

I tell you this because of what happened next. While making certain that there was plenty of food for everyone at the Matthews's home during the days before the funeral for all three, I also did door duty. That means I was standing at the threshold when the neighbor across the street came running toward me, screaming at the top of her lungs, "Margaret can't be dead. Tell me she's not dead. I saw her and I talked to her when the sheriff's deputy said she had died. That's not possible. She was here and I talked to her." All of us did a double take and gathered around.

The woman's story told with utter conviction and backed up by the deputy's log of her telephone call, went like this: She was outside sweeping her stoop when she looked up and saw Margaret walking along her front sidewalk. She yelled at her and asked how she was doing. Margaret stopped, faced the woman, smiled, and said was just fine. She smiled again, turned around, and kept walking to the door, unlocked it, and disappeared inside as the door closed. The neighbor thought nothing of this exchange until, after finishing her chores, she turned on the radio in her kitchen and heard the bulletin. She called the sheriff's department to see if the broadcast was a prank and learned, much to her shock, that the time she and Margaret had been visiting *was the exact same moment Margaret was killed.*

I asked the neighbor if she had ever before experienced anything supernatural. She said, no, then she stunned the crowd that had gathered by saying: "A couple of weeks ago, Margaret and I were talking and I told her that I wanted more than anything else in the world to know if there was life after death. She promised me that the proof I needed would soon be coming. Then she smiled that special smile of hers, just like she did when I saw her yesterday."

This isn't all that Margaret did after her death. She manifested countless times, always seen as fully alive and responsive, whenever she could help another or be of service. These appearances of hers, plus other types of after-death communications from her went on for almost a year. Seven years later, she reappeared to fulfill a prediction she had once made to me: that when I enrolled in a certain class on the power of affirmative prayer, I would look up and see one of her daughters looking back at me. That did happen, even though her family and I had not communicated since the funeral. Several class members saw Margaret in the room before I did, then the lights went out. They did not come back on until Margaret's presence was acknowledged.

Can the dead return after they die?

You bet they can.

For a period of time after death, it is a commonplace for the dearly departed to return home or stick around that which is familiar. Unfinished business draws them back, or simply the desire to let their loved ones know they're okay. Once satisfied that they have done all they can for the living, most of them complete their transition into the spirit realms.

Incidents do occur, however, in which the dying do not merge with their soul but remain a disembodied ego floating around or simply existing until someone or something wakes them up. That's why prayer is so important at the deathbed and afterward. As powerful as the soul is, its memory can cloud or at times seem forgetful. Even a soul can use a little help.

My Brother Joey,
the Angel

<hr>

Toni DiBernardo–Jones
Pennsylvania

My mother was a wonderful mother, daughter, sister, and grandmother. She had a way about her, and she would help anyone she could anytime that she could. She loved her family and most of all her grandchildren. She was the type of person who knew what she wanted and got it. Until the last six weeks of her life she was an independent, active person constantly running here and there; she always loved taking long rides in the car.

The last trip that she made was up to her daughter Mary Jo's house. She always wanted to see her two youngest grandchildren, Brianna and Michael. These two young babies were the light of her life and really kept her going.

Brianna is the only girl among all the boys in the family. She would always be happy to see her Grandma. There have been times since my mother's death that Brianna has said that she saw her Grandma Yooie and has even carried on conversations with her.

In fact, Brianna, who was just three-years–old at the time, would always ask my sister why she couldn't see my mother. At one point, she was pretending to talk on a toy telephone with her grandmother when she turned to Mary Jo and told her "Grandma wants to speak to you now." Unfortunately, this scared my sister, and she threw away the play phone.

If there was some way for my mother to still see these children from beyond, I know she would. She would always say that Brianna melted her heart and that she held a very special place in it just for her.

During her last trip to Mary Jo's, she fell down going into the house. My sister and I had to take her home and bring her upstairs into her bedroom; she never left home or came back down from her bedroom again. This was a very sad time for us; it's hard to see someone who was so full of life and spunk not able to do the things she had always loved to do. She would, at times, put on her makeup and say she was going to see the kids, but she just couldn't do it anymore.

The week that my mother died, I had experiences that were just un-believable as she was communicating with my father and brother Joey who had already passed. One day my mother looked at me and told me that my brother Joey was in the room with us. She said, "Oh, I wish that you could see this beautiful male angel all dressed in white. I'm afraid if you turn your head too fast, he will leave; he is so beautiful."

She went on as if she were having a conversation with this angel. "Did you hear what he just told me?" she asked. Then without waiting for an answer she continued, "I told him to please put me down be-cause I was going to make him fall and he told me, 'Mom, I won't let you fall. You are as light as these feathers on my back.'" I couldn't be-lieve what I was hearing. She then looked at me and said, "Toni, it's Joey; I always knew he was an angel." (My brother passed away when he was just twelve years old.) You could actually feel the energy in the bedroom that day.

Later that day as I continued to sit there, I felt a cool breeze brush up against my cheek. I just knew that it was my beloved father. My mother confirmed this, "Toni, your father just kissed you on the cheek and told me to tell you that he never forgot how you took care of him." I was totally amazed because these were the same words my father had said to me just minutes before he died some twenty years earlier. My father and I were alone in the room when he told me he would never forget how I took care of him and that he would love me forever.

This was a validation of what I already knew. We do not lose our loved ones. This was an experience that I will never forget—a very special memory that I will cherish and carry in my heart for the rest of my life. I am so very happy to have been there with my best friend, my very loving mother. I'll love you and miss you forever, Mom.

I firmly believe that all of the signs my mother and I experienced were due in large part to the power of prayer. I have a strong devotion to Jesus, and I would say the chaplet daily. One day, I was astounded by what happened to my rosaries. After much prayer using these rosaries, the cross turned gold. It was just another beautiful sign from above.

Misty Angel

Summersnow Wilson
Arkansas
sunuluv@aol.com
www.Marysangel.com.

My beautiful daughter Misty Angel died at the tender age of just fifteen. I have since received many signs from my daughter. In fact, I believe my first sign was a couple days before her funeral. I was sitting at my desk trying to write something to be read at her funeral when I clearly felt someone touch my hair. Angel always used to look over my shoulders and touch my hair when she was on this earth. I turned around not able to see her, but I could feel her presence.

One day I did without a $5.00 lunch because I felt it was money I could put toward paying for her headstone. I left the house for a while, and when I came back, Angel's bedroom door, which had been closed, was open. Lying directly in front of her door was a $5.00 bill which had not there before I left the house. And since I lived alone at that time, no one else could have put it there. I took the hint, thanked my daughter,

47

and went out to get myself that lunch.

Angel always used to cuddle next to me in bed. Since her passing, I've felt her cuddle next to me, especially when I've had a bad day.

I had a long-time boyfriend that I never wanted to marry due to my previous bad marriage. He was understanding and just accepted the fact that I was self-supportive and had no plans to get married again. But, after my daughter's death, I began to change my mind. One evening, I spoke to Angel in what I call a sort of spirit telepathy and asked her to somehow lead my boyfriend to want to marry me. The very next day, he asked me to marry him.

On the anniversary date of my daughter's death, several of her friends gathered with me in her memory. We were packing up to go to lunch when I walked out to the road to pick up some of my equipment. Suddenly, I heard Angel's voice, and I looked up noticing that a vehicle was headed straight toward me. At that moment, I felt Angel in front of me holding me in my spot when another car appeared suddenly out of the blue. It diverted the vehicle that was coming right at me and pushed it to the other side of the road.

The vehicle ended up going through some trees and flipping over. I watched in horror as it eventually came to rest upside down three houses away from me on the same side of the road. By this time several of the others, who had joined us for the day, ran to help the driver. The man was drunk and got out of the vehicle without a scratch. When I finally made my way over to him, he looked at me and said, "Where is your little girl?" I was confused and asked, "What do you mean?" He replied, "The little girl that was standing in front of you, where is she?"

I couldn't bring myself to respond so I just turned around and walked away. Afterward, we all proceeded to go to lunch. My daughter's best friend and I talked about what happened, and both of us just started crying. I had no doubt that my daughter had been there protecting me by bringing that other car to divert the one which was in my path.

Angel always seems to find a way to get her messages to me. On my way to work before the Christmas season, I was dreading the holidays and the fact that Angel's birthday was approaching. I spoke to her in the spirit saying, "Angel, please show Mommy somehow that I'm sup-posed to be here continuing this fight. Please show me a sign because

Mommy is tired and doesn't know how to make it through your birthday and the holiday season without you."

Shortly after I got to work, a lady came up to my desk and handed me a flyer. I looked down at it and read something about Christmas on the Square on December 1st at 5:00 p.m. December 1st is Angel's birthday and 5:00 p.m. is the exact time she was born. According to the flyer, the town was celebrating the start of the holiday season with a parade and carnival (her favorite activity). I couldn't have asked for a better sign.

Many months later, I happened to read about another bereaved mom named Ruby who claimed to be in regular contact with her son. I e-mailed her and inquired whether she could ask her son to make sure someone was watching over Angel in heaven. I also asked her why my daughter did not speak with me the way her son seemed to speak to her. Below is her response. Keep in mind that this woman knew nothing about me or my daughter. Ruby had never been to my house. I never told her how my daughter died and that I had found her on the floor in her bedroom. There is also no way she could have known that I had since remarried and that the kitchen is one of the rooms where I miss my daughter the most.

Here's what she wrote:

Last night during our before bedtime chat, my son invited your Misty Angel to join us. It seems that Ben had been looking over my shoulder and read your e-mail. At first, she was very quiet and gradually told me that she watches over you, especially when you're in the kitchen. She said to tell you that her time had been decided before the earth was created.

She completed her purpose for coming and you are to know that's the reason God chose you as her mother. She says to tell you that she's no longer fifteen and that she is growing up but will not grow old so you needn't worry. When you get there, she'll still be your same little girl, only in adult form. Also, she now loves her stepdad and is happy he's in your life. She doesn't want you to be lonely or sorrowful. Ben says your daughter smiles and laughs a lot, and Angel says that's how she wants you to remember her, not in the bedroom.

She couldn't stay to say goodbye because you couldn't have let her go and she had to leave as Jesus, Himself, took her hand and raised her up. You didn't do anything wrong; nothing was your fault. She says, "You're the angel, Mom, not me!" She thanks you for the love you gave that she took with her.

She hasn't contacted you outright because she doesn't want you to put her first in your life the way you used to do. She wants you to live, laugh, and have fun, fun, fun—that's what she wants for you.

One of my daughter's best attributes was the way she always wanted to have fun. She would always say, "Mom, you need to laugh more often and have more fun." Ruby knew nothing about me yet she was able to correctly answer questions I had asked my daughter. I have no doubt that every word came directly from my Misty Angel.

Logan Gets Her Wings

Angela Denes
Ohio
SignsFromHeavN@aol.com
www.geocities/halo4logan.com

I remember standing in our living room when, out of the blue, my three-year-old daughter Logan proudly announced that she was going to be an angel. No one else was around, and we were not talking about anything. In fact, I was quietly dusting when she sought me out.

"I be an angel," she said.
"An angel," I asked.
"Huh, Hun, an ardian angel," she replied.
"Oh, a guardian angel," I repeated correcting her,
Half laughing with my emphasis on the letter g.

In a matter-of-fact and rather serious tone, she answered, "Nues," her word for "yes." Glancing down towards the floor, she appeared some-

51

what ashamed and yet relieved at the same time. Shrugging her shoulder, she walked out of the room with nothing more to say. One week later, my little girl was killed in a tragic accident.

Since her death, I have received many signs from heaven. On one particular night, I had a dream of Logan; only it was more real and not like a dream. In it my little girl came to me for a visit. There was an unmistakable higher presence that accompanied her. I vividly remember being afraid to even touch her because I knew she had died and was in spirit form.

Despite my fears, I still wanted very much to hold her so I asked this presence for permission to hug and kiss my daughter, and it was granted. Logan never said a word. But she let me touch her, and I found myself kneeling down on her level to give her a kiss.

I put my arms around her and gave her a big tight squeeze while I savored the skin-to-skin contact my lips made with her soft cheek. As I was holding her, I acknowledged and thanked this other presence. I couldn't see anyone else but knew someone was there allowing this to take place.

I felt a feeling of urgency rush through me and understood that her appearance was only temporary. As I was hugging her, I remember asking with my thoughts, not my voice, "Please, just one more moment?" It was allowed, and then they both left.

The next morning after awakening and doing my chores, I was interrupted by the ring of the telephone. It was my mother. She asked how I was and then told me, "Last night, I asked Logan to come to you in a dream." My mother now had my undivided attention as she went on to tell me, "I was driving home from work, and I asked Logan to do me a favor."

I was so excited to tell her that I did have a dream—a really good one! But before I could finish, she interrupted me and said, "Wait! Let me tell you what I asked her to do." I thought this was an odd choice of words for my mother, but I let her talk first. "I asked her to go to you and let you hug and kiss her. I asked her to make sure it would be very real, not like a dream."

As she said this, I began crying remembering the dream. After she finished, it was my turn to share the dream I had. I know that Logan did that for all of us. She used my mother and me so that we would have each other to verify for the rest of our lives what had happened.

Several months later, I dreamed that our daughter was holding a cat in her arms when the tow truck ran over her. Next, I found myself at the hospital just like the night she died. The doctors were giving us the bad news, "We're sorry. There is nothing left we can do. She is not going to make it and neither is the cat. We're going to lose both of them by morning." In the dream, my child did die in the morning, but the cat she was holding lived. I remember angrily questioning how they could save a cat but not our child. I was mortified and awoke.

The next day I had to work second shift at the hospital. Toward the end of my shift, I decided to take a break and went outside. I was on the second floor of the hospital at the top of a set of concrete wall–lined stairs that lead down to the main floor sidewalk. A steel door at the top of the narrow stairs gave entrance to the hospital, and I was sitting at the top of them.

As I was sitting outside talking to Logan, God, and the universe, I was aware of the streetlight across the way. While I was sitting there gazing at the light, trying to find a reason for all this pain and misery, I was deep in thought, "Logan, I know you can let me know you're OK. That is all Mommy really needs to understand. I can deal with the pain of living without you as long as I know you are safe and are being taken very good care of. Could you please find a way to let me know that you are alright? Please? I promise you that if you can give me a sign, I will never doubt it. I promise with every fiber of my being; no matter what anyone ever tries to tell me, I will not disbelieve it. People can call me crazy or say anything they want, but I will never question that you did this for me; I promise!"

As I was enchanted by the streetlight, pledging my promise, I remembered about electricity and understood how we are all part of it and that it is related to energy. From a scientific aspect, energy can never disappear; it can change only from one form into another.

I asked her to make the light blink. I told Logan to just flicker it and that would be my sign that she was OK. Most newly bereaved people want to know that their departed loved ones still exist and that they are OK. Our loved ones are just as eager to offer us some reassurance for peace and comfort. For quite some time, I had been praying to St. Philamena to watch over our daughter. I ordered Logan to go and get St. Philamena or someone else if she could not do it herself. I could feel a struggle of energy when all of a sudden the light went off!

I could not believe my eyes. Then it came back on. I was like, "WOW!" I shot straight up from a sitting position, rubbing my eyes in disbelief and looked once more. Again, the light went off and came back on. By now, I was shaking, crying, and practically jumping up and down thanking Logan and God. The light started going crazy: on, off, on, off, on, off, on, off, on, off, on. Almost as if she was as thrilled as I was that we were somehow communicating. Oh, how my heart had been set free. I knew she was fine.

I stepped inside the building and yelled for Sally, a co-worker. She came to see what I was so excited about. As we ventured out onto the landing of the second floor, a cat jumped out of nowhere from behind the steel door. Sally is a feline lover and thought I was excited about the cat. "Oh, a cat, a cat!" she said. I answered in kind of a frustrated tone, "No! Not the cat, the light, the light!" We were both surprised because a cat could have only gotten on the landing by climbing up the stairs, but this one had jumped out from behind the door where nothing but a wall of concrete stood.

I had forgotten about the dream until on my way home from work that night when it hit me like a ton of bricks, "The CAT!" Oh, my goodness, it was the cat from my dream that my child was holding. My dear, sweet, clever little girl and my precious Savior both knew me too well. They knew that although I had made a vow, I was only human and would still have doubts. Therefore, they gave me extra reassurance or what I refer to as a double sign!

A Visit from Denise

M. G. Raub
Washington

When I was a junior in high school, I had a friend named Denise. We shared art class together. She had been absent from school for several days when I decided to go visit her at home to see how she was feeling. We had a nice visit, and she seemed well enough to return to school. She told me that she'd had a cold, but now she felt better and remarked that she would be back at school the following day. I remember that she was smiling when she told me that. I visited with her for a while, then went home, did my homework and other activities before going to bed.

That night I was asleep in my room when I awoke for no apparent reason. My dog Duchess was also awake and stood beside my bed looking toward the door to my room. I sat up in bed and looked toward the door and there stood Denise. She was standing in the corridor facing my doorway.

She was not misty or glowing or anything. She appeared to be just as real and whole as any living person. I did not feel any fear when I saw her, only mild confusion as I asked her what she was doing there in my house. She was smiling as she said, "I just wanted to stop and say 'Goodbye.'" I said "Goodbye" to her but did not ask her where she was going. My sixteen–year–old mind seemed satisfied with her answer. She turned as though she was going to walk on down the corridor toward the stairs. I did not see her disappear or fade away. I glanced at my alarm clock noting that it was 4:30 in the morning. I settled in and soon went back to sleep.

The next morning I woke up and thought about Denise's visit. It had not been a dream so I was at a loss to understand it. I decided to tell Denise about it when I saw her at school since she had said that she would be coming back that day. As soon as I got to school, another friend walked up to me. She asked me if I had heard about Denise. I said, "No." Then she told me that Denise had died earlier that morning.

Later I was told that her cold had suddenly developed into a very severe, virulent form of pneumonia and that she'd been rushed to the hospital where she had passed away. It was all very sudden and totally unexpected. I was absolutely stunned! At that moment, when I'd heard the news of her death, I experienced emotions that I still cannot describe. Afterward I found out that she had died at 4:30 a.m. which was the exact same time when she had come to visit me in my room! She'd visited me before I knew that she was dead.

This happened many years ago, but I still think about Denise from time to time. I will always be grateful for her visit because in some ways, by doing what she did, she gave me one of the best gifts that I have ever received. This is the gift of assurance that there is life after death and that we do go on. This knowledge has been a great comfort to me over the years.

The Rose Petals

Phil Whitt
Ohio
philwhitt@sbcglobal.net

I have been experiencing "visits from heaven" since I was about twelve-years-old. I would hear voices and even wake up to see the silhouette of someone in my room. Back then I was afraid of these experiences, but now I realize that these phenomena are a blessing.

My stepmother crossed over when I was fifteen-years-old. I was staying at my dad's house in Niles, Ohio for three days during the funeral. And I was not prepared for what would take place at the house during my visit.

I was lying in bed when I clearly heard footsteps climbing up the stairs to the top landing just outside the bedroom that my brother and I shared. I quickly woke Rick up, but the noise stopped. A few minutes later my brother fell back to sleep, and the footsteps started again. I was scared and tired but finally fell back to sleep with the covers over my head.

The interesting thing was my stepmother always wore shoes with small hard heels which made the exact sound I had heard on the stairs. The following morning I asked my father to take me back home to Cleveland, Ohio, which he did. Two weeks later my stepmother paid me another visit. I was lying on the couch watching television when I dozed off. Suddenly, I sensed that I was not alone and could have sworn I heard someone say, "Phillip." I opened my eyes slowly and yelled, "NO." There standing just a foot away from me was my stepmother.

She stood there smiling at me wearing a pink nightgown which is what she was buried in. As soon as my yelling brought my younger brother Rick running into the room, she was gone.

I didn't mention what had happened to me in either Niles or Cleveland until years later. When I did, Dad told me that he, too, heard the same hard-heeled footsteps and that this is what prompted him to eventually move. I spoke to people who had moved into the house after he left and found that the sound of hard-heeled shoes was still being heard by the new occupants. They were as amazed as I was that my stepmother's footsteps could still be heard a decade after her death.

During another "visit," I had a vivid dream about my grandfather a year after he passed away. In the dream my grandfather and I were on a bus from the 1950s or '60s. Back then these buses contained pull cords so that passengers could alert the bus driver when their stop arrived.

My grandfather was sitting down, and I was standing up holding on to keep myself balanced. He looked up at me and asked, "Peno," a nickname he had always called me. "Is this my stop?" I replied, "Yes, Grandpa," to which he stood up and walked to the back of the bus. He then took off running into darkness.

I woke up with tears in my eyes. What I found interesting about this dream is that he had broken his hip when I was little and could never run after that.

My grandfather came to me again. Only this time, he gave me what I would later find out was a validation. He simply said, "Go to see your grandmother. She is going to be with me soon." This was all so real, and I knew it was my grandfather speaking to me. So I did as I was told and paid my grandmother a visit. Two weeks later she had a stroke and died.

Years later my mother crossed over after a long illness, and I ordered a spray of flowers for her casket. The spray was made up of an array of multi-colored carnations. But in the midst of the carnations were two pink roses and one white rose to represent my mother's three children. The pink roses were from my sister and me while the white rose was in remembrance of my younger brother who had crossed over three years earlier.

After the funeral service, I wanted to remove the roses from the spray and keep them in remembrance of my mother, but they were gone. I asked my sister, the funeral director, and others if they had taken the roses, but no one had. The funeral director told me that they had been there when the flowers were brought to the cemetery. No one could figure out what had happened to the roses.

A few days later strange things began to happen. I kept finding single pink rose petals everywhere. I found a pink petal lying peacefully on my computer keyboard on two separate occasions and then later found another one lying right outside my backdoor. At first, I couldn't figure out where these rose petals were coming from. I was the only one who had keys to my house so no one else could have been leaving them.

The rose petals continued to show up in unusual places. About a month later my girlfriend Sandy and I went to the cemetery to visit my mother's gravesite. The ground was covered with leaves, and we were cleaning up around my mother's headstone. I happened to look down and noticed a red rose petal lying right there at my feet.

Before I bent down to pick up yet another hello from my mother, I asked Sandy who was standing a few feet away if she could see any new gravesites in the area. I wanted to make sure there was no chance that it could have blown over from another gravesite fresh with flowers. She looked at me like I was crazy wondering why I would ask such a thing. I explained what had happened and asked her to come over to look at the rose petal. We were both in awe.

Even though I had no doubt that these rose petals were from my mother, I decided to visit with a local medium. You can just imagine my excitement when I was told, "Your mother says she is leaving you rose petals."

I haven't received any more rose petals from my mother since that day in the cemetery. Perhaps, she doesn't need to leave them anymore since I get the message. Her spirit is alive and well. And as for that last rose petal, it remains in an airtight bag . . . a very special reminder that we do receive "visits from heaven."

Healing Hands from Heaven

Carolyn B. Coleridge, LCSW
California
carcole9@hotmail.com
www.intuitivesoulhealing.com

When my maternal grandmother Frances LaMaizon Jervis passed on, she promised me she would come back to visit. Frances lived with my family and me in New England and was a second mother to me.

Grandma was a very spiritual woman with a pure devotion to God and a determined will. She had many spiritual experiences and even with limited education could memorize Bible verses. We shared a lot of similarities, especially our love for angels and cats. She was an amazing healer in her own right.

I grew up listening to many accounts of her incredible life experiences. She once told me that she was a fast runner in her homeland of South America. One day she fell while running in a race, hitting the back of another athlete's shoe. As a result, her eyes were spiked by the shoe, and she was blinded. Determined not to be blind for the rest of

her life, she prayed to God to help heal her eyes when she felt a presence and miraculously regained partial sight. She believed, and it happened. Obviously, she was a spiritual inspiration to me and was one of
my earliest teachers.

At the age of eighty–seven my grandmother was diagnosed with pan-
creatic cancer. Because this is the most aggressive and deadliest form of
cancer, my family knew that it wouldn't be long before she passed.
Through it all, Grandma always promised me one thing—she would
come back to visit me after she died.

When I saw my grandmother in the hospital during her final days,
she didn't look like herself. She was very frail and thin. The smell of the
cancer eating away at her had enveloped the room. It was painful for
me to see, and I am sure even more painful for her. Eventually, she was
unable to speak as she lay there nearly unconscious. I told her that I
loved her and that I would miss her. Suddenly, all I could hear was her
struggling with her breath. My intuitive voice told me to tell her what
she had meant to me. I knew her spirit would hear me. This was one of
my last chances to express myself to her. I told her, "Grandma, you
taught me about unconditional love." That was something I was not
aware of until that moment.

Even though she was semicomatose, my grandmother coughed
coarsely and tried to speak. I interpreted this as her acknowledging
what I had said. I knew she had heard me. Two days later I had a dream
about her dancing with me. She was at some kind of outdoor gathering
with many elderly and some younger people I didn't know. She was
dancing barefoot in the center of this grassy clearing. (The grassy earth
and everyone being barefoot represented to me that these souls were
close to returning to the earth.) She saw me on the sidelines and ran up
to me, grabbing both of my hands while pulling me onto the grassy
dance floor with her.

Grandma couldn't walk in her last days so I knew the dream was a
premonition of her imminent passing and the ability she would have to
dance again when she crossed over. The next morning I got a call from
my mother telling me that she had transitioned. Her passing left a big
void in my life. She was the first close family member to die. My mother
was always the disciplinarian, but my grandmother was always the

playful "ma" with never-ending unconditional love. I wondered what she was doing and how she was transitioning.

Although I was saddened because she was gone, it was bittersweet. My grandmother had always wanted to return "home" as soon as she could. She had had two near-death experiences prior to her passing. One night, when she was in the hospital, her symptoms grew worse, and the staff called a Code Blue. The hospital staff was able to revive her. When she came to, she said that she went to the Other Side and that there were tons of angels around her. She stated that they showed her a scroll with her name at the top.

She had three more things to do before the golden seal was put on the end of the scroll, indicating that she had graduated and passed onto the Other Side. The nurses thought she was hallucinating and imagining the white uniforms of nurses as angels. Funny, I don't remember nurses wearing white anymore! Mostly scrubs. My family and I knew that she had truly seen her angels.

The funeral was, of course, painful. It was the most difficult when I saw her hardened body lying in the casket. I held onto her hands as a reminder of our dance together and wished her love on her journey. I admittedly felt distraught with the stone-cold feeling of her hands and the lack of warmth. I wondered about her promise to me before she died. Would she find a way to contact me?

My grandmother died on November 16, and my co-worker told me that she had a black kitten that needed a home. My grandmother loved cats, often feeding them outside our kitchen door so I immediately believed that this as a sign and agreed to take the cat. My co-worker said in another couple of weeks the kitten would be ready to leave her litter. When I asked what day the kitten was born, I was shocked to find out it was November 16, the same day my grandmother passed. Surely, this was a sign. She was sending me a black kitten born on the day that she passed. This must be her message that "life does continue after death." I didn't realize it then, but this was only the beginning. I named my cat Lavender because this particular flower is known as being an emotional healer.

A month later I returned to my parents' home in Connecticut for Christmas. I was saddened that my grandmother wasn't there and thought about her often. One night I went to sleep; the room seemed to be filled with unusually cold air. My bedroom was always cold so I always slept in layers and frequently used an electric blanket. On this night I experienced an unbelievable dream and visitation. In the dream my grandmother walked out of the closet and came up to my bed. She was heavyset and looked healthy as she gave me a warm hug that I could literally feel.

I could feel the strength of her arms and the intense sensation you get when you are truly missed by someone. She told me she had come through dimensions and was very happy where she was. She spoke telepathically and told me things about heaven, which I barely remember but was impressed at the time. I sensed she wasn't alone when she stated she had to go because she was still being "adjusted."

She then hugged me again and grabbed my hands, and I immediately felt this warmth of energy penetrate into them. It felt so warm, healing, and heavenly. When she left, I woke up, but it took me a long time to open my eyes. When I finally did open them, I was surprised to find the covers had fallen off of me. My body was fairly cold, but my hands were astonishingly hot! I held onto them and realized they were the only warm part of my body.

I ran out to my mother and told her to feel my hands because grandmother had come to visit. My mother who had numerous mediumship experiences didn't even blink and replied, "What did you expect? She said she would!"

Grandma's healing hands from heaven helped me believe in the afterlife. She kept her promise and came back to visit me. Today, I continue on my own spiritual journey helping others believe in the continuity of life. As a medical social worker, I relay this story to other grieving families as it helps to soothe their soul. Hopefully it will do the same for you.

. . . .

About Carolyn Coleridge

Carolyn Coleridge, LCSW is a psychotherapist, intuitive, and healer. A former voluntary faculty member at the UCLA Pediatric Pain Program, she performed hands on healing for children in chronic pain. She currently has a private practice and works at various hospitals as a medical social worker.

Appearing on several radio and television programs including CNN International, she speaks on a variety of spiritual topics and is the editor of a monthly newsletter. Carolyn wrote a chapter in *The Spirit of Women Entrepreneurs* and is working on her first book about soul healing. For more information, please visit www.intuitivesoulhealing.com.

Lifelong Friends Keep Their Promise

Mary Ellen "Angel Scribe"
Oregon
angelscribe@msn.com
www.angelscribe.com

The first time I realized that there was more to the world and that mystery, magic, and miracles existed was when my grandmother Anne Woods shared her personal true experience.

Each morning, as Grandma walked to the trolley car on her way to work, she would exchange greetings with Mrs. Carmichael over the garden fence. Their friendship started casually this way. And on Grandma's return trip from work, while Mrs. Carmichael was lovingly tending her garden's flowers, they would chat again.

As the flowers bloomed, so did their friendship.

From these early contacts to death of Mrs. C's husband and then her journey into blindness and eventually into a nursing home, my grandmother was beside her friend the entire time.

Mrs. C and her husband never had children, so facing old age, blind and alone, was terrifying for her. My grandmother promised to be her sight and her helper.

Grandma watched over and took care of Mrs. Carmichael for the next forty years. This undertaking included business affairs as well as a close friendship. Grandma rode three buses every day, except Christmas as she was with us, across Vancouver, BC to visit Mrs. C in the extended care residence.

When Mrs. C was in her nineties, she said, "Annie, I wish I could be helpful to you in your old age just as you have been here for me."

Several months later at 2:22 a.m., Grandma woke to strange scratching sounds on her apartment's window. She noticed the time, got up, and checked the window. There was a metal railing around her building, but no trees or vegetation of any kind were remotely close to the window. Nothing was touching it. So my grandmother went back to bed, thinking that the noise was the oddest thing.

At 8:00 a.m. her phone rang, waking her up. It was the nursing home saying, "Mrs. Carmichael passed during the night. We apologize for not calling sooner, but we saw no reason to wake you up."

Grandma asked, "What time did she pass?" And she was told, "2:22." That was the exact time of the scratching on the window! Mrs. C had come by and looked in on Grandma and said goodbye to her faithful and dear friend.

Grandma resumed her life without her friend and missed her very much. Years later when she was in her seventies and had lived in her apartment for twenty-eight years, the building sold. The new managers left a note telling her that they wanted her apartment. She was free to choose another unit or to move out.

Grandma was startled. The notice was unexpected. She did not have the energy to move and had no idea where to go. So she phoned the new owners of the building and began by saying, "Hello, this is the occupant of Apt. 2B. I will move, but I need another month to locate a new apartment building."

Now you have to realize this is a city of thousands and thousands of people, but the new owner instantly recognized my grandmother's voice. "Is this Annie? Is this Mrs. Carmichael's Annie?"

My grandmother faltered and responded, "Yes."

"Annie, this is Nurse Holden from the nursing facility where Mrs. Carmichael lived for twenty years. My husband and I just bought your apartment building, and we hired a new manager. I am so sorry our new manager has asked you to move. Don't you worry; you stay there as long as you like. The people can find another apartment to move into."

So, in a very special way, Mrs. Carmichael's wish for Grandma came true. She did, indeed, help her out in her old age, too. The bond of love and promises was not broken when Mrs. C died.

We never know when an act of kindness will return and will become a blessing to us.

. . . .

About Mary Ellen "Angel Scribe"

Mary Ellen is an award-winning photojournalist, author of *Expect Miracles* and *A Christmas Filled with Miracles*, and a newspaper pet columnist. Through her popular online *Angels and Miracles Newsletter*, she teaches that we all have miracles waiting to be claimed.

According to Mary Ellen, miracles are not always what you might expect. They are often disguised as acts of kindness. You may be an answer to someone's prayers. For more information, please visit www.AngelScribe.com.

The Greater Reality

---•◄∞►•---

R. Craig Hogan, PhD
r.craig. hogan@greaterreality.com
www.greaterreality.com

I was drawn from apathy about spirituality into the study of the greater reality and afterlife through a remarkable series of events. This study began in 1997 when, strangely enough, I found myself meeting psychics, one after another; I had never met a psychic before in my life. At that time I met and had a number of conversations and readings with Greta Alexander, an Illinois woman well-known as a gifted psychic detective and reader. "Put pen to paper," she kept telling me. I would be a water carrier, she predicted, bringing spiritual understanding to people. Unfortunately, Greta died before we could do any work together. But she would later figure prominently in my study and writing.

In early 1998 I was becoming convinced about the reality of psychic knowing from my encounters with psychics such as Greta, but had little understanding of it. I agreed to participate in a psychic reading with my life partner Donna. As I settled into my chair before the psychic, she looked at me intently and said, "Your crown chakra is wide open!" I didn't know the significance of that but later learned that it meant I was wide open to learning about the greater reality and things of the spirit.

She continued, "You are able to do psychometry. That means you can hold an object in your hand and know things about the owner." That was all very interesting but seemed unlikely to me. "When you go home," she continued, "hold playing cards face down on your palm and see whether each feels hot or cold to you. If it's hot, your psychic side is telling you that it's red. If it's cold, it's telling you that the card is black. If you consistently identify more than 50 percent correctly, that will show you I'm right: you can hold things in your hand and get knowledge about them."

Skeptical, but intrigued, I left the reading and went to Donna's home. There I found a deck of playing cards. Without looking at them, I held them one at a time face down on my palm, placing each card, still face down, either into the stack of "cold" cards or of "warm" cards. I tired of the exercise after around twenty or twenty-two cards and turned over the "cold" pile. They were all black! I gasped and said, "Oh no." Donna rushed into the room to see what was wrong. I turned over the pile of "warm" cards and all but one were red. After I calmed down, I realized there really was something to what Greta and the other psychics I had been meeting were telling me; I was being drawn through the entrance into this realm. So began my engagement in learning more about psychic phenomena which eventually led me into learning about spirit and the afterlife.

In April 1998 my newly found interest in psychic phenomena led me to read a book titled *Tracks in the Psychic Wilderness* by Dale Graff, describing remote viewing—the ability to sit with closed eyes and get impressions about things in distant places. I found a Web site with codes for "targets" that were pictures of locations anywhere in the world. Anyone could try to remote view the picture associated with a code before seeing it on the computer monitor. I memorized the target number, closed my eyes, emptied my mind of all thoughts, and focused on the number code, having no idea what location would be in the picture. Within seconds I could see vague images. I sketched an image of a cathedral-like building with smaller buildings behind it. I described it as being gold and made of stone. I wrote that it had a religious feeling. Above it, I sketched an overhang of some type.

I then clicked on a link on the Web site to see the picture. It was a photograph of a jungle landscape with distant Mayan temples; one was a larger temple in the foreground bathed in gold light; other smaller ones were in the distance behind it. Over the scene was a streak of clouds like an overhang. My impressions were startlingly accurate. I was able to do remote viewing, drawing me even more deeply into this fantastic realm of the psychic. My appetite for learning about it was insatiable.

Over the years it became increasingly apparent to me that a greater reality underlies the apparent world we sense. It occurred to me this meant that the afterlife could be a reality. I began to study the literature about the afterlife and to listen to recordings of séances, especially those of Leslie Flint from the last half of the twentieth century. I was enthralled. The afterlife is a real world with people, cities, countrysides, natural surroundings, entertainment, and none of the negative irritations associated with Earth life. I spent several years soaking up any knowledge I could find about the afterlife. By summer 2004, I felt I needed to write a book about what I had been learning.

That September I had a reading with Laurie Campbell, a gifted, well-known research medium. She said during the reading that a woman came through who had been heavyset in life but who was showing her that she could dance now in the afterlife. Laurie described other details about her, and I knew it was Greta Alexander. Laurie said that Greta was interested in helping me write a book from the Other Side. I was delighted but unsure about how that might happen. She also said a team of scientists and writers was there to work with me.

A couple days later, I decided to try to communicate with Greta. I know that I feel inspired when I am writing, as though I am connecting with sources outside of myself. I even know where my focus is when I am feeling the inspiration: in the upper right corner of my mind. I decided to try opening myself up to that inspiration to see if I could contact Greta. Sitting with a pen in hand, I relaxed and focused on that area of my mind where I get the inspiration. I began to write as quickly as words came to me, not slowing to understand. "Greta, are you there?"

I wrote. I felt the words, "Yes, I'm here" and wrote them as quickly as they came. "Do you want to help me with my writing?" I wrote. As the impressions came to me, I scribbled, "Yes." "How do I know it's you?" I wrote. I felt an emphatic "Test me, test me." I wrote, "What will be the headline on MSNBC?" I continued to write as the impressions came to me: "Ivan Targets Cuba." I knew Ivan was in the ocean somewhere but didn't know anything more about the hurricane.

For the next several days, I looked regularly, with great anticipation, at MSNBC online. The headlines came and went. Then, four days after my session with Greta, on September 13, 2004, there it was: "Ivan Targets Cuba," in just those words. I was both exhilarated and awed. I had assurance that Greta was going to help me write from the Other Side, and I now knew I could receive inspiration from her.

I didn't try the writing again for years. I didn't need to. I knew that as I wrote the book, I was getting help from Greta and the team. The book, *Your Eternal Self*, published in February 2008, has as the authors "R. Craig Hogan, *et alia*," meaning "and others." I didn't write the book alone.

Today I am as sure of the afterlife as I am of this life. In fact, I'm more sure. I feel almost as though I'm on vacation in a strange land and will soon return to the place I know well and to where I belong. I learned that through my study of the literature. Now, I'm devoting my time to participating in group meetings to experience the reality of the afterlife.

This is an excerpt from Dr. Hogan's book describing what happens at death:

After the physical body dies, a variety of events have been described by those who have crossed over. Those who have died a violent, sudden death, as in war or an accident, may not realize they have died. They remain in an Earthly "vibration" as they call it, so they can walk on the Earth, sit on chairs, climb stairs, and take busses, but they are spirit, so no one can see them. One WWI soldier described himself running toward the enemy on the battlefield, but noticing that the enemy was running past him as though they couldn't see him. It wasn't until some time later that he realized he had been killed on the battlefield, but was still running on the Earth plane as the spirit person. His physical body was lying on the battlefield somewhere but all the rest— his mind, personality, and memories—were exactly the same.

Another man said that before his death, he was walking down the street with his wife and remembered seeing something coming at him. He then saw a crowd of people standing around staring at something. He "had a look" and saw someone lying on the street who looked just like him. "Could've been my twin brother," he said. His wife was crying hysterically, but for some reason, she couldn't see him. The reason was that he had been hit by a runaway truck and died. He got into the ambulance with the body and sat next to his grief-stricken wife, who still couldn't see him. Then he went to his own funeral. He remarked, "It was all very nice, but it was so damned silly because there I was!"

Others who pass away describe awakening in an open field, where at times a guide comes to help them. Some awaken on a couch in a home where their loved ones are. Others awaken in a hospital-like setting called a "reception area" where people help them make the adjustment to being dead and their loved ones come to visit. It seems that this common period of sleep is around two or three Earth days.

The transition is quite smooth and without incident. The person may not realize he or she has died, however, and needs help understanding the change. Some are bewildered for a period of time until they make the adjustment. A number of those who spoke during séances described how, in the moments after their bodies died, they felt that they must be dreaming and would wake up.

Several of those who spoke in the Leslie Flint séances described being "earthbound." They stayed on the Earth plane for weeks or years, walking about unnoticed by people, trying to communicate. A few described acting as poltergeists, banging things and moving things about to get attention.

After a while, however, most people do leave the Earth plane and go on to higher levels. Some explain that the excessive grief of the survivors depressed them and retarded them from progressing into happier conditions. Their most fervent wish was to reassure their loved ones that they were fine. Some describe the fact that they couldn't reassure their loved ones as the greatest difficulty in making the transition.

Dr. Hogan assures us that our loved ones are fine and only a thought away. "They're also not worried about you, unless you're grieving and unhappy," he writes. "They now know the truth that you and they are eternal beings. You'll live your life and transition into the next plane of life where you'll reunite, but in the meantime, they know you need to continue to learn lessons and they know they can't really do anything to help you with your struggles; you have to work them out yourself. They're happy, and they know you're fine as well. They'll be happiest when you're happy."

About Dr. R. Craig Hogan

Dr. Hogan is the author and co-author of several books including: *Your Eternal Self* and *Induced After Death Communication: A New Therapy for Healing Grief and Trauma*. He holds a PhD from the University of Pittsburgh and has been studying the nature of consciousness and perceptions of reality for several years.

The founder and president of the Business Writing Center, a Web-based school for writers, he has taught conflict management, group dynamics, and a variety of interpersonal development courses. For more information, visit:

www.greaterreality.com,

www.youreternalself.com,

www.wisesouls.com, or www.adcguides.com.

Author's Note: Due to copyright restrictions, I was not able to include the MSNBC screen from September 13, 2004.

Afterlife Encounters with Ghosts

—————··◀◆▶··—————

Dianne Arcangel

www.afterlife-encounters.com
Reprinted with permission from *Afterlife Encounters*, Hampton Roads
Publishing

According to most survival researchers (scientists who investigate the
possibility that some aspect of the living survives bodily demise), ghosts
are the psychical imprints of people or animals that were left in certain
areas while alive, and any sensitive individual can pick up the prere-
corded images and sounds. Unlike apparitions, ghosts are connected to
a place—therefore, each can be sighted in the same location by different
witnesses. Ghosts do not display animated personalities, appear in vivid
colors, emit radiant energy, or interact with observers. And because they
are residual energy only, they have no intentions.

I have been tracking the following case for more than 40 years and it
depicts the common features for most ghostly manifestations.

THE GHOST OF FAME CLEANERS

My family owned a chain of dry cleaning establishments. Seven days a week, Dyer, our dry cleaner, arrived at his spotting board before daybreak and remained there until long after sunset. His family, life, and love revolved around his work. He had nothing else. My dad, Dyer's employer for some 30 years, was concerned. "He swore he'd never love again after his wife ran out on him." Dad said to my mother and me. "Look at him. He's a hermit. He'll be seventy this week and what does he have?"

"Let's invite him over for dinner," mother said.

Dyer accepted the invitation and seemed to enjoy himself, but when Dad invited him again, he said, "Don't try to fix what ain't broke. My life's exactly the way I want it."

"Okay, just consider it an open offer," said Dad.

Seasons changed but Dyer remained the same—that is, until one approaching Easter when he didn't show up for work. Not only was that unlike him under normal circumstances, but the week before Easter was our busiest of the year. Dad raced to Dyer's apartment across the street and returned with grim news. "He must have had a heart attack in his sleep last night. He died the way he lived, peacefully and alone."

It was during the midsummer's heat, when Maria, one of Dyer's coworkers, rushed outside to greet Dad.

"Mr. Davidson! I saw him! I saw him!" she yelled.

"Who?" he asked.

"Dyer! As soon as I walked in I saw him. He was smiling, standing over there behind his spotting board working on some clothes. I smiled and waved at him, and he waved at me. I started walking to my side of the room to put my things down so I could go over and talk to him, but when I looked over there again, he was gone."

"Imagine that!" Dad joked, "Isn't it just like Dyer to leave when he thought someone might talk to him?"

Several customers and other employees reported similar experiences over the years that followed.

Then two decades brought complete personnel shift for Fame Cleaners. My parents retired to another state, and all of their employees had either moved away or died. My husband, Joe, and I purchased the business to keep it in the family, but my time was occupied as a day–trader and Joe was busy with his own company across the alley. Easter was upon us again and the cleaners needed employees, so Joe hired two sisters who had just arrived from Mexico. Neither woman spoke English, but he did not see that as a problem, since they would simply be washing shirts as a team. The following morning, the pair was busy sorting clothes when they saw a man in their periphery. They turned to face him directly, but were stunned by his transparent–blue eyes, pale skin, and white hair. The sisters looked at one another, then back toward the intruder, but he had vanished. "Hombre! Hombre!" they yelled, running out of the building. Joe and passersby immediately searched the premises and surrounding area, but found no one. An interpreter intervened and relayed their story, adding that their fright was mostly due to the man's ethereal appearance.

Meanwhile, Joe built an apartment above the cleaners, wherein occupants of various ages (ranging from four to 40), under varying circumstances (while watching television, cooking, reading, talking, and sleeping), experienced similar but unusual occurrences. They recounted seeing a short, thin man with transparent–blue eyes, pale skin, white hair, wearing a light–blue suit–all of which mirrored Dyer's appearance during life. Numerous occupants complained, even during Houston's searing summers, "One corner of the apartment is always freezing cold." Joe relayed the incidents to me saying, "I can't figure it out. That cool area should be as hot as hell—it's directly above the spotting board" (Dyer's former work station). Neither Joe, nor anyone at the cleaners or apartment, had ever heard of Dyer, and I did not divulge any information, thinking, *This is an excellent way to gather information, especially since Joe's a firm believer that nothing survives death.* We eventually sold the building, but continue to hear when employees or customers sight the figure of a man who meets Dyer's description.

. . . .
About Dianne Arcangel
Dianne is a former hospice chaplain, psychiatric hospital therapist, director of the Elisabeth Kübler-Ross Center of Houston, and president of the Forever Family Foundation. The author of the best-

selling book, *Afterlife Encounters*, she is an international speaker on the topics of death, dying, grief, and afterlife encounters.

For more information, please visit www.afterlife-encounters.com or www.arcangel.net.

An Afghan Hound Named Betty

Agnes J. Thomas, PhD
Ohio
Talktopets@aol.com
www.petstellthetruth.com

A lady named JoAnne called me because her newly adopted dog, an Afghan hound, wasn't eating. She had taken her to the vet, who couldn't find any physical reason for her problem and referred her to me. JoAnne told me that the dog was the matriarch in the family of five Afghans, four of which were her offspring. Her owner was an older woman who was sent to a nursing home, and animal rescue was called for the dogs.

The dog's name was Betty, and she was eighteen–years–old. I asked her how she was, and she told me that she was very sad because her owner had died. We were not aware of this at the time, but JoAnne was later able to confirm that Betty's former owner did, in fact, pass away. Betty wanted to know what had happened to her four puppies. I explained that they were taken from the shelter and placed in new homes.

Betty went on to say that she had no appetite and wanted to go with her owner. I explained to Betty that when humans die, we go into the afterlife where we live on. We humans call this "going home" because that is where we came from. I told Betty that she still has a lot to offer JoAnne, who adopted her, and that JoAnne loves her very much. I also asked Betty to release her mom because God needs and wants her and that it is very nice where she is now. Betty agreed to release her former owner.

The next day I received a call from JoAnne saying that not only did Betty start eating, but she slept in bed with her. The next morning, according to JoAnne, Betty had a bright pink lipstick kiss mark on her face. JoAnne told me pink was not her lipstick color and wanted to know where it came from.

Betty told us that her former mom visited her in the night and kissed her goodbye.

About Agnes Thomas, PhD

Agnes Thomas obtained her PhD in physiological psychology and worked as a counselor for mentally handicapped and brain damaged children and adults. She has twenty-five years of experience in noninvasive work with animals, researching the development of the respiratory control system, learning, and memory.

As a pet psychic, Agnes has been communicating with animals since 1992 and has studied interspecies telepathic communication. The author of *Pets Tell the Truth*, she is a well-known veterinary intuitive and a sought-after speaker. For more information, visit www.petstellthetruth.com.

Nicola's Story

Dr. Claudio Pisani
Italy
www.ampupage.it

When my son Nicola was three–years–old, he was diagnosed with can-cer—a large tumor was found lodged in his bladder. This was the start of a long and difficult journey for my son as he would later endure seven operations, ten chemotherapy treatments, and a month of radiation.

Despite dealing with a terminal illness, Nicola seemed to be happy and more spiritual than you would expect at such a young age. He seemed to be more intelligent than usual and had an intense love for all animals, including insects. He once told me, "Dad, do not kill ants be-cause the little ones will be left without their mothers to care for them."

Once during one of his many hospital stays, he told my wife Fran and me that he had just seen Jesus. When we questioned him about it, he said, "Jesus walked over the floor, and he has yellow hair like mine." Nicola did not know the word blond so he was using yellow instead. I can't imagine how a young boy could imagine something like this, including the way Jesus walks.

When he was feeling better, we had taken him to the beach. My wife jokingly looked at him and said, "Nicola, your mama is aging; she is a rough draft." To this, Nicola looked at her and said, "Don't you worry, when I'm with Jesus, I'll give you another life."

Two weeks before his death, he was very ill and had not eaten for several days. It was early in the morning on Easter Sunday; he looked at the window, and as if he were speaking to someone, he said, "No, go away; no more; give me a bit more time." He then asked his mother for a glass of milk.

Soon after his death, my wife and I began receiving many signs. Some were simple and somewhat vague while others were complicated and more pronounced. I received messages written on bar soap using my bodily hair. Once I picked up the soap and to my astonishment was the word "salve," which means hello in Italian.

Some time ago, I met a medium from Bologna (Italy) at an event called the Congress of Parapsychology. I was surprised when I received an unexpected e-mail from her telling me that she had received a channeled message claiming, "I am little baby, Dr. Pisani's little baby." She also sent a drawing of what she saw—a picture of a blond little boy with a marine landscape in the background.

I was amazed beyond words as this picture resembled a place my wife and I had just visited on the beach where we used to take Nicola and his sister. This medium also went on to tell me that my son had told her that he's still "arricciolato," a word that doesn't really exist but was the word that Nicola made up to describe his curly hair. Fran and I were the only ones who knew of this code word. There was no way the medium could have known this.

Another time we were all very depressed because it was what would have been our son's seventh birthday. My wife and I didn't want to do anything but stay home and think of Nicola. Finally, we decided to get out of the house and go eat at our favorite "pet" restaurant. This was a place we often dined at with Nicola. It is a little restaurant in a hotel by the beach where we spent our last vacation together before his death.

Fran and I arrived at the restaurant with heavy hearts that day, but we were determined to make the best of it. As usual, I ordered fish, one of my favorites, while my wife ordered something small to eat. I always order more than my wife as I have a much bigger appetite.

When we returned home that day, I went to check my e-mail and found another message from my medium friend. She said that she had another message from Nick. His words were, "Sometimes, I can feel mom and dad's sadness in this wonderful place that I now live.

"I want you to know that I love you both; I am living in a world full of consciousness. Daddy, you are always at your computer, and you can feel me whenever you want. I'm there making little noises or playing with the video. You need only learn how to see me."

The medium then asked my son to give her a sign proving that he is, in fact, with us. According to her, his response was, "Well, how was the food at our pet place? Daddy, you ate a lot and Mom lesser than you, as usual. I'm almost always with you, but sometimes I have to go to other places. I can't always stay to help you. I must learn a lot more to be able to help you better.

"Your time will come; life is a short blow of wind, but, even if we live better here, it is worthwhile to live your earthly life. Kisses and hugs to Mom, Dad; goodbye, sweet sister!"

The Purple Coat

John Edward
www.johnedward.net
Reprinted with permission from *One Last Time*, Penguin Group USA

Before my mother died, she made me promise two things: one, that her mother would be treated "like a queen," and two, that the parties would continue. We had always had a lot of family parties, big, catered gatherings in backyards and living rooms with everyone invited, friends, relatives, neighbors. With my mother's dying wish in mind, I began planning a party for my grandmother's birthday in January, even though it was only a month since my mother passed, and the party would take place just three months afterward. But before I got too far I began considering canceling the party. Despite my mother's wishes, I was feeling disrespectful and guilty. I asked my mother if I was doing the right thing.

A few days later, she came to me in a dream. Dreams are spirits' way of communicating with us directly. It is important to say that not every dream of a dead relative is a visit; many are our way of dealing with the loss. But there is a fairly simple way to distinguish between a dream that is a visit from someone on the Other Side and a dream that is just a dream. A *visit* is profound, a gift. It feels incredibly vivid and real, and stays with us much longer than a standard dream. While the details of most dreams dissolve from memory within a few hours, a visit will be remembered clearly years later. But it doesn't mean that everything in a dream–visit will make perfect sense.

In her visit, my mother came to me in a bar. I don't drink. I begin the dream in the downtown area of the town I grew up in, sweeping the sidewalk outside the bar on a crisp autumn day. Several people walk by me as I sweep, all of whom I recognize as people who have passed, including two young people I went to school with.

I go inside the bar, sit on a stool, and order a Pepsi. At the opposite end of the bar are my grandmother and my mother's youngest sister, both still alive. There are others in the bar but I don't recognize them. The door opens and a gust of wind brings in a swirl of just–fallen leaves. They are followed by my mother. She walks through the door looking radiant, glowing, her sickness and at least ten years stripped away. She comes wrapped in a striking purple coat that I recognize.

I don't say anything right away but think, *What are you doing here? You're dead.* She smiles at me and says, "I had to come and tell you I love you and it's beautiful where I am. And that I'm okay."

"But Ma, you're dead," I say again. She looks at me, as if to say, "You should know better—you of all people." Again, I ask her why she's here. She tells me she needed to tell me she is still with me and that she's proud of what I'm doing. I ask her what she means and she says, "The party, I'm so excited. I can't wait to come."

I ask my mother what my future has in store for me. She shakes her head from side to side. She lets me know that she can't tell me, but that she will be with me always and that she will let me know that from time to time.

At this point in the dream, I question what is really happening here. Even though I'd already had many encounters with spirits—including several personal paranormal experiences, such as the episodes with Uncle Carmine—I am skeptical that this is anything but a dream. (Whether in dreams or through spirit messages, to this day I have different standards for myself. I am not nearly as skeptical about other people as I am about myself because I am always wondering if I am somehow tricking myself.)

"Am I making this up?" I ask. "Is this my subconscious giving me permission to have this party?" My mother looks at me and says, "This party is going to be great."

Now she walks toward my grandmother. And my grandmother starts to disappear. My aunt grabs on to my grandmother and screams, "No! You can't have her!" The next thing is wordless. It is my mother saying *I'll leave her now but I'm going to have to come back for her.* My grandmother begins to reappear.

At this point, I say to my mother, "I know you're here. But what is this really?"

My mother smiles. "Johnny," she says, "this is *your* one last time."

She lets this sink in for a moment. It's been two years since we had that conversation when I said that everyone should get "one last time" to connect with their loved ones after they've gone to the Other Side. And she had just smiled and told me how cute I was.

As I'm taking all this in, she starts for the exit. When she gets to the door, she turns around, runs her fingers up and down the collar of her purple coat and says, coyly, "Would you pick up this coat?" Ending this profound interlude on that cryptic remark, she smiles and walks out the door.

As my mother left, I bolted up in bed. It was morning. I realized I had been crying. My pillow was soaked. I was soaked. I ran downstairs and told my grandmother and my aunt what had just happened. (Everything except the part about my mother coming for my grandmother.) We were all stunned, but still I wondered: was that a visit or just an episode my psyche dreamed up —literally—to make me feel better?

Half an hour later, I had a sudden urge to go to the deli in town for an egg sandwich, the kind you just can't make as well at home. The deli was in a strip mall that included the video store where I worked and a dry cleaner. As I pulled into the parking lot, I saw the woman who ran the dry cleaner wave to me, and I waved back. Then she motioned for me to come inside. I thought she needed change—we were always going back and forth when we needed change—but when I went inside, she came out of the back carrying a garment in a plastic bag. It was my mother's purple coat. I was speechless. (I still am when I think about it.) "Where's your mom been?" the dry cleaner asked. "She brought this in back in April"—April was when my mother was diagnosed with cancer—"and never came for it. She paid for it."

I remembered that my aunt had noticed the purple coat was missing when we were going through my mother's clothes after she passed. We assumed my mother had given it away, and my aunt joked that she wished it was still in the closet: she could have used a nice winter coat like that. But it seems my mother had more important plans for the coat. I thought it was very interesting that she had paid for the dry-cleaning in advance.

The purple coat was, and remains, the most profound personal validation I have received. Without it, to this day I would question whether my mother had actually come through with my "one last time," assuring me all was well on the Other Side and that we should go on with our lives, starting with the party for my grandmother. The way she playfully fingered the coat and then arranged for me to "pick it up" was her way of saying, "This is real. And I'm going to prove it to you."

In retrospect, I now see how my mother's passing showed me how important after-death communications are to those left behind. If I needed it, I assumed most people do. This was more than fun and games, entertainment at psychic "fairs." And in that way, my mother showed me the path I needed to be on. But while her visit did mark a turning point for me, I also have to say that I didn't fully realize it right away. That didn't come until I got past the anger that over-whelmed me during those months. Though the purple coat dream was an exhilarating moment, it did not diminish the rage I felt that God had taken my best friend, and that with all my supposed abilities I could do nothing to stop it, just as I had not been able to intervene in my uncle Carmine's passing.

My mother's doctor had told me that if her cancer had been detected earlier, she would have had a better chance. That's not something you tell a psychic. It was especially disturbing because she had gone months with pains that were misdiagnosed. Why hadn't I seen it? Why did God give me this ability if I couldn't use it to help those closest to me? Was this some kind of cosmic joke?

I was so confused and hurt that I stopped my psychic work altogether. When a regular customer came into the video store and asked for my help—her brother-in-law was missing—I coldly said, "No. I don't do that work anymore," and walked away. But as I was driving home a few hours later, I replayed that abrupt conversation over in my head and immediately heard my mother say, "Johnny, God granted you a beautiful gift. Use it wisely. You won't be able to make everyone happy, but if you can help just one person in your lifetime, then it is all worth it." Damn, I thought. I didn't want to hear it. I turned the music up in the car to stop these thoughts.

When I got home, I saw my next-door neighbor, Lisa, beckon me over. Before I could even get out of the car, she tossed an orange jacket in my hands and asked, "What do you get?" I was in no mood for psychic parlor games about the next guy in her life. As I went to put the jacket down I heard the word "missing." It was as if someone had pressed the "play" button on a tape recorder. I got a man's name, the fact that he drowned, that he was married and was out with another woman, that she also drowned, and when they would be found. It turned out that this man was the same missing person the woman in the video store had asked for my help in finding. He was an old friend of Lisa's parents. All the messages I received turned out to be accurate, and when I met the man's wife, she thanked me. Though the circumstances were of course painful for her, she said it helped bring her closure. She told me, "You have a remarkable gift. Use it wisely and know that even if you can help one person, it's worth it." Was this echo my mom's way of letting me know she had orchestrated the whole thing—and that the message was worth repeating? What I do know is that this experience helped me get past my anger and guide me back on track.

. . . .
About John Edward

One of the world's foremost psychic mediums, a television personality, and a best-selling author, John Edward has captivated audiences with his uncanny ability to predict future events and to communicate with those who have crossed over to the Other Side. Millions tune in to watch his internationally distributed talk shows, *Crossing Over with John Edward* and *John Edward Cross Country*.

John has made several television appearances including everything from CNN's *Larry King Live* to *The Today Show*. He is also a regular guest on New York's WPLJ and other radio shows. For more information, please visit www.johnedward.net.

A Message in
the Garden

---··⟨∞⟩··---

Mitch Carmody
Minnesota
heartlightstudio@aol.com
www.heartlightstudios.net

My son Kelly James Carmody died from a recurring malignant brain tumor; he was nine–years–old. The two years prior to his death were filled with pain, pills, surgeries, radiation, chemo, hardship, love, faith, and a little magic. When nothing else medically could be done for Kelly, we turned to our faith, the power of the planet, its people, and our Creator. We sold our home and our belongings and traveled to Mexico where Kelly had experienced a miracle healing during which his grape-fruit–sized brain tumor disappeared.

Months later the cancer returned, and so did we. The malignancy was spreading throughout the rest of his tired body; we found our-selves back home without a home. We quickly found a place where our son could die and say goodbye. After his death I wrote him a series of letters directly from my sinking heart.

In one of those letters I clearly stated to him:

> If you can arrange for a sign from you this spring,
> like something growing from our yard, that would be
> neat and I WILL notice. I will write again later some-
> time. Know that I love you and still need your love,
> Dad. (Page 42; *Letters To My Son, A Journey Through
> Grief ©*)

A few months later in the dead of winter we bought a new home. Soon the warm vernal winds of spring brought rebirth to our home and our yard, but not to our hearts. I believed Kelly would send me a sign; I just hoped that I would not miss it. I soon discovered that there were three cornstalks growing in the dried up lawn of our backyard. My son answered my request; the poem I have written below sums it all up best. Yes, there is life after death, and our loved ones, who have passed on, can communicate back to us in many ways. We just have to believe, to look, and to listen for their whispers of love. These are the best medicine in the world for the grieving heart.

THE THREE CORNSTALKS

In December of last year
my young son passed away
I wanted proof that he survived
so I would talk, when I did pray.
I asked him for a sign
that would grow in our yard this spring
not a timely rainbow
or a bird on a wing.
I requested a living indication
that Kelly would manifest
growing from God's green earth
a portent at my request.

That summer we had a drought
the ground as dry as bone
but yet from the parched & dried up lawn
three plants grew all alone.
Three corn stalks grew
where none had grown before
no seeds were ever planted
amongst the weeds galore.
These three corn stalks formed a triangle
its terminus pointing southwest
toward the land of Kelly's healing
and the miracle that we knew best
Later in the summer
the northwest corn stalk withered and bent
like the loss of Kelly's childhood
before his life was spent.

A few weeks later
the northeast corn stalk died
just as Kelly's physical body had
where his soul had chosen to reside.
The last corn stalk survived
and bore fruit for all to see
a sacred symbol of Mexico
are the corn stalks three.
This year on the first of December
a mourning dove sat at our door
beseeching us to watch her
for the message that she bore.
This bird captivated us
as she hopped across the lawn

then flew over the lone corn stalk
and in a moment . . . was gone.
I trudged through the snowy yard
anticipation thick in the air
my intuitive senses reeling
in hopes of what could be there.
I examined the dried and withered stalk
for a message it might contain
and near the bottom nearly covered with snow
one last ear did remain.
I plucked this last and lonely ear
pulling its yellowed husk slowly back
within I found a tiny cob
with mold of green and black
This putrefaction of the cob
imprinted a word that could be read
stained clearly on the yellow husk
the word " DAD" was all it said.

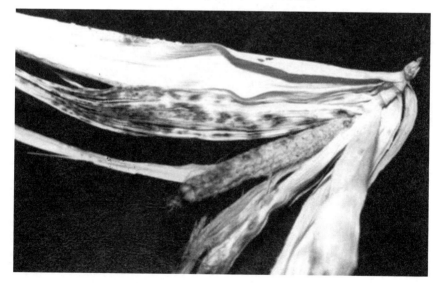

. . . .
About Mitch Carmody
Since the death of his son, Mitch has dedicated his life to helping those individuals and families going through the grieving process. He has conducted a variety of workshops with The Compassionate Friends and Bereaved Parents USA and is a sought-after speaker for many keynote presentations.

Mitch is the author of *Letters to My Son, A Journey Through Grief* and a frequent contributor to TCF Atlanta On-line and currently a staff writer for *Living with Loss Magazine*. He has joined forces with singer/songwriter Alan Pedersen to form, "Two Dads," a partnership for grief support. For more information, please visit www.heartlightstudios.net or www.proactivegrieving.com.

The Boy

Jen–Irishu
Australia
inharmony7@hotmail.com
www.jen–irishu.com

I had been having a relationship with a married man, whom I called The Boy, for ten years before his untimely death. Six months prior, our affair ended, but we still loved each other very much. It was after our decision to have time apart that I began to receive messages through my dreams. One particular dream "haunted" me, though because I was given the day of The Boy's death. At the time, I didn't know what to do or what to think. I was in turmoil.

As the day drew closer, I became extremely agitated and desperately tried to get in touch with The Boy . . . but to no avail.

It was a beautiful, starry early summer evening—too beautiful a night for someone to die.

As I lay in bed exhausted with worry, I heard a car pull up in front of my house. I'd know the sound of that car anywhere. It was The Boy.

Something was strange though; he'd sold his old red Ford and bought his brother's new white one. But, no, it sounded just like the red one.

I jumped out of bed to make sure the front door was locked. Although part of me wanted to see him, I didn't want to let this man back into my life. I had come so far over the past six months; I couldn't! Quickly returning to bed, I buried my head under the sheets with a hand in my mouth to stop the shuddering.

I heard the front door open. I knew I had just locked it! This was alarming!

The Boy walked into my room and got into his usual side of the bed. I felt the doona [duvet] go back as he slipped in beside me. I asked what he was doing and told him that I couldn't go through all the hurt again.

He begged me to help him. Something had happened and only I could help. I told him this was one time I couldn't help him—he was dead. He didn't believe me. He pleaded. Yet, how could he be dead? He was right there with me, just like the old times. We lay together until dawn, never expecting the new day would herald the call I was about to hear. That call ended my life as I knew it. Nothing would ever be the same again.

The next morning I awoke and was sitting up in bed writing in my journal about what I thought was a very bad dream. The phone rang. It was my friend Mandy. She was sorry, but my man was dead. Although I am a clairvoyant and know that death is not the end, I was devastated beyond words. My heart was shattered into a million shards.

When I was later told the details of his death, I was surprised to hear that The Boy died around 12:15 a.m.—the same time he had come to me. So it was him . . . I didn't make it up after all.

His passing has taught me that whether dead or alive, there's no real division between us. We're never alone. We have the spirits' love. They have ours. If it's done with an open heart, then the Universe is one magical place. Death is nothing; our loved ones have only slipped into the next room.

The Boy has given me many validations and messages of love. To name a few I have: found numerous white feathers around, many falling from the sky like soft, fluffy snow drops; heard songs of significance to him on the radio at the most opportune times, have smelled his cigarettes, and have often felt his side of my bed go down. But his greatest gift to me was helping me to understand that when my time comes, I'll have no more fear. I told my friends that if I pass tomorrow, don't be sad. No tears, just celebrations!

About Jen-Irishu

Jen is an author, spiritual counselor, and speaker. She began her spiritual awakening a short time before the passing of her "other wing," known as The Boy. Although she always had the gift of "knowing," she never truly understood it until later in life when The Boy returned to her to share a glimpse of his life on the Other Side and to prove that love has no end. Jen shares their true, unforgettable story in her book, *Messages of Love: My Spiritual Awakening*.

Her children's books, *The Angel in my Dreams* and *The Adventures of Angela and Eli* were given to her in her dream state. She is also the publisher of an e-magazine called *Spirit Whispers*. For more information, please visit her Web site at www.jen-irishu.com.

A Greeting in a Candle Flame

Janice E. Burpee
Maine
Janeeka2@aol.com

During a recent time of meditation and prayer, I gathered pictures of my parents, my best friend, my grandmother, and other loved ones who had passed.

I lit a candle in front of their pictures and began my meditation by giving thanks for all the wonderful people in my life and even slipped in a request for guidance for some troubling things that were occurring. I then focused on my pictures and sent feelings of love to all those who had passed on. I thanked everyone for what they'd meant to me and asked them to be a continual guidance in my life.

Towards the end of my session I was particularly missing my mother. I gazed into her picture and said (telepathically), "Ma, could you give me a sign? I'm ready. I'm not scared. I miss you and would be delighted to hear from you."

Suddenly, the flame on the candle shot high in the air. It started to dance from left to right, really wildly. I looked around the room to see if a window was open or a draft was coming from somewhere. Nothing. My heart started to beat faster. I said, "Ma, is this you? If it is, do something different, right now."

The flame stopped. It stood eerily still. It no longer moved or danced or went high in the air. I had such a great feeling at this point. It was like a warm coating of love slid over my head down to my toes. I felt as though her spirit was hugging me. The hair stood up on my arms, and it brought tears to my eyes. I feel so blessed to have had such a wondrous experience.

A Kiss of Love

Lois Brunet
Canada

Although I have always been strong in my faith and prayers, I must admit I wasn't sure about our ability to communicate with deceased loved ones. Something happened, however, that forever changed my mind. Now, my belief in afterlife communication is as strong as my faith.

My girlfriend Gloria and her sister Joyce and I were sitting in a hospital room watching her husband Allan dying from cancer. We prayed at his bedside. The three of us sat there reminiscing and talking about the good times we had shared when suddenly Gloria started crying and bowed her head saying, "I will never receive anymore kisses from him again."

My heart ached for her. Gloria and Allan had had such a wonderful life together. You could honestly say that their marriage had been a gift from heaven.

Allan had been in a coma for three days, and we were waiting for him to take his last breath. Early the next morning, we all couldn't believe our ears when we heard him whisper, "Get me up." Although we were quite startled, we did as he requested.

Gloria gently held his hand and asked if he knew who she was. He looked at her and whispered, "Gloria Brooks." He then turned very slowly, kissed her, and lay back down once again unconscious.

I walked over to the window as I didn't want Gloria to see the tears running down my face. I knew Allan heard her comment about never receiving anymore kisses. He passed away a few hours later.

The next day I was at church when I clearly heard Al ask me to tell his beloved Gloria that that was his last kiss goodbye. I truly believe that after his goodbye kiss, his spirit was leaving his body to be with the Lord.

Allan has communicated with me several times since he passed. Another day when I was again in church, he told me to tell his wife that she was a very stubborn person. He assured me that once I told Gloria this, she would know it was he giving her signs.

Well, it's a little weird having to tell your best friend that she's a very stubborn person, but I knew that I had to do it. I approached her laughing as I said it, "Just remember, what I am about to say is from Al not from me. Al said you were a stubborn person." You can just imagine my delight when she began to laugh telling me that her husband said that to her all the time. She now has no doubt that her beloved husband had been sending her heavenly signs.

I will cherish these "visits from heaven" for the rest of my life. God has not only shown me that there is life after death, but He has made me believe that death is a beautiful experience.

Get Rita to Say the Word Duck

Reverend Rita S. Berkowitz
Massachusetts
www.thespiritartist.com

We have all lost loved ones and the pain is real, but when we are able to connect with them, an amazing healing happens. One morning during a phone reading while working with Sally, a client from Pennsylvania, the image of a young man came through. He showed himself as a very relaxed dresser—the outdoors type. I proceeded to do a color drawing. As I was sketching and describing the young man, Sally told me that it was her son. About a week later after receiving my drawing, she sent me a copy of the art work and a photo of her son. There was no question; it was her son Danny.

About a year later, Sally called again and set up another session. I didn't remember her or the drawing that she was so thrilled with. I thought she was a client that I had read before but could not remember any details of the session.

At the end of the reading, after asking her if she had any questions,

Sally asked if I could connect with Danny. I asked, "Who is Danny?" She replied, "My son. He is on your Web site." I had a vague recollection of his image, although there were a few young men on the site then. But I described him again and then said, "I know this may sound strange, but he is coming out of the water shaking himself off like a duck." Sally laughed and cried. She told me that earlier that day she sat on her porch and prayed, saying, "Danny, if you are really here during the reading, get Rita to say the word 'duck.'"

I tell this story whenever I am teaching students so they will know that no matter how strange it may sound, they should give out the information they are receiving. We, as mediums, never know how important a single fact can be to validate the presence of a deceased loved one.

During another memorable experience, I had gone to New Bedford, Massachusetts to do a group of readings and drawings when an unusual thing happened. Hilda had booked an appointment for her sister Deborah, who, at the last minute, had decided to cancel. Knowing how difficult it was to get an appointment, Hilda decided to send her husband Arthur instead.

Arthur came into the room with a frightened look on his face, not knowing what to expect. I began to draw an elderly woman with silver white hair, wearing a quite conservative dress. After looking at the drawing, Arthur had no idea who it was. Afterwards, he politely took the drawing home where his wife and mother-in-law were waiting. Upon viewing the drawing, Hilda asked, "Ma, who does this look like?" Her mother was astonished and took a photo out of her wallet. It was Hilda's grandmother, and even the dress matched.

A few weeks later, Hilda's sister Deborah called and said, "You know that should be my drawing. I was supposed to have that appointment, and I was her favorite. She came there for me." I could only laugh.

About Reverend Rita Straus Berkowitz

Rita has impressed audiences worldwide by drawing portraits of loves ones from the Other Side. An ordained minister in the Spiritualist Church of Quincy, Massachusetts, she is a certified medium with a Master of Science in Psychological Counseling.

The author of *Empowering Your Life with Angels* and co-author of *The Complete Idiot's Guide to Communicating with Spirits*, she has been a guest on numerous radio and television programs. For more information, please visit www.thespiritartist.com.

The White Healing Doves

Barbara M. Veillette
Florida

In 1941, when I was eleven-years-old, I had a strep throat infection. Penicillin had not yet been discovered. I heard the doctor talking about me outside my bedroom. He was telling my mother that I was too sick to be moved to a hospital, as my temperature was extremely high. That tonight would decide what would happen. I remember thinking, "I don't feel that hot."

In the middle of the night, my deceased grandmother floated in from the bay window. Her arms were outstretched. On each arm and on the top of her head were perched three white doves. She floated over to my bedside, put her hand on my forehead, and said, "You will be alright now." I was scared. This was the grandmother who didn't like me when she was alive! I did start improving the next day. The next morning my fever broke, and I did, in fact, start to improve. I told my mother about the "visit." She hugged me and started to cry and said that Nana was my guardian angel.

In 1961 I received another "visit" from the Other Side, only this time it was my mother. A week after her funeral, I walked into my bedroom to see my mother standing there, dressed in a long white dress and smiling. She glowed with light. I was both shocked and scared and asked her to leave and not come back again as I was so frightened.

My brother Tom later asked me how I could have said such a thing to our mother. But I was terrified because I was fully AWAKE.

Years later a medium at my church told me a woman in a long white dress was standing by me smiling. She was very happy at what I had done the week before. (I had had my eighteen-year-old grandson christened on Christmas Eve and believe that that is what she was referring to.) The medium went on to tell me that she was holding a single red rose in her hand and was reaching it out to me.

When I told my brother Charlie, he replied, "Give me the rose, it's MINE." I asked, "HUH?" He then told me something I never knew. He was fifteen when our mother died and was the last one to see her in the casket. As they were closing the casket, he slipped a single red rose into her hand! He said one neighbor saw him do it and burst into tears.

The next day as I was driving, I asked my mother, "Mother, how can I give Charlie your rose?" Just then, on the radio, Bette Midler sang, "The Rose." Yikes! I downloaded the song from iTunes and sent it to him on a CD. I think this was her way of giving my brother his rose back.

"Spookyman"

Sheran Wickstrom
Canada
swickstrom@shaw.ca

My twenty–four–year–old son Todd was tragically taken from us on March 13, 1998 in a car accident. Todd was a fun–loving young man, played bass guitar in a band, and was on the verge of a music career when all too soon he was gone.

I have two children; my daughter Janet is married with three girls. The youngest of the girls at the time of Todd's death was Molly who, at twenty–one–months–old, didn't remember her Uncle Todd.

On the eve of the first anniversary of Todd's death, I was speaking with my daughter on the phone, arranging our gathering at the cemetery the next day. My son–in–law had taken the other two girls out for the evening, and Janet was alone with Molly at home. While we were speaking, Molly was acting up something terrible, crying and whining and being a very tired little two–and–a–half–year–old. I suggested to my daughter that we hang up so that she could put Molly to bed.

Suddenly my daughter became very frightened because Molly started talking about "Spookyman." She kept pointing and repeatedly said, "Oh, Spookyman. Oh, Spookyman." My daughter thought there was someone in the house. I stayed on the phone while she checked the entry, but, of course, no one was there. Then Janet surprised me when she suddenly said, "Oh, Mom, it's so peaceful here." I couldn't believe what I was hearing.

Molly, then, climbed onto my daughter's lap and began playing a game that Todd had always played with the older girls—she would giggle and wiggle her fingers and clutch her tummy and giggle some more. Todd always used to say, "I'm going to get you, little kid" and wiggle his fingers at their tummies. How could Molly have known this? She didn't even remember Todd.

Suddenly Janet said, "Oh, my God, Mom! Todd is here . . . I just know it's him." Molly was no longer agitated. She was playing the game that Todd had played with her a year ago before he died. As fast as it began, it was over. Molly got off her mom's lap and said, "Spookyman gone now." Janet asked if it was Uncle Todd, and she adamantly said, "No, it Spookyman." Janet and I were both crying at this time. In our hearts, we knew he had come to visit.

The next day Molly was dancing around the house and suddenly walked over to a picture of Todd and said to her mom, "He Spookyman. He nice. He play with me." She told us what we knew. Todd had given us one of our many gifts on the first year of his passing.

On the evening before the second anniversary of Todd's death, my daughter and her family came to our home. When Molly walked in the door, she had her hand behind her back.

No one had noticed that when they left home, she had brought a gift with her. She had it in her pocket. It was a ceramic figure of a little girl kneeling at a cross. My daughter later reminded me that I had given the girls each one a year earlier. I didn't remember it at all . . . grief does that to you.

I thanked Molly for the gift and noticed it was bound with scotch tape—the wrappings of a child. I sat it on the kitchen cupboard and promised to open it, but in the confusion of the evening, I totally forgot.

The next day I saw it sitting there. As I began to unwrap it, my phone rang. It was my friend Helen Fisher who was calling me because she knew that this was a difficult day to get through. It was the anniversary of the loss of my child. She had lost her daughter Erin in 1989, and we had that horrible common bond. I was telling her what I was doing, all the while unwrapping my granddaughter's precious gift. From within the confines of the scotch tape there were three pennies.

As I looked at the pennies, I nearly fell over. Now you must realize I am speaking to Helen on the phone while this is happening. The first penny had the year 1998, the year of Todd's passing. The next penny had the year 1973, the year Todd was born . . . before I could examine the last penny . . . Helen said, "Oh, Sheran, do you think it is 1989, Erin's year of passing?" Well, it was exactly that year 1989. Helen and I were both crying and laughing and crying and laughing because in that moment through the gift of a little child who would not know these years, she showed both Helen and me what we always knew and felt. Our children, both now in Heaven together, brought their mothers together to live and survive in this world without them. Love never dies and neither do we.

Timmy's Gift

Mark E. Miller
Maryland
mark.e.miller@hotmail.com
www.timmysgift.org

This is the story of my son Timothy and the gift that he gave to me and the whole world. This is also the tale of how a child's love can span all dimensions of space, time, and beyond if we choose to keep an open mind and an open heart.

Timmy was born into my very normal and average world on a blustery March day in 1998. He emerged from the womb as a happy, healthy baby eager to get started on this grand adventure we call "life." His big sister, his mother, and I, his proud father, lovingly bundled Timmy up and drove him home from the hospital to our comfortable suburban home and our dog Buddy to begin our new life together.

Our first year together was a wonderful time, watching my son grow from a tiny, helpless infant to an assertive and independent toddler. Timmy sported an infectious smile and a gentle demeanor that quickly endeared him to anyone in his presence. He was a healthy, happy, blossoming young man who played hard, explored his environment with a voracious curiosity, and utilized the daylight hours fully and completely. In retrospect, it now seems as though he knew that his time with us was limited as he would consistently awaken the entire household at the crack of dawn, fervently announcing the start of a new day.

During the short time that Timmy was with us, I was blessed with the opportunity to witness my children grow not only in physical stature but also in their love for each other. Emily was three years older than Timmy so, naturally, she cherished the opportunity to serve in the role of "big sister." It quickly became obvious that Timmy and Emily shared a strong connection in ways that are difficult to describe in earthly terms. They developed a special language as evidenced by her ability to make him laugh a big, hearty, guttural laugh in a way that could not be duplicated by anyone. And she would tolerate his wily antics and occasional hairpulling with a patience and understanding beyond her years. They spent many hours together every day, sharing the intimate innocence and the unconditional love of sibling soul mates.

Shortly after Timmy's first and only birthday party, he began to show worrisome signs of becoming withdrawn, submissive, and lethargic. The doctor said that there was no need for concern and that there was nothing to worry about because he was probably just coming down with some sort of standard childhood illness. Over the course of the next week, these symptoms became more and more pronounced. I soon developed a burning and undeniable suspicion that something drastic was happening inside of his body, but the doctors could find no evidence of this.

Then, on a Monday morning at work which I'll not soon forget, I suddenly felt extremely nervous and agitated and almost nauseous. I instinctively drove home to find out that Timmy's appointment that morning with the pediatrician had revealed some neurological damage and that he needed to be transported to Children's Hospital in Philadelphia immediately. Thus began Timmy's slow deterioration from unbounded, youthful vitality to a heart-wrenching comatose state within a matter of days. Countless tests and body scans and needle pricks later, all that remained was the lifeless shell of my son, lying motionless in his hospital bed with only a maze of tubes and assortment of machines keeping him alive. For some unknown reason, his brain had swelled, and the doctors were powerless to stop its relentless stranglehold on my son. The swelling within Timmy's skull had become so intense that his brain soon became damaged beyond repair.

To watch your child die in his mother's arms is an experience that goes beyond words. In many respects, I was fortunate to have had some time to prepare myself emotionally for the inevitable, and I was blessed with the opportunity to say goodbye. But nothing could fully prepare or shield my heart from the almost surreal scene that was unfolding before my eyes. The sound of his final breath and the simultaneous relaxation of his tortured body were the mortal signals that his spirit had finally broken free of its earthly shackles. He was now in the caring arms of beautiful angels.

My heart lay shattered and withered, as if crushed beneath the weight of unbearable agony. My ordinary life had suddenly become inexorably extraordinary. A part of me died along with Timmy that night, and, along with our family and friends, we were suddenly thrust face-to-face with the dark emotions of guilt, grief, and despair. I thought that we had lost Timmy forever, but as many of us soon discovered, Timmy had patiently begun the arduous task of opening our eyes to the possibility that love could transcend the seemingly insurmountable barriers of death.

The first sign that Timmy was still with us came from my brother and his family who live a day's drive away in western Pennsylvania. My brother has three children, Timmy's cousins, whose ages at the time were five-, three-, and one-year-old. The night that Timmy passed on, the children reported seeing "lights" dancing on the walls and around the windows of their dark bedrooms. Interestingly enough, Timmy's cousins had no idea that he had died that evening as news of his passing did not arrive at their house until the next day.

When Emily woke up the next morning, she nonchalantly reported that she saw Timmy flying outside her window during the night. Her tone implied that this was to be expected and that we should not be surprised! Needless to say, the experiences of Emily and her cousins were met with a certain level of skepticism and confusion. What in the world was going on here? Emily continued to see Timmy in her room flying around at times in the days and weeks immediately following his passing. At the time, I did not know what to make of this.

Then, about one month after Timmy's passing, I experienced the most vivid, colorful, and lifelike dream that I had ever experienced. The dream was short, yet profound. Timmy was sitting on the floor by the bed with the most heartwarming smile imprinted upon his face. An intense yet pure white light surrounded Timmy and lit the room with a soft glow. He did not say a word, but I could feel the warmth and love and serenity emanating from his being. It was a feeling I shall never forget. I awoke with a jolt, almost breathless, in a state of disbelief because the dream had seemed so real. I later learned that this type of dream is a "visitation" where our deceased loved ones come to us while we are in the dream state. These dreams are somehow very different from the normal and usual dreams. In my heart, I was sure that Timmy was trying to tell me that he was fine and still with us, even though I could no longer physically touch and hold him.

Now my curiosity had definitely been aroused. From my research on the Internet I had learned that psychic mediums can somehow communicate with our loved ones who have passed on. A multitude of very gifted mediums have been able to bring back messages from our deceased loved ones with evidence that cannot be explained via earthly terms. So I decided to find a reputable medium with an outstanding reputation to see if I could receive some sort of communication from Timmy.

As it turns out, I was fortunate to experience a number of compelling sessions with six outstanding mediums—some of them world-renowned—over the next few years. They were able to relate heartwarming messages from not only Timmy but also an entire group of deceased relatives—many of whom I had never met in person. Interestingly enough, the messages from Timmy were consistent from medium to medium:

*   The mediums say that he appears older to them, like a "wise" young person.
*   Timmy stresses that I should not feel guilty as it was not my fault that he died.

*   Most of the mediums were able to accurately describe his physical symptoms leading up to his death.
*   Timmy almost always comes at the end of a reading, waiting patiently for his turn to communicate.
*   The mediums say that one of the many reasons that Timmy came here was to open my heart and he was meant to be here for only a short time.

One medium, in particular, told me that Timmy likes to leave signs in photographs. Initially, I had no idea what this meant. But then I started to analyze recent family photographs and I noticed a number of "orbs" surrounding both Emily and me in three photographs, in particular. Orbs look almost like swirling soap bubbles, and they are believed to be a manifestation of spiritual energy. Large, prominent orbs appeared in front of Emily, [see inset] and smaller orbs could be identified above my head. So now, when an orb appears in a picture, I tell Emily that Timmy is hanging out with us. She agrees wholeheartedly!

Timmy also likes to play with numbers, and his favorite number is obviously "3." Timmy was born on 3/3 and died on 3/31. Timmy's dog Buddy was also born on 3/3, three years before Emily was born, and she was born three years before Timmy. In the months following Timmy's passing, I would frequently wake up exactly at 3:33 a.m. To this day, I occasionally wake up at that same time, and I know that Timmy is around. During one memorable reading, in particular, Timmy showed the medium the number "6." Later, I realized that the date of that reading was exactly 6 years, 6 months, and 6 days since his death!

Many people who lose a loved one will often begin to find coins in unusual places. Timmy likes to occasionally send me pennies, especially 1998 pennies (the year of his birth). Recently, in early March, I moved into a new residence. On March 3rd (Timmy's birthday), I noticed a penny lying on the concrete patio that was definitely not there when I moved in. In my heart, I knew it was a 1998 penny. I picked up the penny, and I felt a warm, comforting wave of energy wash through me when I read the date—1998!

But the story gets even more interesting. I vowed to keep that penny as a special keepsake, so I stored it in a safe place. Days later, it was gone. I could not find it anywhere. About one week later, as I was cleaning out my car, I noticed a penny tucked away in one of the many crevices. It was the same 1998 penny! But, wait, there's more—four weeks later on March 30th (one day before the anniversary of his death in 1999), I walked into the living room and noticed a penny lying in the middle of the room on the carpet. You can probably guess the date on the penny. Yes, it was a penny minted in 1999!

Our loved ones, who have passed on, like to send us "messages" with the help of birds as I discovered later in my research. The summer after Timmy died, I was hiking along a scenic trail in upper New York State. I can clearly recall just how dejected and heartbroken I felt knowing that Timmy would now be riding proudly in his carrier upon my back, occasionally tugging at my hair had he not died. The trail soon passed by an old cemetery out in the middle of nowhere. Suddenly, a small bird flew past me and landed on a headstone almost within my reach. The bird looked directly at me and began chirping and chattering loudly in what seemed like an urgent, almost scolding, tone. I was quickly jolted out of my grief, and I laughed to myself because, at some deeper level, I knew that Timmy was telling me to snap out of it and enjoy all that life has to offer while we are still here.

In yet another unusual set of circumstances, the neighbors across the street moved away not long after Timmy died. When the new neighbors moved in, I was shocked (but not too surprised) to learn that the names of the father and son were Timothy and Timothy, Jr.! After you experience a number of interesting coincidences like this, you soon begin to realize that there is more going on "behind the scenes" than we can know. And when you hear enough of these stories and experience them for yourself, then the evidence of life beyond life becomes insurmountable.

In retrospect, there was definitely something very unusual about Timmy—it was almost as if I was in the presence of an older, wiser being housed in the body of a toddler. It is difficult to describe this phenomenon with mere words, but many parents and family members who have lost children have experienced these same feelings, and many members of my extended family have made similar comments regarding Timmy. In some cases, in the days or weeks leading up to a young child's death, the child will express, in no uncertain terms, that he is going to die soon. Although Timmy was not old enough to express himself in words, I believe that he was preparing me for the tragic circumstances that were about to unfold by reaching out to his family in a subtle, yet powerful way which must be personally experienced in order to be truly understood.

Other members of my extended family have also reported unusual occurrences, almost too numerous to recount here, which they attribute to Timmy. Nearly ten years later, Emily still sees Timmy occasionally or hears his voice or feels his presence. Through the summation of all these experiences, I have learned that Timmy is still with us—not in a form that we can see or touch, but in a form that can only be felt with the heart. Ask your loved ones who have passed for signs—some signs may be obvious but most are subtle, so please keep an open mind and an open heart to the limitless possibilities. Only then will you be able to sense more clearly an unconditional and divine love that often seems so far removed from this frantic, fast-paced world of ours. This realization and knowing is Timmy's gift to me and to the world.

I Can't Go

Santina
New Jersey

My Uncle Angelo was well liked and was always there when you needed him the most. It was emotionally draining for me and my family when he lay in a hospital bed dying from colon cancer. Knowing there was nothing more we could do for him, we waited and prayed.

It was a Monday morning when my father and I went to the hospital to visit him. Although he was in a comatose state, we were told by hospice that he could still hear us and we were encouraged to talk to him.

Upon seeing my uncle in such a dire state, I could not approach the bed and asked my aunt to let him know we were there. When she told my Uncle Angelo that my father and I were there to see him, he made a desperate moaning sound as though he wanted to say something. So although he could no longer speak, I knew he was still aware of his surroundings.

The next night I had a dream. In it, my Uncle Angelo and his late wife, who died twelve years earlier, were sitting at my kitchen table, smiling happily. I walked in surprised to see them both and told them apologetically that my kitchen floor was dirty. I then picked up a broom and started sweeping.

I remember waking up and noticing that it was around 4:00 a.m.

The following night I couldn't sleep once more and was surprised when I looked at the clock and it read 4:00 a.m. At some point I fell back to sleep, only to see my Uncle Angelo appear to me yet again in my dreams. Only this time he did not come with his wife; he was alone, standing next to this massive white light saying, "I can't go."

I tried to reassure him, telling him that everything would be fine and that he needed to go to the Light. Suddenly, I felt like I was being pushed into the beautiful bright Light. I felt myself going forward, but I didn't want to go. I told my uncle that I wasn't ready to go, but he did need to go.

I then began yelling for help calling my mother, "Mom! Mom! Mom!"

That Thursday morning I went to my parents' house and told my mother that Uncle Angelo was going to die on that day. My mother looked at me perplexed and wanted to know how I knew.

I told her about his "visit" to me the night before and said I knew it meant that he was already in heaven. His body may have still been here, but his spirit had already left him. A short time later we got a phone call telling us that my uncle had passed.

Looking back I'm sure my uncle couldn't go into the Light until he reassured his family one last time. He was always here for us while on earth. Now the only difference is that he is watching over all of us from above.

A Text Message from Heaven

Elly Vahey
Pennsylvania

My family and I have dealt with a number of deaths throughout the years—three uncles, two grandfathers, a grandmother, and an aunt all passing before I had even become twenty-years-old. Death itself wasn't new to me. What was new was the feeling of dire despair that came with losing the man that I had planned to marry.

I really felt as though I was losing my mind. I could not take a deep breath; it was almost like I was afraid to deal with the reality of the situation after the exhale. But with time and great amounts of support from my family and friends, I learned to smile more often than cry when thinking about my fiancé, Gerald August Cooper.

His death brought me unanswered questions and worries, and I started questioning my idea of us as a whole. I needed to know if he had died quickly or if he had been in pain. I wanted desperately to know if he had felt what we shared as deeply as I did, and as selfish as it sounds, I wanted to know if he still thought about me in heaven.

Gerald had passed away in June 2005 after an ATV accident in the hills of West Virginia while visiting family. I had never seen that area or its beauty until going to his deathbed to be by his side one last time.

After the funeral ended and the flowers all dried up, I went home to Erie, Pennsylvania where my family and friends were waiting to see me through this difficult time. Much to my appreciation, they would hardly leave my side.

Some months went by, and I met a guy in town who looked a lot like Gerald. Gerald had known of this guy who resembled him, and we had talked and joked about their similarities before he passed. At the time I was moved by very little things that seemed to be similar between the two. On our first trip to a restaurant, we were seated in the same booth that Gerald and I had been seated before his death, and now just like Gerald, this man was giving me tips on how I should've shaken the salt right into the salsa as opposed to on the chips.

He would also say some things just as Gerald had—not big things, just normal conversational things, and I would translate them into something much more meaningful in my mind. Whereas Gerald and I had a lot in common, such as music and the fact that both of us played in bands, this man did not even come close to being my type. We really had nothing in common, but the city we lived in. However, at the time, I thought that God had intentionally sent him into my life, almost like an angel, to help me smile again because of his resemblance to Gerald.

The new man moved right into my life like a train—fast and abrupt. After just a few months, I found myself in the midst of a full-blown abusive relationship, and I truly was becoming the stereotypical battered woman. You may wonder how one would let herself get into a situation like this; it just seemed to happen overnight. It was as though after Gerald passed, I went to sleep, only to awaken in the midst of a terrible dream. Nothing seemed right. Then I found out I was pregnant with twins.

My entire life I had dreamed of the day that I would become a mother. Gerald and I had talked to no end about having children. His mother, the doctors, and I even talked about it when he was on his deathbed; I couldn't believe that I now was going to have children by someone else. I still rejoiced in the news, calling it the biggest blessing in my life!

The months slowly passed; all the while the abuse continued in my home. I was given a black eye two days before my baby shower, at which time I was six months pregnant. I would sit in the tub every night, rubbing my huge belly just praying that my unborn babies inside couldn't feel the stress their mother was under. At times I would try to convince myself that I was delusional and that things were wonderful, just to calm myself down.

On a sunny day in October 2006, I gave birth to twins Kateri and Tobias. I have never felt so blessed; their coming into this world was absolutely the best thing that could ever happen to me.

Eventually the babies' father finally left us. I was utterly relieved yet I couldn't shake my inner feeling of fear. One night the babies and I were sound asleep when their father showed up on my doorstep, ringing the doorbell incessantly while calling the house from his cell phone. I was petrified knowing that if I didn't open the door, he'd gladly break it down. I opened the door and what followed was a belligerent verbal assault. He had been upset about an argument that he had earlier that night at a bar. I stood there staring, nervous, and going through all of the motions, just waiting and watching his every move to brace myself for what might happen. The difference that night was that he only talked about what he was going to do, (break down the kitchen cabinets, etc.). But he never actually did anything. He just threatened that he wanted to. This was so unlike him that I even told my innermost circle of girlfriends about it the next day. I was shocked while I stood there watching him. It was as though there was a greater force holding him back.

The second anniversary of Gerald's death was creeping up, and two of my girlfriends Kristy and Jill wanted me to join them at a taping of show by a local celebrity spiritual medium, named Natalie Smith-Blakeslee, that was airing on our local cable access channel. It was the evening before his anniversary. I was still in my work clothes, had just finished feeding my babies dinner, and was not in the mood to leave my house. My friends picked me up, and just before leaving, on a whim I put Gerald's old bracelet on just to feel closer to him.

The show "Messages from the Light" turned out to be an unbelievable experience for me. Natalie told me everything I had desperately wanted to know and more.

She started by bringing through an aunt who wanted me to say hello to my mother. She then went into the fact that my grandmother, who had passed away when I was a year old, had been witnessing all the violence and didn't approve of the situation, but was glad that things were on an upswing. Natalie said that when looking at me, she saw a big "DV" which stood for domestic violence. I started to cry out of embarrassment and shock.

Natalie went on to ask me if there had been a time, somewhat recently, when the guy seemed to hold back from doing his normal, violent thing. She pulled her arm back to demonstrate him preparing to throw a punch. I immediately knew the exact time she spoke of as did my girlfriends who were there. She continued by telling me that it was my loved ones in heaven who were holding him back that night. I felt unbelievably grateful to think that they "had my back" from heaven. I couldn't believe it, and I was in awe, to say the very least.

Next Natalie mentioned the bracelet I had on and asked to whom it had belonged. I answered and she immediately said, "He's here." I asked her in disbelief, "I'm sorry, what did you say?" She said again, "He's here." At that point, I just lost it! I cried like a baby delighted to be in his presence even if I couldn't actually see him. I listened to what she had to say harder than I've ever listened to anything in my life. It's funny, though, even with that being said, I remember only the things that stood out the most for me, like the fact that he said to tell me he passed away quickly; he's seen me cry at night and watches over me; he does still think of me and love me, and he cuddles in bed with me. She also said that Gerald wanted me to pick up a musical instrument (his guitar still stands next to my bed), and he wasn't mad at me for having babies. I was just overjoyed and since then have felt a renewed sense of peace.

Ever since he died, there were things that happened which made me wonder if it had been Gerald trying to communicate with me. He had bought me a beautiful white gold necklace with a little diamond "E" charm. While he was in West Virginia, I threw a birthday party for my girlfriend Lisa. The next morning the necklace was missing; my friends and I suspected that it may have been stolen the night before. Later while I was in West Virginia for his funeral, Lisa had come to my house, scrubbed it from top to bottom, done laundry and gotten the house spic-and-span to try to make it all the more comfortable for me when I came home. A few days after I came home, we ordered some food. As I went to answer the door, I stepped on something and looked down to see what it was. Much to my surprise, it was the diamond "E" charm! I screamed to Lisa, who was also moved to tears, knowing that it had not been there before.

Moving ahead . . . Natalie told me to get in touch with a friend of hers Josie Varga, who was writing a book about evidential "visits from heaven." She thought that Josie would like to hear about my story. I wanted to call her but kept putting it off not wanting to stroll down memory lane. When I finally did call, Josie and I had a wonderful conversation. Josie answered something for me that I had wondered since Gerald's passing. She confirmed to me that our loved ones in heaven can hear our thoughts. That had been a question of mine for so long; I was glad someone had finally answered it. She assured me that our loved ones are, in fact, with us.

Josie was giving me some examples of stories that she wanted to include in her book and one of them had to do with a butterfly. She said that butterflies are often thought of as a symbol of our loved ones coming through to say hello. I listened, and as I did, I recalled having many odd instances with butterflies myself. When I first came home from West Virginia, I took some pictures to get developed. While looking through them, I found a very prominent butterfly in a picture.

Then, when I returned to work one month after his death, I found a real butterfly just sitting in front of my chair. None of my co-workers had any idea how it had gotten there. Although it was dead, I took the butterfly home and put it in front of a picture of Gerald's final resting place that I have on display. There were three other times when I would see a butterfly and say, "Hi, Gerald." All the while, I felt crazy for doing so. Each time the butterfly landed right on my hand which had never in my life happened before. Each time I would acknowledge Gerald, but as I said, I felt a little crazy for doing so.

I told Josie that I felt bad because I had some children visit over the summer and the butterfly that I had brought home from work ended up broken. She said some things that I will never forget. She told me that signs are presented to us when we truly need them, but most importantly when we open ourselves up to receiving them and pay attention enough to notice them as signs. She said, "If you really want another sign, all you have to do is ask for one." Now as she spoke that sentence, I thought to myself, "I probably don't really have to ask out loud because if what you said earlier is true, he should just already know!" However, in my normal way, I said jokingly to her, "Yea, I will definitely be asking him for one as soon as we get off this phone." I was talking to Josie on my house phone while my cell phone sat nearby.

As I spoke to Josie, my cell phone buzzed letting me know that I had received a text message. I picked up the cell phone to try to look at the text but couldn't because I was receiving a phone call on my cell as I tried to open the text. I missed the call but figured I'd get right back to the other call and text message in a minute. I thanked Josie for the great conversation and told her that I would, in fact, start writing this story for her to include in her book. What happened next was the biggest validation that I have ever received! After I hung up with Josie, I checked my text message inbox. My new text message was from my friend Chantel who had also been a big help to me after Gerald's passing. Chantel and I hadn't talked for a little while, and I found it odd that she would send me a text message at 10:30 at night.

I opened the first "layer" of the text message inbox, which lists the first portion of words that you will read when you open the text. It read, "<FWD><FWD><FWD>" leading me to believe that, like other texts, those "FWD's" would be the first things I would read when I opened up the message. When I opened up the text, however, those "FWD's" weren't there at all. The screen, on which the texts appear on my phone, is normally silver, but in this case it was white and the only thing that appeared, much to my surprise, was "G." This was Gerald's nickname; everyone called him "G Coop," to be exact. I was utterly dumbfounded but didn't want to get my hopes up just yet. I immediately picked up my house phone and called Chantel who assured me that she hadn't sent me a text message at all! "What?!" I told Chantel I'd call her back and immediately called Josie to tell her what had just happened. I wiped happy tears from my eyes and excitedly told her this exact story; we both got the chills.

To make it even more strange, the "backlight" on my cell phone is set to go off after sixty seconds. With that particular text message on the white background, the phone stayed lit up until the next morning when I started getting ready for work. I couldn't believe it! It was truly remarkable to me. It made me think that he wanted me to know he had stayed by my side all through the night.

Some of you may not believe this whole story, and that's okay. I know it really happened, and that's all that matters. I can't think of a greater gift that any of us here on this earth can receive from our deceased loved ones. I feel so humbled and grateful that someone up in heaven would love me enough to take time out of his heavenly schedule to make my heart smile. And to me there's nothing better for a grieving soul than a happy, smiling heart.

I'm Here to Get Mama

Cindy Bigham
South Carolina
csutton16@charter.net

My son Michael passed on February 9, 2002. Later that year on October 31, he came to me in a dream. In this dream he was pulling up to my paternal grandmother's house in a red car, and I said, "Michael, what are you doing here?" He looked at me and replied that he had come to get "Mama," but she wasn't ready yet. He then said that he would be back to get her when she was ready. He took a shower and left.

I have always kept a journal, so I wrote this down. A few weeks later, I was telling my dad about my dream. He looked at me with a strange look and said, "Call your grandmother and ask her about her dream." I called her and said, "I heard you had a dream about Michael. Will you tell me about it?" My grandmother then went on to tell me what had happened on Halloween. She said she knew it happened then because she remembered the kids coming to her house and that she was out of candy.

No sooner had she fallen asleep than she dreamed that Michael came driving up to her house in a red sports car. She said that he was wearing a grey sweater and khaki pants, the clothes we buried him in, (though she didn't get to go to his funeral and we had never discussed what he had on), and she related that he said, "Mama, are you ready yet?" She said "No, Michael. Just need to take care of a few things; then I'll be ready." He then replied, "OK, I'm going to take a shower." She said when Michael got out of the shower, he said, "Mama, I'm clean now, cleaner than I've ever been, washed clean." He hugged her and walked away. After she told me this, she said that she felt her time was near.

She also said that she would try to prove life after death to me and asked me to take a picture of her in her casket at the funeral. Well on New Year's Eve 2003, my dad had a feeling that my grandmother wasn't feeling well. He went to her house, and she couldn't even get out of bed. He called the ambulance, thinking she might have a cold or the flu. They got her to the hospital and found out she had lung cancer. Within two weeks she went into a coma. On February 25, the hospital let her come home, and hospice came to help us.

She was unconscious most of the time due to the drugs they had her on. On February 27, she woke up, looked around, smiled, and said, "Well, hey, Michael. I see you're here like you said you would be." She also said, "Hey, George, I have missed you for so long." (George was her husband and my grandfather who had died in 1987.) "Yes, I'm ready."

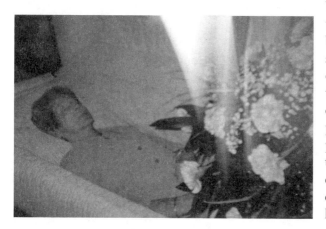

With that she took one deep breath, let out a sigh, and passed on. At her visitation I got a camera and took her picture. In the picture there is a tunnel of light coming from the ceiling into her heart area.

At the funeral I took a picture of her casket and my family members. In this picture is a bright white tube of light beaming down on her casket. I have so many experiences, but this has been the one that proved to the most people that at death we are met by our loved ones and that death is just an illusion. We do continue to live on.

Be Happy for Me

Joyce Keller
New Jersey
www.joycekeller.com
www.youtube.com/user/TheJoyceKellerShow

My mother had a very bad accident while she was in high school and spent the rest of her life unable to walk because she had a great deal of paralysis. She was wonderful about her handicap, never allowing her disability to interfere with our lifestyle. Her heavy, cumbersome leg brace and ever–present crutches were as natural a part of our lives as was the sun rising and setting each day.

When Mom was in her seventies, the sad day came when we lost our shining light. Yet two weeks after her passing, my mother came to me in a dream. She was very happy and filled with exuberance. She showed me her crutches and brace, threw them away, laughed, and said to me, "Ha, Ha, Ha! I won't need these anymore!" She then proceeded to show me how she could run at jackrabbit speed over hills and valleys. After this exhibition she just waved and disappeared after saying, "Be happy for me! Love to all!"

Years later my dad was in a deep coma. My husband Jack and I realized from his rattled breathing that he was getting ready to cross over. Jack and I were concerned that he may have been having some hesitation about leaving his body. As if done in stereo, we began whispering in his ears, "Dad, go in to the Light. Look for it, and go with it. Look for those who crossed before you, who are waiting to greet you and guide you. Go, don't look back, Dad. Just go."

He passed quietly and peacefully that night. A week later he came to me in a dream just like my mother, telling me that Jack and I were so helpful and supportive during his last hours on earth. He told me that he listened to us and did exactly as we suggested and that his transition from the physical had gone smoothly and beautifully.

. . . .

About Joyce Keller

Joyce is an internationally-known psychic, author, radio host, and media personality as well as the author of six bestselling books sold in many countries including England, Greece, Italy, and China. Joyce is a columnist for Lifetime Television and a certified hypnotherapist who has safely and successfully led thousands of people on the healing odyssey of going through their most significant past lives.

She is the author of several books including Simon & Schuster's *7 Steps to Heaven, How to Communicate with Those We've Loved and Lost.* An internationally respected intuitive counselor, healer, lecturer, and hypnotherapist, she is also the host of America's longest-running, live intuitive advice show, *The Joyce Keller Show.* She has been a popular, repeat guest with *Regis, Oprah, Sally Jessy Raphael, Geraldo, TruTV, Entertainment Tonight,* and most other national TV and radio shows. For more information, please visit www.joycekeller.com, www.JoyceKeller.blogspot.com or www.YouTube/user/TheJoyceKellerShow.

Signs from Our Son Billy

Guy Dusseault
Maine
www.oursonbilly.com
info@oursonbilly.com

Our story begins on June 27, 2004, a beautiful Sunday morning at around 10:00 a.m.; our lives changed forever. On that day we received the most devastating news any parent could ever receive—one of their children has died. Our son Billy was killed when the ATV he was riding at night hit a tree and killed him instantly.

For the next eight months, living was just trying to survive the next day. But other than trying to survive, I wanted more than anything to make contact with Billy. For me trying to make a connection with our son was a natural next step. There was no question about it. I had to find a way to connect with Billy. I had no idea how or if this was even possible, but somehow I was going to find a way, no matter what anybody said or thought about it. I prayed to God, read books about psychic mediums, and surfed the Web for information on how to connect with Billy on my own. I had no luck. All that changed when my wife Jo-Anne asked if I would like to visit a spirit messenger named Vicki Monroe. That day was February 16, 2005.

During our meeting with Vicki, we were able connect with our son for over an hour. Billy told us that he was happy, safe, and healthy. He did not want us to worry about him and told us to move ahead with our lives.

Billy went on to tell us about his ATV accident, including the time it occurred and why it happened. He explained that the accident was due to human error but assured us it had been his time to go "home."

Through Vicki he even told me things I had been thinking at the exact time I was thinking them. I was just amazed! For example, he told Vicki that I was questioning how the accident had happened that night. He was right! I was doing just that.

About two months after we met with Vicki, I noticed some of our photos had round white objects on them. I knew through my previous research that these objects in photographs were called orbs. I was intrigued and began doing more research on how the deceased use photographs as a means of communicating with the living.

Billy's physical body may have died on June 26, 2004, but his true form was subsequently released. Now in spirit, his memory is intact, and he is more alive today than he ever was before. With his job here on earth completed, it was time for him to go to heaven.

My son has let us know in several different ways that he is still with us—one is through photographs in the form of " orbs " or as I like to called them "sparks of light."

Often, I can see these sparks of light in the viewfinder as I am taking the photographs. Sometimes there are so

many that they look like all the stars from heaven are in front of my camera. In other photographs there are so many "orbs "that it looks like it's snowing.

On August 20, 2005, for instance, I knew it was going to be a special day. As I was taking pictures, I was astonished by the number of spirit orbs I was encountering in my shots. This was testament to me that there had to be a reason this was happening to me. I was convinced on that day that I wasn't just taking these pictures for myself. I knew then that there had to be a purpose.

As I would later find out through Vicki, my son explained that I was meant to take these pictures so that others would know that our deceased loved ones are always here with us in spirit.

It is important to note that I have taken thousands of photographs using different cameras. Most of them were taken using two different types of digital cameras: a Kodak 3.2 mega pixel camera and a Kodak 6.1 mega pixel camera. I have also taken many with inexpensive disposable cameras and with a 35 mm camera.

When I first started taking these photographs, I could not tell if anything would be in the shot until I would look into the viewfinder to check out the photo I had just taken. As time went on, I would have an idea if there were something in the photo because just as the flash would go off, I could see the sparks of light in the sky or indoors that appeared for a split second.

The only "orbs" that I can see before I take a picture are what I call the large brown ones. When I look through the viewfinder of my cam-

era, I can actually see them appear on my screen, and sometimes I can see many of them popping up on my viewfinder all at once. But if I try to look with my eyes, I can't see them.

Another type of photograph that I have been able to take has streaking lights.

These are lights which may be coming from indoor lights, street lights, our backyard light, our TV light, the moon, or anything that gives off light. These lights can streak in all directions and shapes.

One of the most intriguing types of light photographs

that we have are what I call "angel light." If you take a close look at many of these photos, especially the photos from our backyard light, you'll notice the form that the moving light takes is that of an angel. We have several photographs of these types of angels seemingly using the energy from our light to appear. They may either appear in a long or short streak of light shooting in a straight line or in curve streak of light. Others, who have seen these photographs, mention that the light looks like an angel.

Then we have taken pictures that show the light streaking from the moon. The scene is just amazing. The spiritual energy that appears from the light streaking from the moon can curve in many varieties of angles. Some of the light streaking from the moon seems to reach right to our home. We have a few photographs which show this phenomenon.

 One of our most exciting type of photos contains what some people call mist, smoky mist, or foggy mist, but the term I like to use is spirit essence. While the photos that I have taken are pretty remarkable, the best part is that I can see this spirit essence as the flash is going off. As soon as the flash goes off, I can see where the spirit or spirits are. They don't always show up on camera, but I can see them for a second or two when the flash goes off. It's even more beautiful seeing them with the naked eye than on camera. I can see their texture, color, and size more clearly.

The essence photo can take on any shape or size. My favorite is the heart–shaped photos. These heart shapes have appeared on photographs taken of the moon, street lights, and our Christmas tree lights.

I hadn't noticed the heart shapes in our photographs at first. It was only when I was going over some of the photographs taken on July 12, 2005 that I zoomed in on an orb and noticed that the street lights in the photo took on the shape of a heart. I was dumb–founded and began going through other shots. At this point I came across snaps which contained what showed a heart–shaped moon.

When I looked at a photo taken on October 21, I was stunned at how perfect the heart shape was of the moon. This is my favorite of all the photographs that I have taken over the past three years. People always ask me if I could see the heart–shaped moon with my own eyes when I snapped the pictures. I am sorry to say that I could not. I would (as I do with all of my photographs) just choose a spot at random and take a picture. For the moon shots I would just take a picture, look at the view screen, and see what type of picture came out. Of course, I always want a heart–shaped moon, but it doesn't happen every time. I wish it would; I really love those heart–shaped moon photos.

These heart–shaped images are priceless symbols of love and an important message that love is everything and that nothing else matters. Without a doubt these photos are meant to remind us all of what truly counts in this life and the next—love.

Over the past three years, we have collected about 30,000 spiritual photographs of different types and continue to enjoy taking them. However photographs are not the only way that we have received signs from Billy. I cannot recall the exact day, but it was very soon after Billy crossed over. We heard the doorbell ring sometime after midnight. I quickly got dressed and rushed to the door to see if someone was there, but there wasn't. It is easy to tell because our door has a large window and beside our door is a large window allowing us to see easily anyone approaching or leaving.

I then opened the door, went outside, and walked around in the misty rain. I looked around, but there was no one around. We live out in the countryside which makes it difficult for anyone to run up our driveway, ring our doorbell, and then run away; I think I would have noticed someone leaving our home. Also after looking around and seeing no one around, I walked back to our front door and noticed when I walked back onto our concrete porch that I had left a wet foot print. My footprint was the only one there. If someone had rung our doorbell, he, too, would have left a wet footprint.

It wasn't until we met with Vicki Monroe almost eight months later that Billy told us through Vicki he was the one who had rung our doorbell. He said that he wanted to let us know that he was around. I wished Billy could have picked an earlier time instead of ringing our doorbell after we had gone to sleep, but I guess he wanted to have a little fun with us.

Another way Billy got our attention would be by flicking our lights from time to time, which hadn't happened before his passing.

We also have a couple of motion detector lights outside of our home, and I noticed one day while I was sitting on a bench in our backyard that our outdoor sensor light would blink on and off with no movement of any kind in the area. Again, I never noticed anything like this before Billy's passing.

Vicki also confirmed that this was just Billy up to his usual antics letting us know that he is still with us. I am blessed with the knowledge that my son is still very much a part of our lives—I have thousands of photographs to prove it!

. . . .
About Guy Dusseault

Guy is the author of *Signs from Our Loved Ones* in which he documents the many incredible photographic "visits from heaven" he has received from Billy. For more information or to see more of these photos, please visit www.oursonbilly.com.

Angels Bowling in Heaven

Cherie, "D.J.'s" Mom
Michigan

I lost my twenty-six-year-old son D.J. on January 29, 2006. It was an accidental death due to a combination of alcohol and Xanax which he had been prescribed by his physician. I have had many validations that he is still with me and watching over me. I would like to share with you one of my dreams that I had on the six-month anniversary of his death. This dream was so vivid that I am sure he was letting me know that he is OK.

The night that I had this dream was a stormy one with lots of thunder and lightning. My husband and I were camping. In my dream D.J. and I were walking together down the streets of the town where I live. He was wearing a white sweatshirt, and he looked very healthy and glowing. I don't recall all that was said as we were walking, but I was so happy to see him that I asked where he had been. I then told him that I missed him so much and that it was great to see him. As I said, I don't recall all the particulars of our conversation, but it was like we were catching up on things. We had a very nice time. Then he said he had to go back home, and I asked him where he lived. He told me, "Mom, I live above the bowling alley."

We said our goodbyes just as we always used to with me saying, "Be careful. I love you." I woke up a short time later and felt very refreshed and peaceful. That dream was so vivid and real that I had no doubt D.J. had been with me. As my husband and I were drinking our coffee in the camper the next morning, I told him about my dream and how wonderful it was. I asked him if D.J. had ever lived above a bowling alley since D.J. had lived in various places while working for the railroad. My husband said not that he recalled. Then it hit me like a ton of bricks. I used to take my son camping when he was young. I was a single mom and the two of us would go in our little three-person tent and have such good times.

I remember one time in particular when it was a stormy night and we were both a little scared listening to the thunder and seeing the lightening. I told D.J. that the thunder was actually the angels bowling in heaven—the rumbling was the ball going down the lane and when the ball hit the pins, it caused the big boom. I truly believe that, when D.J. told me he lived above the bowling alley, he was telling me that he lived in heaven.

This dream was truly wonderful, and I felt very good about it. When I returned home that day, I called my mother who was also having a very difficult time grieving for my son, her grandson. I told her, "Mom, he is okay; he came to me in a dream, and he looked great. He is happy and fine." After talking to my mother, I went to visit my son's grave, because it was the six-month anniversary of his passing. I brought a special balloon for him. As soon as I got to his marker, I heard a train whistle blow. Because my son was a railroad conductor, I feel like D.J. is saying hello to me whenever I hear the sound of a train whistle.

As I stood there in front of his grave, I told him that I felt it was he who had visited me in my wonderful dream the night before. I then sat down on a little bench by his gravesite. Just as soon as I did this, a big beautiful white butterfly came right by me. I was very amazed as we don't usually see white butterflies where I live. I truly believe with all my heart and soul that it was D.J. validating my dream and saying, "Yes,

Mom, it was me who visited you last night, and I am okay." The white butterfly was also significant because he was wearing a white sweatshirt in my dream, and I don't ever recall him wearing a white sweatshirt while here on earth.

"Hi, Baby"

Cynthia D. Landrum
Indiana
kenthia50@yahoo.com

About six months before my mom passed, we were talking about God, life, and fear of the unknown. She was afraid that maybe her beliefs, which were more on the spiritual side as opposed to organized religion, weren't correct as she got closer to dying. Although she knew that only 10 percent of her heart was functioning, we never told her that she was given only a few months to live.

I told my mom, "Whichever one of us gets to the Other Side first, let's promise that we will somehow come back and let the other know that we are alright." She needed a new purse so I had gotten her one for Christmas. Although she never got a chance to carry it, she did put her things in it. A month later she passed away, and I took the purse home with me and left it in a rocking chair. At the time I wasn't able to really grieve because we were so busy taking care of the funeral arrangements and financial issues.

So one day I started having a crying jag and couldn't stop. Her purse fell from the chair. Cold chills covered my body as I remembered the conversation we had about letting the other one know, but I thought maybe it was on the edge of the chair which made it fall. I picked up the purse, put it back in the chair, and started talking to her, "If this is really you, please give me another sign." The purse fell again only this time the contents spilled out. This was the most comforting feeling I had felt since her passing. I knew she was letting me know that she was alright.

Sometime later my husband Kenny became ill and also passed. I never had a chance to say goodbye to him as he died before I could get back to the hospital. I felt so guilty about not being with him that day because I had left to take care of our personal things. I couldn't help but cry out every time I thought of him dying alone. But he would soon let me know that he was OK and still with me.

One night he came to me in a very real dream. I told him to squeeze my hands so that I would remember when I woke up and could prove to myself that his spirit was really there. Well, he did. He squeezed so tight that I felt myself waking up and could still feel the pressure. It was such a wonderful warm feeling that it is hard to put the experience into words.

Another time I was having a very emotional day and was talking on the phone when all of a sudden I noticed fingerprints on my television screen. I was watching the screen closely and all of a sudden, the letter "H" appeared. Then a few seconds later this was followed by an "I" and then a "B" and so on until it read "Hi, Baby." I was so shocked that I got off the phone and just stared. I couldn't believe my eyes, but there it was.

Kenny continued to give me additional signs like the scent of his cologne that I knew all too well. Then one morning my alarm clock sounded at 7:00 a.m. I hit the snooze button, planning to nod off again when all of a sudden I heard peeing sounds coming from the bathroom and for a moment I thought he had gotten up to use the bathroom. Just as this thought came and went, I realized I was not alone in bed. I got the biggest hug from behind and a sideway kiss. I felt my head turning to give Kenny a kiss like we always had done when saying good morning to each other. I was not afraid. It felt so good, and I awoke feeling like I normally would when he was alive.

I'm Happy Here

Carole Bellacera
Virginia
www.carolebellacera.com

The instant message flashed across my computer screen on the morning of December 14. I recognized my sister's screen name, and my stomach tensed. "I need to talk to you right NOW."

I knew the message had to do with Mom. She'd gone into the hospital the day before to have a shunt inserted into her brain so that chemotherapy drugs could be injected into the tissue that had been invaded by cancer cells. For six years Mom had fought a gallant battle with non-Hodgkin's lymphoma, but now it looked as if she was about to lose.

On Sunday night before she'd gone into the hospital for the surgery, we'd spent forty-five minutes on the phone. She'd sounded so positive and energetic—and not a bit nervous. "The doctor says they do this kind of procedure all the time," she said. "It's no big deal."

I wanted to believe that. And I guess I allowed her optimistic tone to waylay my fears. "No need to come out," she insisted. "I'll be home by

Christmas, and we'll do our family gift exchange."

All three of us girls were planning to spend Christmas with Mom and our stepfather in Kentucky. We would come from different points of the country: Kathy from Las Vegas, Sharon from Indiana, and I from northern Virginia. Mom was really looking forward to having all of us together for the first Christmas since 1991.

So, instead of talking about the surgery, Mom and I discussed what we'd make for Christmas dinner and who had whose name and what so-and-so needed. It was a wonderful conversation. I had no idea it would be the last real conversation I'd ever have with her.

The phone rang as soon as I signed off the Internet. Kathy was crying. "It's Mom. She's not doing so well."

At nine o'clock that night, I met Kathy at the Nashville airport. My flight had arrived two hours earlier than her flight from Las Vegas. Since Mom's illness had been diagnosed, Kathy had kept a used van at a friend's house in Nashville to drive back and forth from Mom's hometown in Kentucky. We didn't speak much during that hour's drive to the hospital in Bowling Green where Mom lay in an unresponsive state in ICU. I guess we were both in shock.

When I caught my first glimpse of her, I knew it was bad . . . very bad. She gave no sign that she knew we were there or that she knew anything at all. Sharon and her two teenage daughters had arrived before us, and they all looked tired and distressed. Apparently Sharon had driven the five hours from Indiana, crying the entire way.

The next day the three of us stayed with Mom—holding her hand, stroking her head, talking to her. As time passed, it became harder and harder to believe that she heard us, that she'd ever regain consciousness. It was like she was already gone.

On Wednesday afternoon, I stood at Mom's bedside. Kathy had left the room in tears, and Sharon was just as disheartened. We were giving up because Mom had apparently given up. Then the miracle happened. I was holding her hand, telling her that we were here, that we all loved her and wanted her to get better so that she could come home for Christmas. Suddenly I felt movement. She squeezed my hand! My heart jumped, and hope swelled in. She could hear us. She was still with us!

I stayed with her for another fifteen minutes, and she continued to hold my hand tightly. When I tried to disengage it to go tell everyone the good news, she didn't want to let go. But I had to share my new sense of hope with the rest of the family.

For the next three days, Mom continued to improve. Although she never woke up completely, she answered our questions and responded to our "I love you" with "I love you, too." She was aware of how many days she'd been in the hospital. She told us our stepfather's shoe size when we discussed buying him slippers for Christmas. She murmured that she was craving our grandmother's cinnamon rolls. We had the television tuned to CMT (Country Music Television), and when a Vince Gill video came on, Mom said, "That's a pretty song, but it's not on my new Vince Gill CD."

We were thrilled to hear her talk. It was proof that even though she looked so ill, she was still with us. The essence of mom was still there.

On Saturday afternoon at the end of the visiting hour, we kissed her and said we were going out to get some lunch. We told her we loved her.

"I love you, too," she said haltingly, her eyes closed.

It turned out to be the last words we'd ever hear from our mother. When we returned from lunch, the oncologist gravely told us that while we were gone, she'd suffered a stroke and that her prognosis was extremely poor.

Mom died that night about eleven o'clock. Kathy and I along with my Aunt Patty and Uncle Avery were at her side when she took her last breath. I was honored to be with her at that moment. I feel a great deal of peace knowing that the last words she heard in this world were words of love.

I believe—truly believe—that she is in a better place. I believe in God, and I believe in an afterlife. But it's human nature to want to be reassured. For almost two months after her death, I prayed for a sign that she was okay. But nothing happened. Yes, a miracle had occurred once. I think Mom was on her way out before we arrived in Kentucky. But our voices and our love brought her back for only a short time, but long enough to give us the peace of being able to say goodbye.

But now I wanted another miracle. I needed one desperately. During the daylight hours Mom was on my mind almost constantly. So why wasn't I dreaming about her? Or if I was, why couldn't I remember the dreams?

I began to read books about death and the afterlife. A common thread ran through them—the idea that spirits often communicate with loved ones through dreams. A friend of mine told me about a dream she'd had a month or so after her father died. He appeared very vividly, and she said, "Dad, it's good to see you." He smiled and replied, "It's good to be seen."

After reading a section in one book that told how "new" spirits want to communicate with their loved ones but often have trouble doing so and that the easiest way for them to reach us is through dreams, I prayed fervently that night for God to allow my mom to visit me in a dream and to please let me remember it clearly.

Within moments of falling asleep that night, Mom was there. She was dressed in red, her favorite color, and her hair was full and dark brown just as it had been in her younger days. She was smiling and radiant. As soon as I saw her, I began to cry. She came to me, and she took her hands and gently stroked my hair away from my face.

"Everything is fine," she said. "I'm happy here, and I want you to know that I'm always nearby."

We talked for a little while about mundane things. She asked about Kathy and Sharon and said she hoped they were not grieving too much. She mentioned my first novel that was coming out in the spring, (that I'd dedicated to her, *Diamond Lil*) and suggested I should invest my earnings from it.

Too soon she said she had to go. With one last touch of her hand on my cheek, she turned and walked away.

I woke up slowly but with a sense of euphoria. The alarm clock on my bedside table showed it was only 12:30. I'd been asleep for a little over an hour. I settled back in bed and smiled up at the ceiling.

"Thank you, God," I whispered. My heart felt as if it were about to burst from joy.

The next morning I awoke, still surrounded by a sense of quiet joy. I remembered the night's dream with vivid clarity. And I'm convinced it was so much more than a dream. It was a message from God.

That "visit" with my mother was the miracle I needed at the very moment I needed it most. But as it turned out, it would not be her only visit. I thought about her frequently on the first anniversary of her death, but I waited until the hour of her departure before I really gave in to my need to reflect upon how much I missed her.

A few minutes before 11:00—the exact time she left this world—I stepped out onto the deck of my house for a moment of solitude and meditation. It was perfectly still out there—not a breath of a breeze whispered through the quiet, overcast night.

"I know you're better off, Mom, but I still miss you so much," I whispered to the dark night. Tears streaked my face as I remembered holding her slim, beautiful hand as she slipped away.

Then it happened.

My Claddagh wind chime began to ring softly, and then one after another, the other chimes joined in until they were all ringing a beautiful song. I stood, transfixed, smiling through the tears blurring my eyes. She was here with me!

The wind chimes rang for about ninety seconds. Then just as suddenly as they started chiming, they stopped, and all was quiet again.

I waited a moment longer in the stillness. She was gone. But I felt fulfilled and joyous, knowing that she would always be near and that God had answered my prayers and had given me this very special moment with her.

"Goodnight, Mom," I whispered. "I love you."

I stepped inside and closed the door. For a moment I stood there listening for the sound of the wind chimes but not a single breath of air stirred the night. Smiling, I turned off the lights and left the room.

About Carole Bellacera

Carole is an award-winning novelist of several fiction books including *Border Crossings*; *East of the Sun, West of the Moon*; *Understudy,* and others. Her work has also appeared in magazines and various anthologies including *Chicken Soup for Couples*.

Her latest hobby (therapy) is making semi-precious stone jewelry which she sells at craft fairs and online at www.beautifuleveningbead.etsy.com. For more information, visit www.carolebellacera.com.

More Than
Mere Curiosity

Anthony Quinata
Colorado
www.anthonyquinata.com

I was once contacted by a scientist named Trish. She commented, "As a scientist fully aware of the nature of science, I know there are always going to be more questions than there are answers; there are areas that the laws of science just can't adequately explain, if at all. Yet this doesn't necessarily mean they don't exist or aren't real. Personally, I would like to explore this further to see what this (mediumship) is all about."

Trish's scientific mind was definitely on alert, but she had a bigger motivation than mere curiosity. She was also the mother of two young boys. "Science teaches and I believed that once someone dies, that's it. It's over. Now that I'm a mother, I can't bring myself to accept that."

I suggested that Trish come to a small group session I was going to be presenting rather than booking a private appointment. I felt that this was a good way for her to objectively observe what I do while someone else was in the "hot seat." She agreed but did not know what to expect.

When the night finally arrived and she had witnessed several readings, the look on Trish's face went from that of skepticism to bewilderment.

Finally it was her turn, and I looked at Trish and said, "You're here to reconnect with a female. Yes?" She looked at me astonished and could only nod her head, "Yes."

"I'm feeling an impact. My neck is hurting." I continued as I rubbed my neck, "The pain in my neck is so sharp it makes me want to wince. I want to say this person is in a car accident and either gets whiplash or a broken neck. I want to go with the broken neck. She passes from a broken neck. Yes?"

Trish nodded confirming that it was indeed from a broken neck as a tear rolled down her check.

"This woman is coming across as older than you," I continued smiling. "No offense, but she's kind of pushy, like she's used to having her way. I'm asking her for her name, but she's like, 'Just be quiet and tell her what I tell you.'"

Trish started laughing, "That definitely sounds like her."

I continued, "She's coming across as older than you and she makes me feel as though you two were close. Does this make sense?"

"Yes."

"She's making me feel like she's your sister, but I want to say she's more like a cousin."

"She was my cousin," Trish sniffled. "But we were more like sisters."

I kept getting more details. "She's telling me that she has two children, a boy and a girl, but that the girl is there with her in spirit. Do you understand this?"

"Yes," Trish replied as more tears came.

"The girl is older than her brother. Yes?"

"Yes."

"I'm feeling as though the girl passes young, but not young like in a miscarriage or abortion or infant. She passes as a young girl. Does this make sense to you?"

"Yes."

"Did you two go to Disneyland?"

"No."

"Huh? She's showing me Mickey Mouse. I thought your families went to Disneyland because I'm seeing Mickey Mouse. You must have gone to Sea World in Sand Diego with her then."

Trish confirmed that they did, in fact, go to Sea World but not Disneyland together.

"Okay, because I'm seeing Shamu, the killer whale. I saw Shamu when I was young and my family went to Sea World," I told her smiling at the memory.

"Why is she showing me Mickey Mouse?" I wondered out loud. Suddenly, I saw (psychically) a map of Florida. "Was your cousin vacationing in Florida when she passed?"

"Yes," Trish said stunned.

"Mickey Mouse shows up again," I went on. "I hear the sickening sound of metal crashing against metal, and my neck once again feels as though it's being whipped to my right." All of a sudden everything became clear to me. "Your cousin was vacationing in Disneyworld with her family when she died. She was in a car when it was hit by another car that ran a red light."

Trish nodded, her face hidden by the tissue she was clutching; her shoulders going up and down.

"Her daughter was in the car with her when it happens. But she doesn't pass away right away. Your cousin waited to cross her daughter over."

"She and her daughter were in the back seat when they were hit by another car," Trish offered. "It hit them right where my cousin was sitting. Her daughter didn't die right away. She died a few hours later."

"Was her daughter a ballerina?" I ask. "I see her wearing a tutu. She was taking ballet dancing lessons. Yes? She says she is dancing for Jesus now. Your cousin's husband is remarried."

"Yes."

"He has kids with his new wife," I continued.

"Yes."

"His wife is happy that he's remarried. She's happy her son has a new brother and sister."

"OH, MY GOD," she almost shouted now. "He does have a boy and a girl with his new wife!"

I felt their energy pulling away. "Please tell him and his son that you heard from them, and they send their love. She also sends her love to you. They're pulling away now."

The room was very quiet with the exception of tears as others in the room cried along with Trish. "Any questions before we end tonight?" I asked. "Trish?"

"That's just it," she said, "I have more questions now than I did before I came here!"

"Please know that this is their way of letting you know that they aren't really dead," I said in conclusion. "They haven't died, not really, and you and your loved ones won't either. If you walk away tonight understanding that, then I've done my part. God bless you all."

. . . .

About Anthony Quinata

Originally from Guam where it is considered disrespectful and immoral to talk to spirits, Anthony is an acclaimed medium and clairvoyant. He admits he had never planned on becoming a medium but says his calling came after a number of convincing incidents including the appearance of a deceased friend who told him to tell her family that she was alright.

Eventually he realized that he was meant to be an instrument to those trying to connect with their loved ones. For more information, please visit www.anthonyquinata.com.

The Mess on the Floor

Ann Albers
Arizona
www.VisionsOfHeaven.com

I am blessed with a strange career. I live with a foot in two worlds—one firmly upon the earth and the other side of me tuned into the heavens. You see the heavens are not far away. They are simply a different frequency. Just as television and radio waves pass through us on a daily basis, so do the signals from those in the heavenly vibrations.

Although I started adult life as an electrical engineer, God had His way with me, and I am now an angel communicator, medium, author, and spiritual instructor. I didn't ask for this career. It found me. Or more accurately, I prayed for my calling, and God answered. The subject of how I began to talk to the heavens takes up an entire book, but suffice it to say, I started doing "readings" and began to communicate with the dead. The first time I was aware of a verifiable spirit was with a beautiful young woman who sat in front of me asking the angels about the various details of her life. All of a sudden I was interrupted by a completely different feeling in my body and in the energy around me. I shut my eyes, got quiet, and felt to see who was there. An elderly woman appeared in my inner vision with graying hair, small curls, and a mischievous grin. She wanted to thank the young woman in front of me for taking such good care of her and for "sneaking her chocolate bonbons in the nursing home." As I dutifully reported her message, the young woman in my chair began to sob. She had loved and cared for her elderly friend, and no one on earth knew their little chocolate secret.

Perhaps the most awfully humorous confirmation I received was when a gentleman in spirit showed up to talk to his wife. "Tell her I'm sorry I left the mess on the floor," he chuckled and then showed me an image in my inner vision of him passed out on the floor after he died of a heart attack. I was mortified! I couldn't repeat this to his dear grieving wife who was sitting in front of me choking back tears.

"Say it," he commanded rather forcefully, still with that grin on his face. And so, since my policy is not to filter the words of spirit, I repeated his message. His wife started laughing and crying simultaneously, both so hard that I thought she would split down the middle. "He left EVERYTHING on the floor," she cried and laughed. "Everything. So it's not a surprise that after me nagging him his whole life to pick up his clothes, his final joke would be to leave himself on the floor." I laughed so hard with her that I nearly cried as well! He smiled in the other realms, happy to exchange his warped sense of humor with his beloved wife one more time.

"Tell her I'm still eating my pink grapefruit out of a china dish for breakfast every morning," one lady told her daughter, and the daughter confirmed that this was her mom's favorite breakfast. "Tell her even though I was forty-years-older, I still had a thing for her," a former boss told his younger friend who confirmed that they could never figure out why there was such an attraction between them. This job isn't just to serve others. It helps me in my own grief when friends and relatives pass away.

The deceased are not always calm and peaceful. One night I was in a large convenience store shopping for household items when the breath suddenly got knocked out of me as strongly as if someone had punched me in the stomach. I doubled over and looked around instinctively, but, of course, no living person had done this. "Wait until I get home and I'll talk to you," I snarled telepathically. "That hurt!"

I got home and immediately went into meditation, asking rather angrily, "Who are you and what do you want?" "I am SO mad at Louie," an older woman kept repeating. "What does that have to do with me?" I asked, surprised that I could hear a name. I'm not the best at names with either the living or the deceased. She just kept repeating her angry statement. "Look, I don't know who you are, and I'm tired, so you have to go away," I said. "I'll talk to you in a reading if your loved ones pay a visit."

I didn't realize that my first client the next morning was this woman's daughter. The deceased lady showed up right on time at 9:00 a.m. sharp the next morning to speak with her daughter. "Tell her I am SO mad at Louie!" she exclaimed. "It is not my fault he's handling the will that way." She was concerned that her ex-husband was trying to screw the kids out of the money she left them in the will. Her daughter and I calmed her down, reassured her that they would handle it, and urged her to please go into the Light as all souls really should do after death. She finally did so, and we all felt greater peace!

Perhaps the most important communication I had was with my own grandmother. She was getting near the end, and the family was well aware of the fact, but we didn't know exactly when she would leave. I was cleaning my house early one morning when she appeared to me in spirit, rather strongly and told me, "It's your grandmother, and I'm up here with Jesus and the Virgin Mary, and I'm fine. You had better check your e-mails. Your mother needs you."

I turned on the computer, checked e-mails, and sure enough, there was the news from my dad that my mom's mother had indeed passed away. The message asked me to call as soon as I could. I picked up the phone, called home, and blurted out to my mom, "Grandma told me to call you." Silence. "Yes, I know she's dead, but she came in loud and clear, and she's doing great. She's speaking really clearly again, and she's feisty!" My mom cried and laughed with me. For the last three years of Grandma's life, she couldn't speak well due to a stroke that occurred while she was pruning her yard at the age of eighty-seven.

I now know beyond a shadow of doubt that there is life after death.

Every day that I see clients, I get wonderful little validations. The deceased love to let their loved ones know that they are alive and well. People can get this proof if they desire it. They can learn to silence their minds, trust their first thoughts, feelings, or visions, or at least, to be aware of the silly little things that happen around them signifying their loved ones' presence. The angels have a little joke that they don't have to prove life after death . . . According to them, "We'll all find out anyway!"

. . . .
About Ann Albers

Ann Albers is a popular spiritual author, lecturer, angel communicator, and medium. Her passion and purpose is teaching others to tap into the power and beauty of their souls, as well as helping people connect with the love and wisdom of their angels.

She is the author of several books and meditations, including: *Bridging the Gap between Christianity and Mysticism, Love is the River: Learning to Live in the Flow of Divine Grace*, and *Whispers of the Soul* which documents her journey from avionics engineer to angel communicator. For more information, visit www.VisionsOfHeaven.com.

Tell Mom and Dad I'm OK

Lynne Gawley–Hofstetter
Canada
supercalynne@sympatico.ca

I had just returned from a weekend in Atlanta at a Dynamic Essentials seminar and had sat down to read the paper with the thought in my mind, "Are we doing enough, are we telling everyone the benefits of a chiropractic lifestyle? Are we really changing lives?" When I say "we" I am speaking of the chiropractic profession as a whole. Every speaker that weekend seemed to ask that question.

When I opened the paper, I saw the face of an angel . . . a tiny baby boy, who in the first eleven months of his life, had fought harder to survive than we will ever have to do in our lifetime. Josh was born by emergency C-section and due to complications was without air for eight to thirteen minutes at birth. He was diagnosed with severe quadriplegic CP, was partially deaf, and was possibly blind. At eleven months he weighed only twelve pounds, the weight of a two- to three-month-old. When I saw the pain on this baby's face, I knew we had to do something.

Chiropractic does not cure anything; I knew that, but I also knew that if Josh were under chiropractic care and his little body were free of nerve interference, his quality of life and health had to improve. I took the newspaper article into work and asked Dr. D what we could do. We immediately wrote a letter to the family offering to help.

When I called Josh's mom to follow up on the letter, she had just opened the mail, looked up in to heaven, and said, "OK, God, I hear you." Apparently that Sunday at church one of our patients told her she thought Josh would benefit from chiropractic care.

The letter was sent out October 19, and by October 22 Josh and his family were all under our care. After Josh's third adjustment, he slept through the night for the first time since birth. We went to his house every day at lunch to adjust him as his family couldn't afford the taxi fare to come to the office. Dr. D was adjusting Josh for no fee.

Within the next couple of months Josh started to gain weight. You could just tell he loved getting adjusted. By May his weight had doubled. He still had many medical problems; it took everything he had just to breathe. But his quality of life was definitely better.

I received a terrible phone call from Dr. D at the end of May; Josh had passed away in his sleep the previous night. My hair stood up on end, and I had a sick feeling in my stomach. My heart ached for his family. I dreaded the thought of going to the funeral home the next day.

That night I was fevered and had a fitful, dream-filled night. What I thought to be the same recurring dream I now know was a "visit" from Josh with a message I had to deliver to his family. The dream went as follows: I walked into a large cathedral type building; at the front of the large room was a tiny white casket, and beside the casket stood a beautiful luminous man (who I believe was Jesus). I was drawn to the beautiful light at the front of the room. When I got up to the casket, Josh sat up. I was shocked and said, "Josh, how are you? What are you doing?" He then replied, "I'm hungry, but someone is going to feed me now," and he looked at Jesus and smiled. "Tell my Mom and Dad that I am OK."

Josh had never been able to eat except through a tube in his stomach because his swallowing reflex had never developed. This always bothered me because I wondered how they ever knew if he was really full. I guess this was his way of letting me know he would be full, and I was to be a messenger to his parents.

The next day when I went to the funeral home (I had never been in this funeral home before), I was surprised to find that it was just as I had seen it in my vision. My hair stood up as I approached the casket. It seemed to be glowing, and Josh had on what he was wearing in my vision. WOW! Talk about being the most awake I have ever been in my life. I now knew my purpose.

Normally I would have just kept this to myself; I have had a lot of vivid dreams or visions. Whenever I spoke of it before, my mother would say, "Oh, Lynne, you are such a dreamer; you have such a vivid imagination." So I would just forget it but not this time.

I told Dr. D and his wife about it that day at lunch. They asked me if I was going to tell Josh's family, and I said I wasn't sure yet; I didn't want them to think I was crazy. As usual I was worrying about what people would think of me rather than doing what I knew was right.

I continued to have parts of this vision for the next month, and then one morning at work I decided that this was the day. I phoned Josh's parents only to find that their phone was busy. I then went to lunch planning to try them again later when I came back.

Later when I returned from lunch, Josh's father coincidentally walked into the office. I hadn't seen him for a month, and he just dropped by to thank us for being such a big part of Josh's life and to tell us all how much better his son's life had been because of our help.

I knew it was now or never, this was a definite sign. I had to tell him. "Glenn," I said nervously, "I have something to tell you, and I hope you don't think I'm nuts." I told him about the vision, and he started to cry. He then thanked me saying that my message is what they had been waiting for. He became very emotional and quickly excused himself so he could go home and tell his wife.

I felt this tremendous rush of excitement come over me. I had done the right thing.

Since that time, my best friend has lost her mother, and a similar thing happened. Her mom came to me in a vision. My friend was going through a break up with her husband at the time of her mother's illness but kept hanging in there in order to spare her mother any additional pain.

In the vision her mother asked me to tell her daughter that she was doing the right thing and to go on with her life. I told my friend about it the day of her mother's funeral. It helped her get through that very rough time and reminded me time and time again that those who have crossed over can and do communicate with us.

A Touch from Beyond

T. Edgar
Western Australia

I was living in Los Angeles with my girlfriend Mary when she took me to meet her seventy–two–year–old father for the first time. Her dad Bill, a lifelong heavy smoker, was in the hospital due to complications from emphysema. Bill and I instantly got along with each other. Mary's dad told her later that he liked me, and she said that I was the only boyfriend he had met whom he had immediately taken to. I was pleased.

After his release from the hospital, Bill came to our small North Hollywood apartment for dinner. But he had a disagreement with Mary shortly after, and we didn't see him again until he fell ill about eight months later. He was back in the hospital, but this time it was very serious. When we went to see him, he was in intensive care. He had a breathing tube in his throat and, although conscious, was unable to speak or otherwise communicate.

Before we left the room, I leaned over to him, looked in his eyes, and said, "We'll be back." He was clearly distressed, which I put down to his physical condition. He died that evening before we could visit him again.

A couple of days later, Mary and I went to his small apartment in Burbank to box up his few possessions. We were there for an hour or so, had loaded the car, and were just preparing to leave when I had to use the bathroom. As soon as I went in the room, I felt a strong presence. The air seemed suffused with brightness, and my skin began to feel prickly. I left the bathroom and closed the door behind me.

At that moment the energy presence I had felt in the bathroom became very intense, and I was frozen to the spot. Suddenly I felt what I can only describe as some kind of energy on the back of my neck pushing my head down. My attention was instantly riveted to a small, otherwise unnoticeable built-in wardrobe drawer near the floor. I knelt down and opened the drawer. In it was a lone object: a passbook for a bank account containing Bill's life savings with Mary as a co-signatory. Since he had not made a will and had not told us about the bankbook, it seems he wanted to be absolutely sure that she received the money.

Prior to this, I had not given a lot of thought to the existence of a life after physical death, but this was very convincing. Bill not only clearly still existed, but he was able to have an effect on me in order that his intent to help his child could be fulfilled. It was an extraordinary, undeniable, and profoundly affecting experience.

Pushed Out of Heaven

Phyllis Hotchkiss
Florida
AngelPM7@aol.com
http://duane-hotchkiss.memory-of.com/About.aspx
http://www.geocities.com/Heartland/park/4746/brian.html

When our son Brian was murdered at the age of nineteen, we had no idea the impact he would have in the lives of his loved ones many years later.

Brian never lived to see three of his nephews and his niece. His youngest nephew Jared was seven-years-old when he had an incredible experience that saved his life. The parents of my daughter-in-law Sheryl were over at their house for Sunday dinner and Jared's grandfather gave him a lifesaver. Jared, being an active child, jumped up on the couch. When he did this, the lifesaver went down his throat the wrong way, and he was chocking. Mike, my other son, grabbed him and tried to get Jared to cough the lifesaver up. Jared lost consciousness for a few seconds.

Mike was able to get Jared to spit the lifesaver up, and when Jared

came to, he told his parents that he was falling into heaven and someone who looked just like Daddy pushed him back and told him that it was not his time. Sheryl looked at my son Mike and told him it had to be Brian. She got Brian's graduation picture and showed it to Jared and asked him if that was who pushed him out of heaven. Jared said yes, but he wasn't wearing a suit. Sheryl asked Jared what he was wearing and Jared said a red T-shirt and jeans. That was what Brian was wearing when he was killed. No one else knew that but my husband Duane and I. Until that moment, Jared really had no idea who Brian was; all he knew was that he saw someone that looked like his father.

Jared then went on to tell his parents that he sees his uncle all the time. He said Brian wakes him up every morning, goes to school with him, and plays games with him. His mother said she often walks by Jared's bedroom door and hears him talking to someone. She asked him who he was talking to, and he said Brian.

When my daughter Lisa came to visit with her family, we all got together. Jared and Ryan, my oldest grandson who also sees Brian all the time, had a lot to talk about. Neither one knew that the other saw and felt Brian before that day. They compared their experiences; it was great that they both had something in common even though there is nine years between them.

After everyone left that day, Jared told his mother that Brian was in the house and had a great big smile on his face. He was very happy to see everyone together. Keep in mind that Jared was just eight years old at this time.

I believe that prayer had a lot to do with this. Jared told his mother that he prays all the time and that he loves God a lot. He is a very spiritual child.

These experiences have been very comforting to everyone in the family. These "visits from heaven" validate to all of us that Brian is still with us. Out of five grandchildren, two have had experiences with "visits" from Brian. I find it interesting that my son chose one child from each of his siblings to come to. I also thank God for all the precious heavenly validations that our family members have received.

Quit Kissing My Ashes

Judy Collier
Louisiana
jkc42@aol.com
www.quitkissingmyashes.com

My son Kyle had been driving fast and did not have on his seat belt. He apparently was reaching for a CD on the floorboard of his Bronco when he slid onto the shoulder of the road. In his attempt to regain control, he overcorrected, hit a bridge railing, and was thrown eighty feet, land-ing between two bridges.

Hitting his head upon landing, Kyle suffered severe head trauma. After spending two days in intensive care and undergoing tests that showed there was no oxygen getting to his brain, we decided to take him off of life–support and to donate all of his organs.

Shortly after his death, I received a phone call from Bennie, a casual acquaintance of mine. She said she had to see me immediately; she had to tell me something. She said she'd come to my house, but since she was at work, I offered to meet her at her place of business instead.

When I arrived at her office, she leaned over her desk and grabbed both of my hands, proceeding to tell me what had happened the night before. She woke up around 1:30 a.m. and started receiving messages from Kyle. She said she didn't see his body, but he was connecting to her through some sort of telepathy. She noted that he talked on and on for at least three hours. She showed me notebook paper with notes scribbled on them. There were pages and pages of them.

The first thing Kyle told Bennie to tell me was that he was happy where he was. He explained that if given a choice, he would not come back. He felt that my grief was holding him here, and it would continue to hold him if I didn't let him go.

At the time she was telling me this, I had mixed emotions. It felt good to hear that he was happy. Every parent wants to hear that. But the part about my keeping him here upset me. I wondered how she knew what I was going through. She has never lost a child. What am I supposed to be feeling? Just say, "Goodbye, Kyle," and be over it? No way!

I told her I missed him so much. I did want him to be happy, but I couldn't help my grief. It had only been two months.

The next words stunned me. She said. "He wants you to quit kissing his ashes. He's not in there." I knew she knew we'd had Kyle cremated, but how did she know I was kissing his ashes every morning and every night? No one knew that I was doing this.

During the days that followed my son's death, I had several readings with Mary Jo McCabe, a medium who founded the McCabe Institute in Baton Rouge.

Three years after Kyle's death, Mary Jo called me one evening. She asked if Kyle had ever had a green and yellow parakeet. I wondered why she wanted to know. I told her I didn't think so, unless he had had one that I didn't know about when he was in college. I told her I'd check and see. She told me he'd come to her and had shown her a green and yellow parakeet. We talked a bit more and then hung up.

Since I'm an itinerant teacher, I travel from school to school through-out the day. The day following my phone conversation with Mary Jo, I had finished teaching my classes at one school and was driving to the next one. I happened to drive down the street where my daughter's friend Wendi lived.

I turned into Wendi's driveway. I had never been inside her house before as I had just recently found out where she lived. She seemed surprised to see me. I was even surprised that I was there, having no idea why I had stopped. She invited me in, and I told her I could stay only a minute or two or I'd be late for my next class. I remarked how nice her house looked and asked her if I could take a quick "peek."

We entered the den, and Wendi commented, "I feel like Kyle's here."

It was then I spotted a green parakeet sitting in the corner in a cage. Reminded of Mary Jo's call the previous night, I said, "Oh! You have a green parakeet!"

"Yes, "Wendi said. "And there's a yellow one in the cage below."

I learned down and couldn't believe my eyes. I told her about Mary Jo's call.

The next time I saw Mary Jo, I told her about Wendi's green and yellow parakeets. Mary Jo told me it was Kyle's way of letting me know he is aware of everything going on in my life.

. . . .
About Judy Collier

Judy is the author of *Quit Kissing My Ashes: a Mother's Journey through Grief*, the uplifting story of her son Kyle's death which shares her personal experience and realization that death is only the beginning, not the end.

She is a popular speaker and has appeared on several radio and television shows helping the bereaved understand that our loved ones are always with us. For more information, visit her Web site at www.quitkissingmyashes.com.

Nanny and the Cockatoos

Michelle Leech
Australia

My grandmother Lily died after a long battle with Alzheimer's. I sat and held her hand, talking to her and sleeping next to her for six days, twenty-four hours a day. I loved her very much.

The morning she passed I asked her to give me a sign when she got to heaven (she could not respond as she was semiconscious). After she was gone, I went outside her room to let my other relatives have a moment with her. I looked up toward the sky and said in my head, "If you're OK, show me a white bird or even a white feather so that I can't mistake it is meant for me."

Later that day I was standing outside of my house crying with my dad and my uncle, when a flock of about a hundred cockatoos flew approximately one meter above our heads. They were so extremely close that if I had reached up, I could have touched them all. They just came out of nowhere!

For those of you who are not familiar with cockatoos, they are large white birds native to Australia and nearby islands and are known to squawk loudly. But for some reason this time they were not making a sound, not one of them! All you could hear was the flutter of all their wings.

They flew really low over our heads and then flew into the trees surrounding our home. Once in the trees they started to squawk and lots of feathers began to fall from the branches. I was seriously overwhelmed but filled with peace at the same time. (My father was a bit freaked out!)

I have no question in my mind that it was my Nan soaring above us, showing us how free she is now. The setting was at dusk with a beautiful sunset of pinks and purples, and the event was just one of the most beautiful things I have ever seen.

Then in 2008, Nan paid me another "visit" after the birth of my first child. It had been a long and very difficult labor. After I gave birth, they took my son to the nursery, and I, relieved that it was all over, was lying in my room waiting for the doctor to come back.

I happened to look up toward the ceiling and couldn't believe my eyes. There was a white feather hanging from the vent in the ceiling directly above my bed. How did a white feather get into a hospital? There are obviously no animals or birds allowed in a hospital room, especially not in the sterile delivery rooms!

My heart skipped a beat. I just smiled and said hello to my grandmother. I thanked her for letting me know that she was there with me.

Tigger's Forewarning

Karen Christopherson
Michigan
www.trilliumconsultants.com
TrilliumConsult@aol.com

The spiritual bond between our beloved cat Tigger, my son, and me was as solid and as meaningful as any I've known between humans—a connection that had been strengthened by each of the experiences we'd shared over the years. The one that will always stand out the most in our minds dealt with her forewarning us of her own death.

It all began with my "just browsing" in pet stores when I was newly married and living in a rented home where no pets of any kind were allowed. Since the time I was a child, I had always been a rescuer of strays and had from one-to-three cats at any point in time. Now that I had a home of my own (albeit rented), I started longing to have a feline friend once again —after many years of apartment living.

It was on one of these walkthroughs that I spotted Tigger in all her regality. At six months she was larger and more magnificent than most full-grown cats. She paced the cage in a graceful manner until she saw me. Our eyes fixed upon one another; we remained frozen in a gaze that seemed to last several minutes. I can describe it only as though we had instantly recognized each other from some other time and place. We knew we were finally meant to be together again. I told the pet shop owner that I "had to have her" and begged him to hold her for me until I had the details worked out to bring her home. He excitedly shared her story: the original owner, a family friend, had developed allergies and had given specific instruction to not let her go to anyone who didn't "fall madly in love" with her. He said that a deposit was unnecessary and assured me that he would reserve her for me.

I was "beside myself" as I rushed home to talk with my new husband, who was a "by-the-book" kind of guy. He reiterated to me "the rules" laid out by the landlord and cautioned me against talking with him. It didn't dissuade me. I set an appointment with the landlord for that very evening where I emotionally shared my experience with him and his wife—outlining for them all of the precautions I would take to ensure that they would incur no damages. They immediately said, "Yes!"

That was the beginning of our lives together. Tim, my son, was born several years later and grew up with Tigger as his constant companion. Even as an infant, she was as protective of him as a mother bear with her cubs and would lie with him for hours as he slept. When he became an active toddler, she trusted him not to be rough in his treatment of her. She continued this pattern throughout her life, eagerly waiting at his side to see what new game he'd devised for her and sleeping either under the covers with him or at his feet.

In the middle of the night on an August day in 1985, my son Tim, then nine-years-old, came to me teary-eyed to relate a dream he'd just had in which Tigger had come to him to foretell her own death. Tim described how Tigger had approached him in the dream, breathing in a "panting" way, common to dogs but not to cats. She had looked at him longingly, told him that she loved him very much, and would miss him terribly, but that she would die soon. She wanted him to understand and accept that it was her time to go.

Although Tigger had been diagnosed with feline leukemia several years before, her veterinarian had consistently marveled at her complete lack of symptoms and at how she had outlived every other cat with the same diagnosis. There was no reason to think she would suc-cumb at any time in the near future.

About six months after the dream on an early morning in February of 1986, Tim came running to me sobbing, saying that Tigger had just approached him, breathing in this panting way and looking at him right in the eyes —just as she had done in the dream. Tim said he knew she would die that day and wanted me to accompany him to his room to see her. Sure enough, Tigger was there panting, something she had never done before.

We sat with her for hours, talking with her about favorite memories and explaining how much we loved her and would miss her. We thanked her for her warning in the dream and told her we understood that it was her time to go. Although she didn't seem to be in pain or to have any other symptoms, she did not want to be held and simply sat facing us, listening intently to everything we had to say. There was no doubt in our minds that she fully understood us.

In the evening, we called the family together to bid their goodbyes and then decided on the night's sleeping arrangements. Tim finally de-termined that he wanted to sleep downstairs on the couch where Tigger liked to lie at his feet while he slept. Tigger was obviously in favor of this plan and readily accompanied us downstairs. However, unlike her normal behavior, it was apparent that this time she did not wish to lie on the couch. Instead she sat on the floor right in front of Tim's face, so that she could watch him fall asleep.

At 2:30 a.m. Tim awakened me in quiet tearfulness to tell me that Tigger had gotten up on the couch at his feet after he had fallen asleep and that he had just found her dead.

We knew that Tigger had made her transition and that our love and strong spiritual connection would last until we could all be together again.

Moo

Artie Hoffman
New Jersey
www.artiehoffman.com

A girl who had lost her mom, dad, and sister all within a year's time came to me, yearning for some sort of validation that they were all OK. She was the only one still living and was very depressed; she needed to know that her family was still around her spiritually.

I looked at her parents' picture and asked her, "Your dad had an incredible sense of humor, didn't he?"

"Yes," she answered while a smile slowly began to form on her face.

"Your parents are telling me that you will receive a sign from both of them on the same day. A bird is going to crap on you; this will be a sign from your father. Your mother will show a beautiful white feather. You will know immediately that it is from her. It's not going to be a typical bird's feather just lying around; it will stick out at you."

I could tell she was confused wondering how this was going to take place. But I explained to her that I just relay the information as it is given to me.

A year later I bumped into her friend, and she reminded me about the reading described above. She then told me that her friend did, indeed, receive the validations her parents had promised her during the reading.

Days, weeks, and months went by, and nothing happened. She hadn't received any signs from her parents and wondered if she ever would. Then, while on vacation in Mexico, my client was lying on the beach when a bird suddenly crapped on her; she was dirty but nonetheless thrilled! Later that same day she went to pull the cover off the bed to go to sleep and on her pillow lay a beautiful big white feather. The pillow was not a down pillow so there was no explanation of how it had gotten there.

Needless to say, she had gotten her signs from heaven. She now knew that her mom, dad, and sister were still with her and would always be.

My clients are not always receptive to the messages I give them. On one memorable occasion a very tense, skeptical woman, seemingly with a very arrogant type A personality, walked in wanting to connect with her mother. I get skeptics coming to see me all the time, but this woman was visibly angry and just wouldn't relax.

She handed me a picture of her mother, and I started to give her the information that I was getting from her mom. Her mother was concerned about her daughter and wanted her to create a better, happier lifestyle for herself. Personally, I knew that the information I was getting was very important, but her daughter wasn't impressed. She just looked at me and subliminally shot back, "Yeah, yeah, yeah, tell me something from my mom that I will know is from her, and stop giving me all this general advice about my life."

As a medium, I have grown used to skeptics, but this woman's attitude was really starting to agitate me. Her body language was as cold as ice.

During the final minutes of our reading, I looked at her and said, "Your mom is showing me a bunch of cows."

Finally I seemed to get through to her. She looked at me wide-eyed and asked, "Yeah, so what?"

"I don't know why I'm doing this," I continued. "But moo . . . " I began to moo like a cow as my once arrogant customer broke down in tears. She pointed to the picture of her mom I was holding in my hands and joyfully told me, "That's her name."

I looked at her confused and unaware of what she was talking about. "What's her name? What are you talking about?"

She looked at me as the tears continued to come and said, "Her name is Murial, but everyone called her Moo."

I never know why I say the things I say to people at times. I merely repeat what I see never knowing how much of an impact it will have.

About Artie Hoffman

Artie is a gifted medium who not only helps people by connecting them with loved ones on the Other Side but also by lending his love and support to the people who need it most. As a hospice volunteer, he goes to Central Park in New York City a few times a year to hand out money, food, and water to the homeless.

He is the host of *Angels & Answers* on www.nytalkradio.net. He is also a frequent radio guest and is working on his first book, *Down to Earth with Artie Hoffman*, which is a humorous look at his life as a medium and the many life lessons he has learned. For more information, please visit www.artiehoffman.com.

Dad Makes His Presence Known

William
metasuccess1@msn.com

When my wife's brother was terminally ill, my wife and her sister were with him. They stayed with him all day Friday and Saturday morning as he was fighting for his life. Trying to comfort him, my wife told him on Friday not to be afraid and to go toward the Light, but he became very agitated at the suggestion, so she quit saying anything like that.

He was communicating with her by squeezing her hand. During their Saturday morning visit, it was clear to both sisters that he was concentrating on them and on what they were saying. But about 10:00 a.m., he began to focus on the ceiling above the bed and away from his sisters.

Two safety pads were leaning against the wall behind my wife and her sister. They were to be laid on the floor at night to protect a patient if he fell out of bed. The pads had been leaning against the wall all morning and the previous day, since they were used only at night. They had not moved an inch all day Friday or Saturday.

My wife's brother was extremely close to his father. He had lived his entire life with his parents. When my wife noticed that her brother had begun focusing on the ceiling, she asked him what he was looking at and if he saw their dad, who had died many years earlier. Just then one of the pads fell away from the wall. It did not slide down the wall but fell away in a forward motion as though it had been pushed.

The noise startled my wife and her sister. Her brother moved his gaze back from the ceiling to his sisters in the direction of the safety pad that had fallen. Then, slowly, he looked back again toward the empty side of the hospital room, and my wife asked him a second time, "What do you see? Do you see our dad in this room?" At that instant the second safety pad fell forward, away from the wall. This really shook the two women up. Both pads had fallen from their place next to the wall at the exact moment my wife asked the question, "Do you see our dad in the room?"

After this second incident my wife's other sister came into the room, and their brother tried very hard with his frail voice to tell them that he loved them. When this second sister bent down to kiss him, she said, "He looks at such peace now." Later a nurse came into the room, and the women were asked to take a break. When they returned, they discovered that their brother had died while they were gone.

After the pads fell, he was noticeably calmer and seemed to have lost his resistance to going toward the Light. Since he died only minutes afterward, I suspect that he saw his dad in that room and was ready to give up his physical life. It is also significant that he died ten years to the day from the time his father had died and at the same time of day.

When one person sees something like this, we might chalk it up to stress or hallucination, but my wife's sister was with her and saw the same phenomenon.

Flick the Lights

Maria Campanella
New Jersey

On November 16, 2003, my father died after a long two–year battle with glioblastoma, the most common form of brain cancer in adults. Three weeks later I went to the hospital to have a colonoscopy. While I was under anesthesia, I had a dream or what I now know was a "visit from heaven."

I saw my father; he appeared in such high spirits and was sporting a broad smile. He said, "Maria, why are you so sad? Look how happy I am. I'm here with everybody. Don't feel sad for me. We are all happy."

He opened his arms wide, motioning to the people around a long table behind him. There I noticed many of my deceased relatives including three of my uncles: Carmine, Angelo, and Pellegrino. They were all sitting around a table, eating and enjoying each other's company.

Then I noticed there was an empty chair at the table and wondered why it was there. I felt as though my father wanted me to pay attention to the empty chair. Once I did, I heard the sound of the nurse's voice trying to wake me up.

I remember not wanting to wake up. I felt so peaceful and calm. I felt such warmth and love and I wasn't ready to let go yet. It was as though a huge weight had been lifted from my shoulders. But I reluctantly woke up, and after a brief recovery, my husband drove me home.

When I arrived home, I was told that my neighbor Barry had passed away that same day. I was stunned. Could this have been the meaning of the empty chair? Barry had been suffering from melanoma. Even though there was a twenty–three–year age difference, he and my father had become friends as their cancers had created a special bond between them.

Before explaining what happened next, I need to go back two weeks prior to this day. Barry showed up at my front door and told me, "Maria, this is the last time you will be seeing me." I was surprised and said, "Oh, come on, Barry; you are going to be fine." But he insisted that he would not be getting better. He told me that he was leaving to take his children on a trip to Hershey Park in Pennsylvania. The following week he returned from this fateful trip by ambulance only to be welcomed by hospice.

During this time, I went over to his house to see him, and he seemed lifeless as he lay unresponsive in the hospital bed which had been placed in his living room. I walked over to him, remembering this scene all too well having just lost my father. I leaned close to him, and for some reason I cannot explain, I telepathically communicated with him saying, "Barry, when you get over to the Other Side, send me a sign that you and my father are alright. Flick the lights." I have no idea why I chose this method of communication, but it was the first thing that came to my mind.

On the night of his death, the same day as my colonoscopy, I could not sleep. I found myself tossing and turning and finally decided to get out of bed noticing that it was just 3:00 a.m. I made my way downstairs as my mind flooded with thoughts of my father and Barry.

I walked over to the window and stared across the street at Barry's house. All of a sudden, his porch light flicked on and off. I stared in disbelief but thought it was just a coincidence. Then, again, his porch light flicked on and off. My heart was racing as I remembered my words to Barry, "Flick the lights."

I quickly dismissed the thought and went back to bed feeling a bit unnerved. The next night I still could not sleep, and when I turned to look at my alarm clock, I was surprised to find that it was once again 3:00 a.m. As the night before, I made my way downstairs and over to my window to look at Barry's house. Again his porch light flicked on and off.

This time I felt overwhelmed and quickly ran back upstairs to bed. The following night I was not surprised to wake up at exactly 3:00 a.m. for the third night in a row. This time I was anxious to make my way over to the window. I now had no doubt that Barry was communicating with me.

Sure enough, his porch light flicked on and off as I stared in amazement. At this point I prayed and told Barry that I knew this was a sign from him and that I was sure he and my father were OK.

The following night I slept like a baby. I did not wake up at 3:00 a.m. I never saw his porch light flicker on and off again, but I didn't need to. I was now a believer. I had asked Barry for a sign, and he gave me one. I'm sure Barry was welcomed by my father and is now seated at that table in a chair that was once vacant.

Many months later I was speaking to Barry's wife and asked her if she happened to have a motion sensor light for her porch. Her response shook the very core of my being. "No," she replied. "In fact, the porch light hasn't had a bulb for years." This was yet another validation that those in heaven work in mysterious ways.

The Address on the Mailbox

Donna A. Bowman
North Carolina
treasuredwords@msn.com
www.walkingwoundedauthordonnabowman.blogspot.com

On January 17, 2007, we lost Ashley, my twenty–three–year–old son. I was devastated, but God's mercy is wonderful. God gave me a wonderful gift, and I refuse to see it as anything other than that.

I remember every detail of what God did and all the glory that goes to Him. God has his ways of comforting us, and he comforted me and my family in a way that I had never experienced before.

Ashley had passed away and been with the Lord for about eight months at this time, and I still had days when I would cry a lot. I just could not get over the fact that my baby was gone. I believe God saw my pain and was slowly bringing me toward a healing period with all of this.

Many times in my walk with the Lord, he has dealt with me in dreams, but this was the first time I ever had something like this hap–

pen. I went to sleep one night, and I was immediately in the spirit and walking in heaven. I was walking down a road and looked to my left as I came upon a house. There was a young man sitting on a bench outside, and although he had his back to me, I knew it was Ashley. He had a knife and a piece of wood in his hands which he was whittling.

I heard a voice tell me to look to the left and behind me. That is when I saw a mailbox, and the address on the mailbox was 000–000–0000. I thought that was really odd. I woke up and looked at the clock, and it was 3:00 a.m. I felt a great sense of peace and the presence of the Lord. I knew that this dream was from him and was a way to comfort me as well as speed my healing process.

The next morning I called my daughter Teri and told her I had something to share with her that I had dreamed about last night. She interrupted me (something she never does) to tell me that she got the weirdest phone call last night. The number showed up on her caller ID as: 000–000–0000, and it came precisely at three in the morning. Well, I just about dropped the phone. Before I could tell her anything else, she told me as she walked out of her bedroom, she happened to glance up towards her bookcases. These bookcases are very tall, and you cannot see anything on the top shelf unless it is something large. She saw something sticking out that looked like a small piece of wood. She got a chair and climbed up and got it. It was a piece of wood that Ashley had carved our names in years ago.

I just about fell out of my chair and then told her the dream I had. We cried and laughed together realizing this was just another way that God can and did comfort us. That "visit from heaven" started not only a healing within me but with our children and my husband. How much does God love us? I don't think we will totally grasp all of it until we are in the arms of Jesus. There is no rational reasoning behind my daughter's dream or my dream. Some people will say we are crazy. But I know in that dream God sent comfort, tranquility, and healing to all of us.

About Donna Bowman

Donna is the author of *The Walking Wounded*, a compelling true story about her own experience with child abuse told through the eyes of an abused little girl. For more information visit www.thewalkingwoundedauthordonnabowman.blogspot.com, or e-mail her at treasuredwords@msn.com.

Siena

Patricia Federico
Arizona
Patricia@mymadretierra.com
www.mymadretierra.com

I was born with the gift of *el don* (touch healing) and the gift of second sight. In March 2005, a friend invited me to a retreat called the *cursillo* in Phoenix, Arizona. I was really afraid to go due to the fact that I hardly ever went to church and I had heard that the Roman Catholic Church did not approve of people like me.

I found this disapproval ironic since I feel very connected to God and I use my gift to help others. Yet the Church made me feel afraid to tell the truth about who I was and what I did for a living. So going to this *cursillo* meant finally opening up and telling the truth.

My friend Mona told me that I need to join a parish since you had to be sponsored by a church in order to attend the retreat. So I set out to find a parish to sponsor me. I went to two different churches, and neither one would sponsor me for one reason or another.

At this point, I became discouraged and thought about giving up. But, then, I suddenly thought about my spiritual guides. When I do my healing work, I often feel the presence of three female guides.

There was one spiritual guide, in particular, who was very powerful; her energy stood out and was just amazing. I had asked for her name many times telepathically but never received it. So I thought, perhaps if I attended this retreat, she might reveal her name to me.

I then decided to try one more church, St. Catherine di Siena in South Phoenix. As soon as I asked to be sponsored, the woman in the office said, "We would love for you to go to the *cursillo*." She allowed me to join their parish and sponsored me as a member so I could attend the retreat.

A short time later, I went to the retreat and had many beautiful experiences. One was seeing a vision of Jesus walking through the desert, asking me to stay on path. However, I was a bit disappointed because I did not receive the name of my guide (or so I thought). But I quickly put it out of my mind, telling myself, "You are blessed, and you were accepted by the church. Be happy. How could you ask for more?"

I returned home and continued my healing work, feeling refreshed and renewed. Then in late 2005, I received another invitation to go on a tour of Italy with a group of people. I really could not afford this trip but decided I would manifest my trip with sacrifice and prayer. I saved money by working more and giving myself less, and I prayed to my guide to help me.

In March 2006, exactly one year after my visit to the *cursillo*, I found myself touring Italy with a group of wonderful people. It was an amazing three-week tour including Rome, Florence, and Siena. Ah, yes, beautiful Siena. I smile as I think of it now because I felt such a warm and deep connection there.

Our tour included a stop at every church on our path. So while I was in Siena, we stopped at the Basilica of San Domenico. It was there that I was given one of the most blessed validations that I have ever received. But before I go on, I need to explain the significance of this church.

In the spring of 1380, St. Catherine of Siena died of a stroke in Rome at the young age of thirty-three. As the story goes, her body remained in Rome, but the people of Siena wanted to bring her back to her hometown. Knowing they could not take her whole body out of Rome, they took just her head which is entombed in the Basilica of San Domenico.

Getting back to my experience, as I entered the church, my body began to vibrate with an energy I had never before experienced. It felt comfortable yet chilling, and then bliss came over me.

Then telepathically I heard the words, "I am here to guide you; this is your home; you asked for me. I am your sister in spirit. Do not sacrifice yourself; love yourself, and I will guide your hand in holy love."

As tears rolled down my face, I trembled with joy and love. A couple of my friends, David and George, became worried and asked if everything was okay. I told them that I had just received a message and now knew that St. Catherine was one of my guides. They hugged me with joy.

But, as you would know, there are always unbelievers. One woman in particular came over and said, "OOOHHH" as she waved her hand like I was some kind of freak. I just closed my eyes and asked God to forgive her. When we finished our tour of the Basilica, there was a small gift shop attached to the church so we went over and bought souvenirs. I bought the book of St. Catherine's life so I could learn more about my guide.

As we were walking out of the church, my friend David yelled from a distance in front of me, "OH, MY GOD, Patricia! Look at your bag!" As I lifted my bag filled with my souvenirs, I noticed that the bag contained a picture of St. Catherine on the outside. By itself this was not significant, but directly below the picture of St. Catherine was printed the name "Federico," my own last name! I couldn't believe my eyes.

The next day I found out that the family who owns the gift shop also happens to be named Federico. What a confirmation! I like to think of it as a very special "visit from heaven" in Siena, Italy from my guide St. Catherine.

. . . .
About Patricia Federico
Patricia is a gifted intuitive and an empath. She is one of the Southwest's most trusted stress-management consultants and alternative healers. As a practitioner of the ancient healing arts, she has mastered techniques developed over millennia and handed down through generations of *Sobadoras/Curanderas* (women who heal with and through their hands). For more information, please visit www.mymadretierra.com.

Dad Came for Mom

Sheila Upton
United Kingdom
sheiladevenport@btinternet.com

My dad passed away in May, 1996. He often visits me. I know it's him and have had it confirmed by a medium. Four years ago my mom was diagnosed with Alzheimer's disease. Her decline was rapid. It was hell and heartache watching as the disease took hold.

During this time I had a dream. In the dream I walked into a pub looking for my dad. I saw him standing a few yards away from me, but he did not look like the dad I had known. He looked to be in his thirties and was dressed very smartly. As he wrapped his arms around me, I said, "You have to come home, Dad. Mom is very ill, and she needs you." He looked at me and said, "I can't, Bab." (the name he used to call me).

I turned to walk away and saw a woman sitting at a table. She had black hair, was dressed really smartly, and wore red lipstick. She smiled at me, raised her hand, and shook her head slowly. I was livid and thought, "Why is my dad with her when my mom needs him so badly?"

This is when I woke up.

The next morning I was crying and trying to work it all out, when suddenly I thought about some old photographs. I got them out and sorted through them until I found one that made it all fall into place. The man in my dream was in his thirties, and Dad in the photo was in his thirties, dressed exactly the same as I had seen him in my dream. The woman in my dream was my mom. It meant that Mom was already with him. I told my dream to a medium, and she said, "That was not just a dream, Sheila. You were meant to see that your mom is with your dad 95 percent of the time."

In my mom's last months, she slept for most of the day, but at 4:30 every morning she woke up and stared at one corner of the room, talking to whomever she could see. Two days before she passed away, my sister and I were holding her hands when the area around us became cold. I started crying and said, "Dad's here. He's here." I could feel overwhelming love. It was pure unconditional love from my father to his three special girls. This feeling lasted for only a short time, but we knew he was there with us.

That same night we could smell a strong perfume. Kath, my sister, said that it was our aunt's perfume. We had just been told that she had passed away. Aunt Nell had come for Mom. The next morning at 4:30, Mom started talking to "the corner" again, but this time every name she

mentioned was the name of a relative who had "passed"—her mom and dad, our dad, her sister and sisters-in-law.

At one point, Mom started making funny faces and laughing, so I got my camera and took photos of her laughter and also of Kath and me kissing Mom's cheek. The first photos are lovely and clear, but, when Kath and I are kissing her, Dad's spirit is visible. There is a white mist all over the picture. I look at the photos and can see him as clearly as I see Mom.

Ricotta Cheese

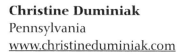

Christine Duminiak
Pennsylvania
www.christineduminiak.com

My dad and I were very close. In February of 2000 he was called home to the Lord. After he passed, I started to notice that when I was preparing dinner for my family, I would feel someone gently massaging the top of my head. Since I consider myself to be rather cooking and baking challenged, I always felt this little massage was from my dad giving me heavenly encouragement in the kitchen. And I would smile and say hello to him. I would also be given a simultaneous thought to call my eighty-year-old mother to check up on her.

One night I believe my dad gave me more than encouragement after I attempted to make some special cookies from scratch.

My teenage daughter had asked me to help her make cookies for her boyfriend for Valentine's Day; I thought to myself, "OH, NO; the blind leading the blind!" But we gave it the old college try, anyway, and hoped for the best.

The recipe called for ricotta cheese—an ingredient I had never bought or used before. We followed the recipe and the "cookies" ended up coming out of the oven looking like an embarrassing mess. They tasted pretty bad, too, so we had no choice but to throw them out. I was left with quite a bit of unused ricotta cheese and wondered what to do with it.

Later I had the most vivid dream of my dad. In the dream I was in an unfamiliar kitchen, making breakfast. Some of the goodies there were buns, bacon, and even those "cookies" that we had thrown out. In this dream I could even smell the aroma of the bacon as I watched it sizzling in the frying pan. I offered all of it to my dad to eat, but he just pointed to the "cookies" and said to me, "You know ricotta cheese goes with manicotti." I didn't know this, but I said, "Thank you, Dad."

While my dad was there, I was very pleased and happy to be able to give him a big hug once again, and during that precious hug I took notice of the familiarity of the distinctive shape of the back of his head and hair.

I woke up with tears streaming down my face because I was so happy. I thanked my dad for coming, and I thanked Jesus for blessing me with such a special visit from my dad.

It was then that I realized that I did not know whether or not ricotta cheese was an actual ingredient in manicotti as mentioned by my dad in the dream. So that morning I called my sister (who is a terrific cook) and asked her about it. She said, "Yes, exactly. Ricotta cheese is what does go into manicotti!"

What a great validation of this dream visit from my dad to let me know he was actually there visiting me from heaven.

About Christine Duminiak

Christine is a certified grief recovery specialist, a spiritual bereavement recovery facilitator, a member of the Association for Death Education and Counseling, and the founder of Prayer Wave for ADCs—a non-denominational worldwide Internet grief support and prayer group with over 500 members from 19 countries. She is committed to spreading the message that our loved ones survive death, are still a part of our lives, and that God, in His mercy, allows them to communicate with us from Heaven in many different ways in order to comfort us.

The author of *God's Gift of Love: After-Death Communications*, she is a certified reflexologist and a certified energy healing practitioner. Christine is the radio co-host of *Ask the Angels* on www.blogtalkradio.com and a sought-after speaker who travels around the country holding her After-Death Communication Seminars and conducting her *Bridges to Heaven—For Those Who Grieve* Seminars. Her latest book, *Heaven Talks to Children*, documents children who have seen the spirits of deceased relatives, friends, pets, angels, or holy beings. For more information, please visit her Web site at www.christineduminiak.com.

Hey, I'm OK

Kathie Carrigan
Maryland
www.angelfire.com/amiga2/ourangelboy2/chrissie.html

My daughter Chrissie, born a preemie at just twenty–eight weeks, was my little miracle and angel. She would later commit suicide at the age of fifteen after dealing with many illnesses including anorexia, depression, and MPD (multiple personality disorder). One of these personalities and its desire to die would eventually overpower her.

Chrissie lived each day as if it were a year. She was an honor roll student the last year of her life, and she was very proud of that. She was such a joy to be around, had many friends, and just loved life. When Chrissie gained her wings, it really tore me up since she was my baby and I was supposed to protect her . . . not have her take her own life. I met a medium by the name of Anthony Quinata at a bereavement group meeting. He was doing readings for people who had lost loved ones, and I thought "Okay, let's try this." I missed my baby girl so much, and it was worth a try.

Anthony knew nothing about Chrissie beforehand, but when he was finished, I felt like he had known her all of her short life. I was told things no one knew about except my family. Anthony told me that her grandparents are with her along with her dog Lacy. He spoke in detail about all the little things that we used to do together and things we now do in her memory. He went on to say that she likes my curio cabinet where I keep the items that were important to her. I was amazed when he told me that I hadn't changed her room since she left. Chrissie told Anthony about the little things she does in the house to let me know she is with me. She also warned me about my having heart problems. After the reading I found out that my blood pressure was sky high and later ended up in the hospital with chest pains.

Soon after the chest pains, I was diagnosed with supraventricular tachycardia, a form of heart rhythm disorder. At this writing I have not had surgery to correct the problem, but I will have to have the operation soon.

I take comfort in my reading from Anthony and from the knowledge that my daughter is still looking out for me. It is also comforting to know that she is in heaven, that she is not in pain anymore, and that she sends me her love. I continue to keep candles burning for her since she said it helped her. Anthony was so correct when he told me what Chrissie was saying to me. There was no way he could have gotten the information beforehand.

When Chrissie came through, she totally showed her personality. She called Anthony Mr. Man and would not talk at first; she said, "You know so why ask me?" This was the way Chrissie was—very much to the point and shy at times. Anthony said that she was very precocious. The one thing I had always said about her was that she was an old soul in a young body.

Sometime later I had a reading by another medium named Natalie Smith–Blakeslee who told me that my daughter is with Karen Carpenter. There was a message to Karen's uncle asking that I say hello for her. What is remarkable about this is that no one knew I once worked for Karen Carpenter's uncle and that I had met Karen early in her career. I was told that I would hear a Carpenter's song. The next day out of the blue I heard "Merry Christmas, Darling" on the radio.

My little grandson Petey will often tell us that Chrissie is around playing with him. Petey will seemingly be playing and laughing with someone, but there is no one there. When we ask him what he's doing, he often says that his Auntie Chrissie is tickling him. His baby sister Vanessa will stop to stare and start smiling, but there is no one there. When she sees a picture of Chrissie, she smiles and giggles. It seems like Vanessa and her brother definitely know their aunt even though they had never met here on earth.

Chrissie has sent my family and me many signs, but perhaps the most amazing one was the appearance of a photo in a roll of film taken during her sister's honeymoon. When my daughter returned home, she was stunned to find a picture of Chrissie in the middle of the pile of pictures. The entire family was in shock. Since she was deceased, we wondered how this photo could have gotten there. Obviously Chrissie did not go on the honeymoon. And what got to us is that all the negatives on the roll are numbered except for the one containing this photograph.

She often made the peace sign when taking pictures so it doesn't surprise me that she would present herself in this way. She is also smiling and seemingly very happy. She is saying, "Hey, I'm OK." It's one of the many ways she has let us know that she is still with us.

An Officer's Regrets

Daniel M. Darrow
Rhode Island
she.remembers@yahoo.com

In the early years of my parents' marriage, my father was pretty much like any other enlisted military man with a family and ambitious aspirations. This was greatly admired not only by my mother's family and my mother but presumably also by his commanding officers as the promotions kept coming. Within a relatively short time my father had gone from being an enlisted military man all the way to the rank of lieutenant and later on to lieutenant commander.

I remember my childhood at this point being like what every other kid my age experienced and I was none the worse for wear. That is until I started waking up at night to what were seemingly vicious arguments regarding my father's affairs with other women. After these accusations were made, my father then began to leave the house for work in the morning and not come back at night for days on end. I was quite young at the time so I didn't have a very good grasp of what exactly was going on. Since my mother did a very good job of hiding it from my friends, classmates, and me, everything appeared to be completely normal. At about the age of ten, however, I remember one of the arguments involved something about a possible murder that had occurred aboard ship where my father had been stationed for sea duty. I also remember a lot of discussions on the subject, and to this day the details of these are rather sketchy. My father was never charged with anything. Interesting to note, however, is that my father and this man had shared quarters on the same ship.

It was around this same time that my father began drinking quite heavily and became involved in even more extramarital affairs. This was a known fact within my immediate family as these women with whom he had been involved had no couth whatsoever and thought nothing of calling or even showing up on our doorstep at all hours of the night or early morning hours. They would further hurt my mother's already broken heart by demanding to know where he was. But she was raised as a very strict, by-the-book Catholic. Divorce was not allowed within the church without facing excommunication. Since my mother went to church regularly, the thought that she would no longer be welcome in the very place that gave her any comfort was just intolerable; so rather than get a divorce, she made the decision to stay with my father.

Fast forward approximately thirty years when my father receives the devastating news that he has inoperable brain cancer. He continued with his former ways until the end of his life which I'm sure contributed to the speed with which the disease progressed. Within four years my father had passed away on the floor of the family room. It is also interesting to note that his death occurred at home. I am convinced that because of the life he had lived, his spirit remained in that house after his death due to all of the accompanying guilt that he may have finally felt for the treatment of his wife.

Even more interesting, however, is the fact that shortly after his death, I called my mother. Since we hadn't spoken in a very long time, I assumed that perhaps they had made peace with one another because of my father's illness and that she might be grieving his death. Nothing could have been further from the truth! As I said, "You must miss Dad

. . . " her response, completely unexpected and in a virtual torrent of words as she practically screamed into my ear, "That SOB destroyed my life. Miss him? I hated him, and I'm glad he's gone!"

As soon as this statement was uttered, a rush of deafening white noise came over the phone, and I could no longer hear my mother speaking. It was later established that she could hear me perfectly and couldn't figure out where I'd gone or if I'd hung up! It should be noted as well that this particular phone was a cordless, digital phone with a "landline" phone sharing the same phone number and no "other" lines. We keep this phone in case the other two digital, cordless phones lose their charges or we lose electrical power.

Almost immediately after this white noise experience, the landline phone began to ring in the other room while the line (shared) I was trying to talk to my mother on was still engaged! My wife went to answer this phone even though we both knew it was impossible for it to ring separately because again it is a shared phone number and line. When my wife answered it, however, she heard nothing but this same white noise and a distant "voice." Strangely the words of the voice could not be distinguished one from another.

Within an hour my mother was sitting in the den where she and my father would watch TV. Down a small hallway adjacent to this room is a door that leads to the garage. As my mother was watching TV that night, she heard that door open and a voice saying, "Hi, Mom." For some reason this is what my father used to call my mother. He rarely, if ever, called her by her real name.

This same door was the only entrance he ever used to enter the house. It's also interesting to note that upon the sale of that house and my mother moving into a condo, all paranormal activity experienced by members of my immediate family ceased.

"Visits from heaven" are believed to occur often when souls are trying to express "afterlife regret." Also, earthbound spirits have been said to hold on to or stay on this earth plane due to sorrow or feeling like they are unworthy to enter heaven. I believe this was the case with my father.

Eliphalette Wrench, Mother of Francis

---•◦⟨∞⟩◦•---

Anna O'Donoghue
United Kingdom
DALSOD@aol.com

My son Francis died in a motorcycle accident in 1986 when he was just twenty-five-years-old. One day, on an impulse, I went into a Spiritualist Church in Bristol—something I had never done before. I sat in the back, trying to make myself inconspicuous. However, the medium who was there suddenly looked at me and said, "I have a lady here who is probably your grandmother. She is a little birdlike person and is wearing a Victorian dress with a high lace collar."

The medium then clutched her throat and appeared to be in great pain. She then said, "She died because she had something wrong with her throat." She went on to say that this woman was bringing though a young man who had died in a motorcycle accident. She continued, "The young man is sitting with his head in his hands and telling me to say that he is sorry. He says he had been driving too fast and that the accident was his fault. He says he had just finished studying and had his

whole life before him. Now he is smiling and giving me some red roses for you."

The facts about my son were all true, but we did not know why he had had the accident or that he had been driving too fast. The roses were significant as well because I put red roses on his grave every week. However, I had no idea who the lady was as she certainly was not my grandmother.

Later I asked my mother about her, and she said, "Oh, that is your great-grandmother Eliphalette Wrench who died of cancer of the throat." I was duly impressed and was even more so when I told the story to my cousin who produced a photograph of Eliphalette dressed in Victorian clothes with a high lace collar. On the back of the photograph was written in faded ink "Eliphalette Wrench, mother of Francis." She, too, had had a son named Francis, my cousin's father.

It seems to me that the only explanation for this incident must be that it is a direct communication from my great-grandmother and Francis. I went into a church where I had never been before; I knew nothing about my great-grandmother and all the facts about Francis were correct.

Induced After Death Communication

---···◄⟨∞⟩►···---

Dr. Allan Botkin
www.induced-adc.com
www.healingafterthewar.org

Reprinted with permission from *Induced After Death Communication: A New Therapy for Healing Grief and Trauma*, Hampton Roads

I discovered induced after death communication (IADC) therapy by accident when I was experimenting with variations of a new and very powerful psychological procedure called eye–movement desensitization and reprocessing (EMDR). During EMDR therapy patients track with their eyes an object (usually a therapist's hand) moving in a particular side–to–side rhythmic fashion. It is now well accepted that the movement of the eyes greatly increases the brain's ability to process and integrate information. This accelerated brain activity allows patients to rapidly process both grief and trauma.

After I had made a number of significant changes to the standard EMDR protocol, I was surprised when a high percentage of my patients reported at the end of the session that they had an experience that they believed involved actual communication with the deceased person they were grieving. The eye–movements not only rapidly processed the profound sadness which was at the core of their grief, it also helped patients rapidly achieve a state of openness or receptivity to what is apparently a natural and rather common experience.

The following case is an example of an IADC in which the information obtained during the experience that was not known to the patient, and later turned out to be verified. While it is clear from the thousands of IADCs that I and my trained colleagues have performed that IADCs are consistently and profoundly healing, we do have a number of cases in which verification was obtained. While I have maintained a neutral stance with regard to the issue of whether these experiences are spiritually authentic or not, I have to admit that in every case new information was obtained, it turned out to be accurate.

CASE:

Simon came to see me for grief therapy about one month after his good friend Jim had died. Simon was also very close to Jim's wife, Darlene. During our session I first used my IADC procedure to help Simon process his deep sadness. At the point his sadness appeared to dramatically decrease, I gave him another set of eye movements and instructed him to "just go with whatever happens." He then closed his eyes and sat quietly for a moment. He then said, "I can see Jim. He's smiling and waving."

When Simon opened his eyes, he said "The image was very clear. That makes me feel great. I feel like he's O.K. But you know, I was really hoping to have a message for Darlene. She is not doing well at all." I then instructed him to keep that thought in mind, and induced the experience again. When he opened his eyes he looked puzzled and said, "I didn't see Jim this time. I just saw one hand holding another hand. I could tell the top hand was Jim's because it was broad and veiny, like Jim's were. The other hand seemed to be Darlene's. Now that doesn't mean anything to me. It's not much of a message for her."

When we ended the session, Simon felt both a reconnection with Jim, and a dramatic reduction in his sadness, but he was somewhat confused about the image of Jim's hand holding Darlene's hand.

Later that day, however, I received a rather frantic phone call from Simon. He explained to me that after our session he went to see Darlene and told her about his experience. When he told her about his image of what looked like Jim's hand holding her hand, Darlene began to cry, smiling and nodding her head. Darlene then said, "Last night I had a dream. It was so clear it didn't seem like a dream. I felt, really felt, Jim holding my hand. Simon, he did give you a message for me. He was saying that it really was him holding my hand last night."

About Dr. Allan Botkin

Dr. Allan Botkin holds a PsyD in clinical psychology from Baylor University and has been a practicing psychologist since 1983. A respected after-death researcher, he experimented with variations of a powerful procedure called eye-movement desensitization and reprocessing (EMDR). He discovered that one variation of this procedure results in an experience which many of his patients believe is communication with the deceased.

The co-author of *Induced After Death Communication: A New Therapy for Healing Grief and Trauma* (Hampton Roads), Dr. Botkin uses this treatment because of the healing it offers his patients. For more information, visit www.induced-adc.om or www.healingafterthewar.org.

Tanya's Heavenly Bracelet

Carol Rhodes
Oregon
tanyasmom@tmfineart.com
www.linksandloops.com/tanya

We had moved to Oregon just twelve weeks before Tanya's tragic car accident and death. I hated Oregon for the longest time. I felt that if we had not relocated from California, my daughter would still be with us. But I would later find out that she knew her time was near.

After Tanya's passing, my daughter's best friend Kim related to me that Tanya had told her she felt she was going to die in Oregon. According to Kim, Tanya had also said she would be a guardian angel not only to Kim but also to me, her brother Kevin, her sister Alethea, and Gary, her dad. Did she on some level know about her young death? During a reading with a well-known medium named George Anderson, he said, "It is as if your daughter knew that she would not live to be an old woman."

After her death we began to receive many comforting signs, but Tanya's appearance and hug was the most precious gift of them all. At this point in my life, I did not want to go on living; I missed my daughter so much. She always had a way of giving the best hugs. She'd squeeze real tight and hang on for the longest time. I would go to her grave site every morning before work and every evening after work. Each time I would tell her how much I loved and missed her. Each time I would say, "I'd give anything for one last hug."

One night just before her sixteenth birthday, I walked into my room and sat at the edge of my bed. When I looked up, Tanya was there! She didn't say anything, but her eyes expressed so much love and she had the most beautiful smile.

Tanya wrapped her arms around me. I put my right hand on her left arm. She was cool yet not cold, solid but not quite hard. My hand did not go through her, but it was just so different; it felt kind of like touching "Jell-O."

The texture of her skin startled me. There are no words to describe what her arm felt like. I drew a quick breath, and then Tanya gave me the most beautiful loving smile. She just backed away and was gone. I can't even begin to convey how much her "visit" meant to me.

Tanya would go on to send many messages using the television, computer, music, etc. Several times as I walked passed, the television in her bedroom (now the sitting room) would just turn on. On November 29, 1994, the first anniversary of her entrance into heaven, we got up early to go to the cemetery. Again the TV went on as I walked passed her room. We all went to the cemetery and then out to breakfast. We then did some shopping and other things before returning to the cemetery to light a candle at her graveside.

When we returned home later that evening, it looked like a light was on in the sitting room. When we went inside, we found the light was coming from the TV which was on. Before we left that morning, I had checked to make sure nothing was on. I cannot begin to tell you the comfort and profound sense of love that embraced me.

On another occasion I had found a note Tanya had written about her best friend Kim's birthday. I placed it in my jewelry box, forgetting about it until an amazing thing happened. I was telling Kim about the note and Tanya's plans to buy her friend a ring or earrings with her birthstone.

While Kim was on the phone, I went to my jewelry box to get the note and screamed, "Oh, My God!" I asked Kim if she remembered what jewelry Tanya had on at her service. She said Tanya had on the diamond and ruby pinkie ring I had given her, earrings, a pearl–like bracelet, three sterling silver rings, a necklace, and an angel pin.

I asked her if she was sure about the bracelet. Kim said yes; it was the one Tanya's Aunt Tina had made for her. I then told Kim excitedly that this same bracelet that my daughter was buried with was now lying on top of the note in my jewelry box. I had goose bumps all over.

I quickly called her Aunt Tina. She did not remember anything other than the fact that her niece had jewelry on. I then called my sister Gina in Hawaii and asked her. Yes, Gina did remember the bracelet. I asked her if she was absolutely sure and she said, "Yes."

A few months later I met with a medium named Linda Hullinger. I said nothing to Linda about it so there is no way she could have known about the bracelet. Yet Tanya kept showing Linda the bracelet during our reading and confirmed that she did indeed give it back to me.

At that time family and friends wanted me to seek counseling for thinking crazy thoughts. My mother even offered to pay for the therapy. But I knew Tanya was trying to communicate with me, and I refused to believe that I was crazy.

Then one night my mother woke up to find Tanya standing at the foot of her bed, smiling. Needless to say, she now believes me and no longer thinks that I need counseling. I have no doubt my daughter is as strong in heaven as she was here on earth.

Two Hearts in the Snow

Janice E. Burpee
Maine
Janeeeka2@aol.com

The year before my mother passed consisted of several long hospital stays. I often took her in her wheelchair on a tour of the hospital grounds frequently stopping at the gift shop, her favorite place in the hospital. She was a voracious reader and was pleased to find so many books at discount prices.

One day while waiting for my mother to look through the collection of paperbacks, I wandered around the store and came upon a clock. It was pastel pink, flowery, and covered in cherubs. The bottom was a carousel with little white horses dancing about. My mother agreed that it had "me" written all over it.

When it was time to go, I wheeled my mother up to the cashier. She put her weekly supply of books on the counter and said to the cashier, "I'd also like that clock." Looking at me, she said, "Janice, Merry Christmas. This is my gift to you." It is one of my favorite gifts.

A few months later my mother quietly passed away. That night I took a bath and lay on my bed reminiscing over the past year of my mother's life. The trip to the gift shop popped into my mind, and I looked over at the clock on my dresser. I noticed that the pendulum was not moving. When I took a closer look, I discovered that the clock had stopped at 3:17 p.m., the exact time that my mother had crossed! I have left the hands in that position to this day.

Shortly after my mother's death, my oldest brother Mike celebrated a birthday. Since he was a self-professed "Mama's boy," we all knew that this would be a sad day for him. We gave him a little party, but he excused himself early to go home.

On the way he decided to stop at a yard sale. He browsed through the tables and decided to buy three paperback books. Once at home he discovered that two of them had belonged to our mother. This was confirmed by her initials and by the rating system she used to mark inside the cover of every book she read.

This reduced my big brother to tears. He questioned how books belonging to our mom had found themselves at a yard sale an hour's drive from her home. Our mother had managed to make her presence known in order to wish him a "Happy Birthday."

My older sister Kathy is really quite psychic. She talks to my mother and father and other deceased loved ones all the time. One day months after my mom had passed, she asked her for a sign. She was making her

 bed at the time and something told her to look out her window. There imprinted in the snow covering her lawn were two perfectly shaped hearts entwined together. She was so excited she got her camera and took a picture.

When she told me about this, I initially thought it must have been tire marks or impressions from something falling off a tree. But after seeing the pictures, I was surprised at the perfect heart shapes with absolutely nothing else around them in the snow. Even after her passing, our mother still managed to give her children a piece of her heart.

I'm in Peace

Adriana Martinez
New Jersey

When my mother died unexpectedly from a heart attack, I was devastated. I just couldn't accept my mother's death. During the day I was an active mom with three young children; I was so busy that I didn't have the time to really mourn my mother's loss until the kids went to sleep and I eventually went to bed alone with my heavy thoughts.

Each night I would go to bed and cry myself to sleep, missing my mother terribly. Until one night my mother came to me in an unforgettable dream. She looked so incredibly beautiful and much younger than she had been when she passed. She appeared to be in her twenties and seemed so peaceful and calm as she looked at me and said, "I'm in peace."

Ever since then I have felt a sense of peace and contentment. Although I will always miss my mother, I no longer cry myself to sleep. I know my mother is happy, and I will be forever grateful for her "visit" to me that night.

Many months later while visiting with my aunt in Cuba, I was going through some old family photographs and found a picture of my mother just as she had appeared to me in my dream. I stared at the picture in utter astonishment; I knew this was her way of validating her appearance to me.

She looked so vibrant and cheerful. It's no wonder why she chose to come to me as she had been when she was the happiest while on this earth.

My Benji Boy

Ruby Kennard
Arkansas
ada.rubyk@yahoo.com

On October 6, 2007, my thirty-nine-year-old son Ben died of severe head trauma suffered in a motorcycle accident. His loss devastated our entire family as he was the "glue" that held us all together. He had been a second dad to all seven of his nephews, and they adored him. My fourteen-year-old grandson Logan had received several messages from Ben such as seeing the words, "I love," written on the steamed bathroom mirror while he was in the shower.

On January 19, 2008, I was checking my e-mails just before leaving the office for the day and saw that I had received a new message. After scrolling all the way down to the very last of my old, already read e-mails, there it was—the subject was "You can trust" but the date it had been sent was January 26, 2004. Now, I didn't have this e-mail address four years ago and couldn't believe the message had been traveling around in cyber space looking for me for four years. When I opened the message, it was a picture of all the old cures: Pepto, Vicks, etc . . . nothing spectacular; but the mystery was how did this e-mail find me after four years.

I felt puzzled so I went home, wrote the date down, and put it on the TV console near Ben's picture. Eight days later on January 26, I picked up my two grandsons Logan and Garrett and a friend of Logan's who had come for the weekend. On the way home I stopped by Wal-Mart to pick up snacks, leaving the boys in the car while I was in the store. Afterwards we drove home, and the boys spent a fun weekend together before I took them back the next day.

A few days later I checked my cell phone for messages and found that I'd been sent a sequence of images on the twenty-sixth of January. When I opened the folder, the first thing I saw was Ben's left index finger. Ben's big hands and long fingers were easily recognizable as he was a welder, and both of his index fingers were always getting smashed; he had a permanent bruise on the cuticle of both fingers. Both of my daughters were visiting that afternoon so I showed them the images and they each exclaimed, "That's Ben's finger!" We were all in shock and couldn't figure out what he was doing until I started to fast-forward the images. It hit me that he was using his finger in a left-to-right motion over the boy's face who was visiting with my grandsons over the weekend. It was as if he was shaking his finger saying, "No, No, No!"

The next weekend Logan spent the night at this same boy's house. Sometime during the night the boy's nineteen-year-old brother came in drunk and poured lighter fluid on my grandson, thus setting him on fire while he was sleeping. The kid claimed it was only a sick joke! Logan had first and second degree burns all across his chest. We know now that Ben was warning Logan to stay away from that boy.

Everyone in our family has had some form of "visit" from Ben, usually messages of guidance. But for me, his mom—we have an ongoing relationship. I woke up very early one morning, for instance, to the sound of Ben's excited voice in my head. "Mom, I have a son!" I got out of bed, went to the bathroom, and thought, "Ruby, gal, you are finally losing it big time!" And then I heard his voice again very clearly, "Yes, Mom, I have a little boy. He's been waiting for me for nearly ten years." At that point, I said out loud, "No, no, Ben, you have a daughter, Kendra.

You don't have a son."

Ben does have a thirteen–year–old daughter Kendra he hadn't been able to see since she was a toddler. Though he wasn't able to see her, he loved that little girl and grieved for her until his last breath. Anyway, I then heard him say, "Shut your eyes, mom." So here I am at 4:00 a.m. talking and arguing with myself. But I finally decided to give it a try and shut my eyes. Instantly a video started to play in my mind of many years ago when Ben and his wife came over to tell me they were expecting a second baby. They were so happy. A few weeks later she left him and ran off. Ben wasn't able to track her down for a long time. When he finally found her, she refused to allow him to see Kendra and had already gotten an abortion. He was heartbroken; after the shock was over, we never spoke of it again.

I called my daughters, and they did the numbers, racking their brains to figure out exactly what year and what month this all had happened as they had known about the new baby and the abortion. It was over nine years ago. Two days later I went on an insane quest searching for some totally useless item when I opened an old Bible and found an old letter Ben had sent me in the back cover. For whatever reason, I kept it. I then heard Ben's voice saying, "Look at the post mark, Mom; that's Joel's birthday. It was July 7, 1998. Never would I have remembered such a painful part of his life or mine at 4:00 a.m. nearly ten years after the fact.

Looking back I think the key to our telepathic communication is that while he was passing, I told him if he came back in any form, I'd know him and I'd hear him if and whenever he called or wanted to communicate. My two daughters and younger son agreed. We then told him it was OK for him to leave us and to go to Jesus. We actually rallied him on, saying, "Go, Benji; go now, go to Jesus!" Immediately his heart stopped, and he did just that.

I continue to receive signs from Ben. He wakes me up at night to find lost documents, blows out light bulbs to let me know he's with me when I'm grieving, keeps the house fans blowing when they're in an "off" position, and leaves the scent of his aftershave to linger around me when I begin to miss him to the point of tears. He has answered my questions telepathically and has shown me heaven through his eyes.

He's even preparing me for the different stages of development one experiences on arriving in heaven.

I haven't lost Ben. He's with me always . . . just not in the flesh. He's made it very plain that I'll always be his mom and he'll always be my Benji Boy, even in heaven. His "visits" comfort me, give me the strength to go on without his physical presence, but most of all they reaffirm that Jesus is the Lord and that God really is love. All I can say is heaven is real, and Ben is waiting for me with all the love he took with him when he left.

Our Special Butterfly
...The Swallowtail

Helen Fisher
Oregon
www.helenmfisher.net

Our daughter Erin died from complications of the treatment for Hodgkin's disease on June 18, 1989. She was twenty–years–old.

Since our daughter's passing, butterflies have become very significant in our lives. The first made an appearance several days before Erin's service after we had scattered her ashes, hovering over them for twenty minutes or more. My sisters were with us that morning. They had waited some distance away to give Ron, Erin's sister Lizz, and me the chance to say our last goodbyes in private. When we told them about the butterfly, they both looked shocked, and one looked about to faint. "Tell them about the butterfly," one said to the other. It turned out that the younger of the two was concerned about our choice to have Erin cremated. They had talked at length about this after going to bed the night before. During their discussion, one sister visualized a bright white light and in the light was a butterfly. She told herself that if a butterfly appeared when we scattered the ashes, our decision was the correct one. They said nothing about this to my husband or me until they learned about the butterfly's appearance the following day.

Erin's service was held in an outside amphitheater at Sonoma State University. For a reason I did not understand at the time, I found myself telling everyone who greeted me prior to the service that whenever they saw a yellow and black butterfly (swallowtail) to think of Erin. I soon found out the reason. Just as everyone stood at the conclusion of the service, a swallowtail butterfly flew in a straight line into the amphitheater, then back and forth over the crowd. It was one of the largest swallowtails I have ever seen. The feeling that filled my entire body is difficult to explain other than I was flooded with joy. A friend described my face as glowing.

Our special butterfly showed up when Erin's friends would come to visit, often hovering at the window for several minutes. Her sister was literally dive-bombed by the same type of butterfly several times in the three weeks following Erin's death.

Our basset hound Bridget brought a swallowtail butterfly into the house and laid it on the floor for me to see. It was unhurt, flying away when I took it back outside.

We have continued to have unexplainable events happen in the years since Erin made her transition. For example, a terrorist warning was issued right before Christmas, December 2003, stating there might be an attack involving airlines in the United States. Lizz was scheduled to fly out the next morning to spend Christmas with us but was hesitant because of the warning. She called several times trying to decide if she should come or just skip Christmas. I suggested that she sleep on it and decide the next morning. I then asked Erin to go to her sister, and if it were safe for her to fly, tell her just one word: "Go." I forgot about my request until the phone rang the following morning. It was Lizz calling from the airport, ready to board her flight. She hesitated for a moment, then said, "Mom, Erin came to me last night and said one word, 'Go,' and I knew that it was okay."

One afternoon several years ago when I was rushing around getting ready for dinner guests that evening, the thought "Lizz will have to go to the hospital" popped into my mind. There was no reason why I would think this because when we had spoken earlier in the day she was fine. Within ten minutes after our company departure that evening, the phone rang. It was Lizz calling to tell us that co-workers had taken her to the hospital after she had become ill at work. I have no doubt that the thought I picked up came from Erin because I sensed her presence during my conversation with Lizz.

On yet another occasion the deceased daughter of a woman who contacted me after finding my Web site came to me while I was in the shower. She had a message for her mother: "This is Zoe. Tell Mom I am okay . . . peaches and cream." The latter did not make sense to me. The only thing I could associate peaches and cream with was her skin, which her mom said was beautiful. Zoe's mother and I talked about what the message meant, and she arrived at the following, which I believe was the intent of the communication:

I felt in the end that the message was actually to do with my skin. I had been anxious about my skin as I had had a scare with skin cancer about six years ago. All the anxiety connected to that time had been resurfacing for some reason, and I had asked Zoe to give you a 'don't worry, be happy' type of message. I feel that the message was to say that my skin was OK."

When my husband learned that his only sibling Carol, who had lung cancer, was not expected to live more than a few days, he caught a flight so he could be with her at the end. Ron called me several days later between 8:30 and 9:00 in the morning to let me know that she was not expected to live more than a few hours and that he would keep his scheduled flight home that evening since there were no services planned. After we finished talking, I went outside to bring our garbage can in from the street. I then started to wheel our neighbor's can to their garage. I had taken just a few steps when the thought "Goodbye, sweetheart" popped into my head. This startled me because whenever Carol called and I answered, she would say, "Hi, sweetheart." No one else ever called me sweetheart other than my husband.

Ron called again around eleven o'clock to let me know that she had died just minutes after he walked back into the house from the back-yard where he was when he called me. This would have been close to the exact time that I experienced, "Goodbye, sweetheart."

Ron's sister being ill was just the beginning of a very difficult August. It started out with two very good friends, who are our neighbors, ending up in ICU. We have known the younger of the two, now in his fifties, since 1998. He and his wife and two children are more like family than neighbors. He developed a serious viral pneumonia that was not able to be identified by the excellent hospital where we live, nor by the Mayo Clinic. He went downhill fast. But somehow a miracle occurred, and after several weeks on a ventilator, he started to rally and continued to do so. The other neighbor who was in his mid–seventies also recovered.

It was during this time period that Carol died. While he was in Los Angeles with his sister, I had to call him with bad news about our pet Miss Kitty. She had colon cancer that had spread to her lungs. The vet said to bring her home, and when it was time, he or his partner would come to the house, or we could bring her to his office.

She was a special cat because she had appeared on our doorstep the evening of November 1, 1990, just prior to our second holiday season without Erin and the first that we would not have had extended family with us. The three of us kept stiff upper lips, but we all wondered how we were going to make it through the holiday without falling completely apart. Miss Kitty brought joy back into our lives with her antics. She was about four–months–old when she "knocked" on our door. She and the dog kept us all in stitches during Christmas. They both went wild all day Christmas Eve. Lizz said that if she hadn't seen their antics, she would not have believed it.

Poor Ron came home from Los Angeles to even more mayhem as we found out the next day that my oldest brother was in the hospital with a huge blood clot in his leg and multiple clots in his lungs. We made a quick trip over the Cascades to see him and found him doing fine. He was sent home two days later. We later found out that during this same time frame another friend had had a heart attack and flatlined in the ambulance on the way to the hospital. Luckily the ambulance crew was able to save him.

We delayed taking Miss Kitty for her final visit to the vet for several days. By then it was obvious that she was failing fast and had very little quality of life left. The vet had told us that we would know when it was time. He was right. On Tuesday morning we took her for her final visit. Having to do this was just about all we could take emotionally at that point. The doctor knew that Ron's sister had died, and he said that she would probably meet Miss Kitty when she arrived. I said, "No, it would be our daughter who will meet her." The next thing I knew I was wrapped up in his arms. He was close to tears, saying that it was hard

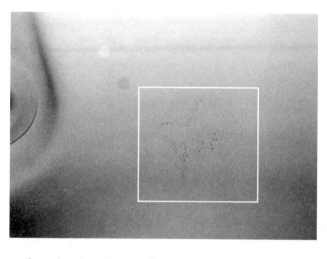

enough to lose an animal, but parents should not lose their child.

The following morning I filled the bathtub and turned on the bubbles and sat there for a long time, not wanting to get out. I didn't have the energy to face the day. Ron and I were both totally exhausted, mentally and physically. I finally reached down and pulled the plug and sat watching the water level go down. Then I saw something that I still find hard to believe even with a picture to prove it. An image of a butterfly started to form at the receding water line [see inset]. I screamed for Ron to come, probably scaring him to pieces. I have no doubt the image appeared to help us get through all that had happened in the past several weeks and no doubt that Erin was letting us know she was with us through it all.

I can almost feel her hand in the middle of my back pushing me to continue when I get discouraged.

About Helen Fisher

After the death of her daughter Erin, Helen M. Fisher says she felt as though there was a hand in her back pushing her to share her "visits from heaven." This led her to write *From Erin with Love* which was her way of turning the terrible negative of her daughter's death into a positive by helping others understand that death is not the end.

She is working on a second book and speaks publicly about her experiences. For more information, visit www.helenmfisher.net.

The Three Validations

---·◄◊►··---

Herbert Hawkins
Alabama

On August 17, 2008, my life changed forever when I lost my loving wife Jimmie to cancer. My children and I had difficulty dealing with our loss and leaned on each other for support. However, we never thought we'd actually be comforted again by my wife. But she consoled us in the most divine of ways.

Shortly after her death she made two amazing full-bodied appearances and another one in the form of a dream. She appeared first to the pastor of my church. The following is Don's account of what happened:

We had a prayer meeting at the church, and everyone had come and gone. It was about 11:00 p.m., and I was the last one remaining in the church. Suddenly, I felt a presence and looked around. There she was standing about thirty feet away from me. Jimmie was wearing a stunning pink gown and looked much younger than she had been when she passed. I would have guessed that she was about thirty-years-old.

I stared at her in utter astonishment as she stood there in full body just glowing with the most beautiful smile on her face. No words were spoken, but I sensed she was telling me that she was happy and that she wanted me to let her family know she was fine.

The whole experience lasted for about thirty seconds, and then she simply faded away. I had known Jimmie for thirty-five years, and I was the one who presided over her funeral months earlier. Yet, there was no doubt in my mind at that moment that I had just witnessed a "visit from heaven."

About one month after her initial appearance to the pastor, she appeared to his wife Geraldine.

It was 5:00 a.m. one morning, and I couldn't seem to sleep. I decided to get up and went into the bathroom to wash my face. Feeling like it was just too early to get up, I changed my mind and went back to bed. I lay there for a few minutes still wide awake when I sensed that I was not alone.

I opened my eyes and was startled to see Jimmie standing at the foot of my bed smiling at me. She looked radiant in a beautiful long, pink chiffon dress and appeared to be about thirty-years-old. The morning light was filtering through the blinds, and I could see her clearly. And since I had been awake and was not sleeping, I knew I was not dreaming. But how could this be possible? She looked just as solid as she was when she was alive. There was a boxed floor fan blowing in front of my bed. I was amazed as I watched her dress sway to the air forcefully emitted from the fan. She was standing there with a huge smile, seeming like she had just walked into my room.

Jimmie and I were friends for over thirty years, and she was always such a wonderful, giving person. On this day she seemed very happy and content. She stood there for what seemed like an eternity, but it was really a little more than a minute's time.

Later that day I received a phone call. My sister had passed away. It was, then, that I realized Jimmie was just letting me know she would there when my sister crossed. It was the most comforting experience and one that I will never forget.

During November of that same year, Jimmie gave us another validation when she came in a dream to her good friend Sheila.

I knew that Herbert and his daughter Julie were hurting. I felt so bad for them that I prayed to God to give them both some relief from their pain.

One night I had the most incredible dream. Jimmie came to me wearing a beautiful white, two-piece suit. She looked absolutely stunning and much younger than she had been when she had passed.

There seemed to be a bunch of people around her, but I had no idea who they were. She looked at me smiling and told me, "Everything is alright with me; tell Herbert and Julie that I am OK; I want them to be assured that I am at peace. I can't come to them, but they can come to me." I had no doubt she came to me in answer to my prayers.

My wife and I were married for forty-three wonderful years, and I miss her very much. But her messages gave me just what I needed to ease the hurting and to go on with my life. As she said, she can't come back to me, but I can go to her and someday I will.

. . . .

Author's Note: After writing this story, Don, Geraldine, and Sheila were shown several pictures of Jimmie to try to determine what she looked like when she appeared to them. Interestingly, all three chose the same picture of her independently of each other. The photo is enclosed with this story.

A Shepherd
Named Titan

Natalie Smith–Blakeslee
Pennsylvania
nataliemedium@adelphia.net
www.loveandlight.com

As a medium I have helped many people connect with loved ones on the Other Side. Those who have passed want to share their love and communicate the faith that we are eternal. I often wondered why I had

been given this gift; every time a parent came to me for information on their lost child, a cold shiver went through me.

I have been blessed with three beautiful daughters and couldn't imagine losing one of them. So here I was counseling others to maintain their faith about what becomes of us when our body falls away releasing our soul to the Light, yet the thought of that happening to one of our children before my own liberation frightened me beyond speech.

The day we lost our twenty–seven–year–old daughter Carrie to leukemia, I was there holding her hand as she drew her last breath. At that moment I could see her going into the Light and those who were there to meet her. I was two different people: one person holding my daughter's hand and one inside myself watching her as she went into the Light.

Having had my own near–death experience, I knew all too well she could hear my thoughts as she left. I, too, could feel her love for me and the love from those waiting to welcome her to the Other Side. I never told anyone about my vision. However, after her passing, I met with a medium who is a friend of mine. He described the two people that I saw meet her in the Light.

Further validation came from her father, my former husband. He had a dream that he was in a room and opened a door to find his mother and my father standing there with Carrie. These were the same two people I had seen welcome her as she passed.

Before her illness Carrie referred to my work as "hog wash." Perhaps it was the influence of the rest of the family, her friends, or her fear of the unknown. I don't know. But for whatever reason, she chose to doubt. However, after her diagnosis, remission, and final relapse, we discussed the subject of death a lot.

She asked me about how long it takes someone to die and if I sincerely believed the information I received from those who had passed. She wondered, if there truly was a heaven, what it was like and why she had to leave her daughter, Morgen—that question ripped me apart. I answered her from my solid belief in an afterlife; and yes, I believe the messages that I receive are real and are from people who have crossed over. I assured her that she would still be able to watch over Morgen and that she would know the answers to all of her questions, and, no, I don't know how long it takes to die. That's up to God and you.

I asked her for a sign, but she never answered. Carrie so loved animals that we always had dogs and cats in our home. From her childhood into her adulthood, we would visit our local pound, often to sit with animals. Carrie always brought treats for the animals. She loved to sit in the large cattery and play with the cats until they were adopted. She would bring dog food for the dogs and hated to leave the pound without bringing one home with us.

When my marriage ended, I spoke to Carrie about getting a dog for protection. We walked among the dogs, and she said, "Hey, Mom, Titan looks like a great dog. I think you should get Titan." This dog was a full-grown shepherd, and I wanted a puppy. A few weeks later, we were back at the pound only to find Titan still there. Again Carrie said, "See Mom, Titan is still here; you should get him." Since her passing I have thought of that scene many times and regretted not bringing him home.

In the first year after her death, my tears were never far from my eyes, arriving without warning and accompanied by a stabbing pain in my heart. How could I continue in my work to assure others about life after death and the validity of "visits from heaven" when I choked on my own grief every time I thought of my daughter?

Time passed; we leaned on each other, on family, and on faith. The pain receded; it lessened in fits and starts with every "message" we received from her. Hope replaced sadness; faith conquered doubt, and here we are more than three years later with a renewed belief in what we know to be true: there is a life after life, and our soul lives on.

Specifically since her death, Carrie has made her presence known in so many ways. She has served other grieving parents by facilitating messages from their children; she communicates through her music as well. There are gentle notes from the piano when there's no one in the room; songs magically appear on the radio station, and the scent of her favorite flowers or perfume often surrounds me as I walk through my house.

On the first anniversary of her death, my husband and I took our youngest daughter Ally and our granddaughter Morgen to the Pumpkin Patch outside of Pittsburgh where her mother spent so many days in treatment. Thinking aloud, I said, "Carrie, we have Morgen with us. Are you around?"

At that time I felt Carrie's hand on my shoulder and her long fingers pressing in assurance of her presence. My tears welled and flowed. My husband Steve glanced over at me, reaching for my hand in support. His touch unleashed days of pent up emotions as I sobbed and thought,

"Carrie, I know it's you. Please give me a sign so that I'll know I'm not losing my mind."

At that moment, Tim McGraw's "Live Like You Were Dying" came on the radio. It was her song; it was the way she lived her life from the day she was born. This was her song even before she received the initial diagnosis of cancer.

We arrived at the pumpkin farm and scrambled out of the car. The girls were really excited and scampered off to the gift shop with Steve and me in their wake. My husband glanced at me and grabbed my hand. I was too overcome with emotion to explain what had happened in the car. All I could do was smile through my tears and nod my head. I was beginning to think that had to have been a coincidence, a product of my yearning.

Pulling myself together, wiping the tears from my face, I plastered on a smile and followed the girls into the gift shop. There was Ally running toward me with a TY "Beanie Baby" dog in her hand. I was about to say "no" when she overruled me with "But you promised . . . " reminding me of what I had said on the way out the door that morning.

Sighing, looking toward the ceiling, I returned my attention to the stuffed doggie in my daughter's hand. My eyes widened as I looked at the birth date on the dog's collar: August 17, 2005. Not only was it Carrie's birthday, but the last birthday she shared with us. Flipping the tag over to read his name, my mouth fell open when I read "TITAN."

Titan, I repeated. That should mean something. I knew it did, but through the tears of astonishment to the tears of joy . . . I couldn't think . . . .just couldn't think as I struggled through the jumbled memories of the shepherd in the pound named Titan.

You will experience "visits" from your loved ones who have passed, if you are aware and open to receiving them. You don't need a medium to facilitate these communications, but often a medium helps to validate what you know to be true in the first place.

Love is so much stronger than physical death; love survives death, and God's love has given us hope to comfort us in our loss. With hope we can see the signs, receive the messages of assurance that although our loved ones are not with us in the flesh, they will always be with us in spirit.

. . . .

About Natalie Smith-Blakeslee

A psychic medium, medical intuitive, pet communicator, and bereaved parent, Natalie realized the purpose behind her extraordinary ability after having a near-death experience followed by the death of her daughter to an aggressive form of leukemia. She communicates with those who have passed, bringing hope and love to the family and friends left behind.

She has been a guest on various radio and television programs and is the host of her own cable television show, *Messages from the Light*. The author of *Close to You, A True Story of Love, Healing and Communication with the Other Side*, Natalie holds a nursing degree and is trained in hospice care. For more information, please visit www.loveandlight.com.

Keep the Family Together

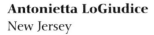

Antonietta LoGiudice
New Jersey

It was nearly midnight on March 17, 2007, when I received a phone call from my sister telling me that my father Paolo Iuliano had been admitted into the hospital with chest pains. She did not sound alarmed as the doctors said he was in stable condition and wanted to keep him in the hospital for observation.

My plan was to visit my father first thing in the morning, but he visited me instead. That night I had a dream unlike anything I had ever experienced before. It is so hard to explain, but let's just say that it was incredibly real and intensely vivid. When I woke up, I remembered every last detail from the faces to the conversations, colors, and emotions.

I can still remember it today. I was taking my entire family to visit my father in the hospital (my husband, mother, children, brother, sister, nieces, nephews, aunts, uncles, and cousins). Since I have worked in this hospital for twenty years, I know my way around. In this dream, however, everything in the hospital was under construction and moved around including elevators, staircases, and hallways. No matter which way I turned, I couldn't seem to find him.

After some time of running around the hospital frantically searching with my very loud and large family, I finally found his room. The room was much different from the patients' rooms at the hospital in that it was set up like a newborn nursery with a large glass window for viewing. Only, instead of babies, the room contained adults.

As we started to enter the room, the head nurse stopped us and said that we could not all go in the room because there were too many of us. I argued with her saying that we were a close-knit, large family and that we all wanted to see my father. She agreed but only if we would go in one at a time.

I began to send my family in one by one, sending my cousins in first. I immediately noticed that my father was becoming angry because he wanted to see me. When I finally went to his bedside, he told me that he didn't want everyone there to say goodbye. He said I should send them all home and tell them to stop crying.

After I did as I was told and sent everyone else home, my father told me that he wanted to make sure I did three things: keep the family together, take care of my mother, and stop crying. It's important to note here that this is definitely something my father would have said. He emigrated from Italy in search of the American dream and settled in Elizabeth, New Jersey. He always put his family first, no matter what. His family meant everything to him so it did not surprise me that he was telling me to keep the family together.

I listened to him intently and wanted to stay with him, but he would not let me. He told me to take my kids home and not to worry anymore because everything was going to be alright. I then drove home with my husband and kids, and as soon as I opened the front door to my house, the phone rang. It was the hospital telling me that my father had passed away.

At this point I woke up and couldn't fall back to sleep. I called the hospital to check on my father and was told that his condition was stable. Early that morning I called my mom who told me that she had just finished speaking with my father and that he was okay. I told her that I would pick her up and we would go over to the hospital. Just a few minutes later, my sister called. My father had had a sudden heart attack and passed away.

Even though I was not physically with my father, he found a way to see me one last time and to give me one last lesson.

I Was Shaken Awake

Marie
Arizona

My mother was a former teacher and remained fairly active in the community well into her eighties. She was president of the residence council at the assisted living facility where she lived and especially loved to play cards. In fact, she would meet with her former teaching colleagues once a month to play bridge.

At eighty-seven, however, she was stricken with a terminal heart and lung disease, and we had no choice but to transfer her to a hospice facility.

One night I believe she came to say goodbye to me one final time before leaving for her next adventure in heaven. It was around 12:00 a.m. when I was shaken awake from my sound sleep by something I could not put my finger on. Initially, I thought it might have been our dog Gonzo needing to go out, but he wasn't there.

For reasons I cannot explain, I was unexpectedly overcome with a sense of loss and heartache and started crying. I had no idea why I was acting this way.

I knew I was missing my mother but wasn't sure why and couldn't stop crying. I bolted out of bed . . . again not sure why . . . as if propelled and went into the bathroom. When I returned to bed, still crying, my husband Mike asked me what the matter was. I looked at him as I tried to calm down and told him that I missed my mother.

At this point I could not go back to sleep and just lay in bed thinking of Mom until the phone rang about twenty minutes later. I reached for the phone claiming, "It's Mom." Something intuitively told me it was hospice, and it was. My mother had just passed.

As I would later find out, my sister Judy was awakened at about the same time. Yet my other sister Pam, who was staying with me, slept peacefully. Perhaps my mother knew I was there to give Pam the news of her passing.

Again I'm sure my mother was just stopping by one last time. As a former teacher, she enlightened many souls here on earth. And she continues to do so from heaven.

An Auspicious Transition

Reverend Juliet Nightingale
www.towardthelight.org

On Thanksgiving I had the honor of being at the home of my friends Patricia and Earl in Nashville, where special friends were gathered all round. What made this so special is the fact that Earl was dying and barely holding on—even as we were there—because his body was riddled with cancer. Another healer and I both gave Earl Reiki and polarity treatments together and something very profound was brewing within all three of us during the treatment. It was such a wonderful day filled with so much love and communion.

After leaving their home that evening, I was very aware of Earl in my space and could feel him reaching out to me telepathically. I kept reassuring him that he'd be all right, and I made that promise to him since I, too, died of cancer but was brought back. On November 27, 2005, at roughly 2:00 a.m., he became so present in my space and was talking to me about our mutual friend Kenny that I was wondering if he was transitioning at that very moment. I was drawn to tears—but tears of joy and gratitude—and feelings of overwhelming love and compassion rather than grief. I made a promise to Earl that I'd pass on his special message to our dear friend and pass the torch on to him.

The following evening, November 28, a friend was at my office for a counseling session as he'd just bade farewell to his beloved fifteen-year-old cat Dirky whom he had to have put down. I was giving him grief counseling as well as teaching him how to be a medium and how to trust his own intuitive and telepathic abilities. It was about 11:00 p.m., and Daryl told me that he suddenly saw something move over my head. I looked up and said, "Earl," wondering if he'd just transitioned. Yet I didn't receive a call, so I didn't pay much attention to it. Still I felt Earl's presence so strongly that I had to wonder.

Finally at 2:15 a.m., I received a call from Kenny, letting me know that Earl had, indeed, crossed over at about 11:00 p.m.! He died at his beautiful home on the Cumberland River, surrounded by friends and loved ones. So, indeed, it was Earl that Daryl had seen after all! In one day, November 28, two souls transitioned—a man and a pet—yet I was able to see both of them and know that they were fine. On top of that I knew that they were utterly relieved to be free from their dense physical bodies, no longer suffering or struggling.

After I received the call from Kenny about Earl's passing, I sat quietly at my desk and focused on Earl, and then I addressed him. "Earl, what do you look like now? I am not asking what your physical body looked like, but what form have you taken on in the spirit world? This is what I want to see," I inquired. Sure enough, after a moment of quiet waiting, I beheld a most beautiful, luminous vision before me. I saw what appeared to be a luminous form resembling a jellyfish or inverted water drop, but it was very intricate with unique detailed "features." The form was glowing and pulsating and, oh, so beautiful!

I then got out my white pencil and proceeded to draw this figure on black paper in order to give it its proper effect. As I drew this beautiful image, I remembered that it resembled another being that I'd seen during my transcendent NDE (near-death experience) in the mid 1970s when a beautiful luminous being stood before me after I was told that I had to return to the physical plane . . . which broke my heart more than I could ever explain. It's as if this beautiful being was a "gift" being given me for agreeing to return to the earthly plane. This being was pouring such deep penetrating love and sound into me that I felt he had promised to be with me forever.

A few years after the NDE, I did meet that beautiful being in his physical form—a most kind and gentle soul with soft features and penetrating blue eyes—and we mutually recognized each other immediately! I initially met him in the spirit world before meeting him on the earth plane, so I saw his spirit form rather than his human earthly form, which would have meant nothing to me in the afterlife. A good point to make here is that we recognize one another by our essences and also by the fact that we're members of the same soul group (or cluster), so it's not the form that generates recognition, but rather one's essence.

We manifest ourselves in different forms when in the spirit world—especially when we're traversing through much higher dimensions or frequencies. While in the afterlife during my NDE, I had a similar form that felt like a luminous bubble—very much like the figures described above. When mediums "see" a human-looking figure of a deceased individual, that's strictly for the sake of recognition and that's not how one actually looks in the afterlife. The one exception to this is when one is traversing in the lower astral plane and/or when one doesn't realize that he has crossed over or when one is "stuck" and still somewhat earthbound. Then one will still have very "human-like" experiences.

When people (and other creatures great and small) cross over, they simply shift into another dimension and vibrate at a much higher frequency. It's like moving up on the radio band. We never really die, but only shift in frequency. The fact that I've seen and communicated with so many individuals in the afterlife for so many years and the fact that I've died several times and come back, I've got no doubt at all the we really do live forever!

How auspicious that as I was teaching someone on mediumship, he had such a wonderful spontaneous moment of seeing someone's spirit right above me there in my office and precisely at the point of his crossing over!

A few days later I did take the drawing of the "spirit portrait" of Earl over to Patricia as a gift. When she looked at it, she was quite struck by it. She explained that it reminded her of the many luminous sea creatures Earl had encountered in his deep sea diving endeavors as a photographer. It bore great meaning for her, and she was moved deeply. Indeed I, too, am reminded of the afterlife—and deep space—when I look at images from deep within the ocean. It never fails to completely take my breath away.

I can't express how much love and gratitude I felt as a result of all of this. The Thanksgiving holiday and tutoring lesson in mediumship had special meaning for me that year, and I am so honored that I was able to be a part of that sacred rite of passage and to assure others that life is, indeed, eternal.

The "Moving" Picture

Christine Sherborne
Australia
chris@colourstory.com
www.colourstory.com

We had just moved into the area and did not know anyone. My ten–year–old son Nicky was killed when he was knocked off his bike by a car and died instantly. A priest happened to be passing by and stopped to pray for him. This same priest later conducted my son's funeral and told us that he felt an incredible sense of love surrounding Nicky.

A few days before the accident, my son told me that he didn't mind if he died young. In hindsight it was as if he already knew. Following his untimely death, my family and I experienced several "visits" from Nicky. For instance one week after he passed, I felt him kiss me just as I woke up in the morning. I also had several vivid dreams in which he would tell me that he had important work to do where he was now.

We had just moved from the UK to New Zealand so my family was overseas and couldn't come to the funeral. Two weeks later, however, my husband's sisters came for a visit. Since we had the funeral service recorded on tape, we started to show them the footage.

As the tape began, my sister noticed that a picture of Nicky sitting on top of the TV was moving. All five of us looked at the picture as Nicky's face jumped out of the frame in 3-D. He appeared to be looking around the room and seemed to be ecstatic. Honestly, I had never seen him look so happy.

He was talking to us, but we couldn't hear any sound. It seemed to us that he was saying he now knew everything and it was fantastic.

This experience seemed to continue for quite some time. Eventually, his face started to fade back into the picture. At this point we all looked back at the taping of the funeral service on the TV screen, and it had ended. Afterwards, we timed the tape and discovered that the experience lasted for about forty minutes.

We were all just dumbfounded by what had just occurred. The next day we were still in shock and decided to write the entire incident down on paper and sign it.

There were five of us in the room that day (my husband, his two sisters, my oldest son, and I). The fact that we all saw and witnessed the same thing at the same time was further proof that this wasn't some mass illusion built out of grief. It actually seemed more real than anything else.

The other interesting thing is the day when this happened was March 21, 1991. He was born on November 11 at 1:00 a.m. and died on March 1, 1991. I often wake up at night and notice that the digital clock reads 11:11. I'm not sure what this all means, but I don't believe it's a coincidence.

As for that affidavit containing all of our signatures verifying what we had all witnessed that day, I will keep it forever as a reminder that my son is still with us. It is not the signatures that count, but the sense of peace that they bring and the knowledge that death is not the end.

One Lone Daisy

Dr. Clark Schmidt
Florida
ritzink@hotmail.com

Being a doctor of metaphysics and a trance medium, I have encoun-tered many strange and wonderful spiritual experiences over the years. In 1993, for example, my mother broke her hip and had to have hip replacement surgery.

I was worried that the operation might be too much for her and decided to go into a trance meditation in order to make contact with a guide I've come to know as Daisy. When I did, I was told that my mother was going to be fine and to prove it she said that there would be a daisy flower growing outside my mother's window.

The next morning I was anxious to go outside and sure enough there was one lone full-grown flower directly outside my mother's window . . . exactly where Daisy said it would be. I was just stunned and ran inside to get a camera to snap some pictures. I had been outside doing yard work just two days prior so I was absolutely certain there was nothing growing in that particular spot before.

When I called the doctor to ask about my mother's condition, I was told that she sailed through the operation without any noted complications. At the end of the day, the flower was still there standing ever so strong and seemingly alone.

You can just imagine my surprise when I woke up the following morning to find that the daisy was gone. It was as though it had never existed. Not even a petal lay on the ground. It just disappeared without a trace.

I do believe that those in the afterlife frequently help us here on earth. This was just one such instance where a very kind spirit was able to give me some reassurance and soothe my worries in regards to my mother's surgery. Help is available for those who choose to accept it.

. . . .
About Dr. Clark Schmidt

Dr. Schmidt is the author of *Tantric Meditation, Function and Purpose of Self* and is currently working on another book. He is also the director of the Universal Parapsychological and Metaphysical Association (UPMA).

At the young age of eighteen, Dr. Schmidt created a psychic phenomena research organization in which members not only researched the paranormal but also worked with doctors in the field of holistic medicine. He later opened the Celestial Visions School of Metaphysical Arts in Fort Lauderdale, Florida.

Joe Passed On

Larry Gibble
Pennsylvania

When I was about five-years-old, I lived with my grandparents. One night I had a very vibrant dream. It all seemed all too real. A man I did not recognize came to me and said, "Tell Francis (my grandfather) Joe passed on." To this day I can still remember how clear and concise his image had been.

My grandfather was originally from Oklahoma, but we were living in Pennsylvania then. He never talked much about his childhood or his siblings with me. I had no idea who this man was or even if my grandfather did have a brother. The next morning I dutifully told my grandfather about my experience and gave him the message. To my surprise I was told he did have a brother named Joe.

He immediately called someone in his family who confirmed that the man who had visited me was my grandfather's brother. Joe did, indeed, pass away the night before.

Grandma Was Just Here

Mindy
Idaho
www.waitingtowakeup.com

I was eleven-years-old, crying and praying for my grandmother who was in a hospital in Oregon. At this time my family and I lived in Wyoming, and I had just spent the previous summer with her.

I was in my room, thinking about my grandmother and lying on my bed with my eyes closed. All of a sudden I felt that I was surrounded by this warm peace. Something told me to open my eyes, and when I did, I saw my grandmother standing before me. She told me not to cry and assured me that we would see each other again someday.

She then told me that she loved me and wanted me to be a good girl. I replied that I would be good, and she slowly started to fade away smiling. About twenty minutes later I heard the phone in the front room ring. My mother answered the phone, and I could hear her talking though I could not hear what was being said.

After my mother hung up the phone, she came to my room. She told me that she had something she needed to talk to me about. To this I replied, "I already know, Mom. Grandma is in heaven." My mother looked at me funny and asked me how I knew. She wondered if I had just heard her conversation.

"No," I told her. "Grandma was just here." My mother stood there confused as my grandmother had died twenty minutes earlier. Though I was only eleven and had never experienced anything like this before, I was sure my grandmother had visited me. It was her last goodbye.

Dad's Promise to Return

Frankie H.
North Carolina

My dad was a very kindhearted, friendly, and jolly man. He had been sick for some time in a veterans' hospital. My husband Pete and I would visit him often. One night, for reasons I cannot explain, I couldn't leave my father.

I had my husband call my brother to come up to see him. My brother said, "I'll see Dad tomorrow. I'm sick and tired of you guys telling me to go and see Dad!" Pete came into the room and, assuming my dad was asleep, told me what my brother said. Dad wasn't asleep and just grimaced.

At this point his breathing became a bit labored, but he was still able to communicate and told us to go to the cafeteria to grab a bite to eat. We were reluctant to leave him, but he insisted. So we left for about half an hour to go to the cafeteria.

After we ate, we started back to his room. Pete said, "Why do you want to stay here tonight? Let's say goodnight, and we'll come back tomorrow." I was as shocked by my reply as my husband was when I said, "Because Dad needs me. He'll be dead by 5:00 a.m. I won't let him die alone." To this day, I don't know how I knew this.

When we returned, the nurse offered to bring in some beds for Pete and me, and we accepted gratefully. My bed was placed right next to my father's bed; I held his hand and told him that I loved him.

Around 4:00 a.m. Dad's breathing became even more labored. My husband ran to the nurses' station to get some help. The nurse checked for a heartbeat and said, "He's gone. I'll call the doctor." The doctor came in and pronounced him dead at 5:00 a.m.

Three days later I was in the kitchen when I felt my father's presence. I could feel that he was trying to communicate with me. I could also feel his frustration at my not being able to hear him. I looked at the location where I felt his presence and said, "Dad, I know you're trying to speak to me, and I know you're there! I love you so much! Whatever you do, please don't appear to me, because I don't think I can handle that!"

A few days later while I was in the office, my husband ran upstairs and said, "I just saw a shadow of a man's head and shoulder in the kitchen!" Being an engineer by trade, my husband is a very logical man. He said that he went into the kitchen and looked at the shadow from every angle to see if it was an anomaly of lighting. I told him, "Oh, that's just Dad." I went downstairs and although I didn't see anything, I could again feel his presence in the room. I spoke out loud, saying that I knew he was there and that it was alright.

Several days later while my husband and I were watching TV in the living room, we heard a crash in the kitchen. We looked at each other, both afraid to move. My eyes followed my husband to the kitchen door-way, and I saw him turn pale as he said, "Honey, look at this!"

There on the cold stove was a small plate. It had broken in half and collapsed onto itself into the shape of a cross! I knew it was my father, a former minister, trying to communicate with us.

Two months later I had a dream about him. In my dream he and I were standing in a wheat field. I could touch and smell him. My father held me in his arms for what seemed like an hour. I said, "Dad, I miss you so much. Why did you have to leave me?" He spoke telepathically, using his pet name for me, "Mouse, I'm okay. Don't be sad. I'll be back soon." To which I replied, "What do you mean? You're dead!" My dad just smiled. That's when I woke up.

About two-and-a-half months later, my sister called and told me that my brother and his wife were expecting a baby. This wouldn't have been noteworthy except for the fact that they had been married for seventeen years and had been unable to have children.

A few months after that, my sister-in-law sent me a picture of her ultrasound. On the picture, clear as day, was an image of the fetus that looked exactly like my father, sleeping in the womb just like he slept in life with his hand under his face. My brother and his wife later had a healthy baby girl.

I have to wonder if my father chose to come back as my brother's child. Was this what he meant when he said, "I'll be back soon"? Regardless of the answer to this question, I know that my father is still with us.

The Winding Staircase

Patty Garris Layne
Virginia
www.nickbockrath.com

Nick was heading back to his Navy base in Dahlgren, Virginia when he ran off the road with his bright yellow 2001 Ford Ranger Edge and overcorrected. Although the Navy said my son died instantly, I later found out that he didn't pass until fifty minutes after the accident.

Although in my grief I thought that I would never hear from my son again, I would soon find out that I was wrong. Shortly before the first anniversary of his death, he visited me in my dreams. I was standing in what looked like a huge mansion with a winding staircase. No words can truly describe just how magnificent this mansion was. It seemed to have no walls holding up this winding staircase. And there were enormous marble columns but, again, no ceiling to hold them up.

I was standing there, waiting by a marble wall but not quite sure what or whom I was waiting for. I can't remember much about the décor, but I do remember that it was beautiful and very bright.

Suddenly I heard my son's voice behind me say, "Hey, Mom!" I immediately turned and said, "Oh, my God! Nick, it's really you; I can't believe it! It's you!"

He was walking past me, wearing a white T-shirt and swinging his dress shirt in his hand just like everything was great and that it was not a big deal that I saw him. When Nick was young, I would get so aggravated with him because I'd spend so much time ironing his dress shirts, only to have him wear them for just a few hours before taking them off and walking around with nothing but his T-shirt on.

I remember holding my hands to my mouth and repeating, "Oh, my God" several times and marveling at how beautiful and happy he looked. He was laughing as he continued walking and started to make his way up the staircase. I felt like he was following someone though I couldn't see anyone.

I was confused and asked, "Where are you going?" I couldn't hear his response and asked, "What?" By this time he was far up the staircase that appeared to be leading nowhere because I couldn't see an end.

Nick then leaned on the staircase and said, "WILL." I said, "What?" And he repeated again seemingly loud, "WILL!"

I was still confused and asked what about Will to which he replied, "Will–Holly." I remember telling him that Holly, his girlfriend, is now with JP and that JP loved Holly and Nick Jr.

Nick looked as if he was going to continue up the stairs, and I said, "Nick, please! Can I just get a hug? PLEASE, I JUST NEED A HUG."

He appeared immediately in front of me and gave me a hug. I could actually feel the warmth of his body as he hugged me. I know it was Nick! I even saw the mole that he has on his left chest. I remember thinking, "Oh, thank you, God. Oh, thank you." And then I woke up.

Since my dream Nick has given me many signs, so many, in fact, that I have begun to keep a journal. On another occasion I was on the house phone with Suzy when my cell phone (Nick's former cell phone) started ringing. When I answered it, Pam was on the line asking me why I had just called her. I explained that I could not have called her because I was on the house phone at that time.

On yet another day I was feeling overcome by grief while cleaning the bathroom and sat down. Through my tears I began to tell God and Nick that I just didn't want to stay here any longer. I had my face in my hands, when for some reason I looked up to see Nick's shower radio moving back and forth on its own.

As accustomed, I tried to reason what was happening. But it finally dawned on me that there was no way a radio could be moving in the bathroom in the middle of a house with absolutely no wind.

I began to talk to Nick telling him how alone I felt, etc. Then, oddly, I heard his voice in my head telling me that I was going to be okay and that we'd be together again someday. I know he's right. We will be together again someday.

The Money is in the Sock Drawer

Glenn Dove
New York
doveinsight@aol.com
www.glenndove.com

Over the past twenty years, I have helped thousands of people connect with their loved ones on the Other Side. Truthfully, though, I didn't grow up wanting to be a psychic medium. I had a passion for music and always wanted to be a musician. But after the release of my first album, a friend who was killed in a tragic accident informed me that I was being called to help others through channeling. The rest, as they say, is history.

Even though I contact spirits for a living, I am just as amazed as my clients are when I receive a validation and even more so when it involves a "visit from heaven" from someone I know and love. One of the most remarkable validations I have ever received came from my father.

I was working late and decided to visit my father in the hospital the following morning. But I was never able to see him again, at least not in his earthly body.

That evening I received a phone call at home telling me that he had passed. Although I know that death is not the end, I was understandably upset, knowing how much I would miss him. But I kept myself busy by making phone calls and the funeral arrangements.

Later that night I lay on my bed awake with my eyes closed when I suddenly sensed my father standing in front of me. The odd thing was when I opened my eyes to see if he was there, the room was just dark. But as I closed my eyes, I once again saw my father standing before me.

The first thing he said was, "Bertha and Ray." I had no idea what he meant and asked him who Bertha and Ray were, but he only laughed telling me that they had come to cross him over and that he was fine. He wanted me to know he was okay.

My father then told me he had money that he wanted to give to my kids, his grandchildren. He told me to go to his sock drawer in his room. There, he said, I would find the money. I was a bit surprised by this because my father never had money on him. My mother always handled the finances and would give him money when he needed it.

The next day I asked my mother who Bertha was, and she looked at me with this astounded look on her face. Bertha, she explained, was my father's favorite aunt. Since he didn't have a close relationship with his own mother, Bertha raised him and was more like a mother to him.

She was surprised again when I told her I didn't know who Ray was and then reminded me that it was my cousin Raymond. It was then that I remembered him. One summer I had gone to visit my uncle and met some of my cousins for the first time. Ray was one of them, only I called him Raymond.

About six months after that visit, Ray died of a heart attack at just forty-years-old. So now I understood. My father was letting me know that his aunt and nephew had come to meet him and to help him transition.

Later that day my son and I went to check my father's sock drawer. We removed sock after sock and couldn't find anything. We were beginning to think there was nothing there until we came to the last sock at the bottom. In it we found about $1,000 just as my father had said.

This may be hard for some of you to believe, but I was shocked. To me this experience was the equivalent of a client coming to me for the first time and getting a long-awaited message from a loved one. It was both exciting and comforting to know my father had come through with a validation for me.

When I do readings, I try not to get emotionally involved. But this was different. This time I was involved. This time it was my own father coming through.

Since my father was in the Navy, his casket was draped with an American flag in the tradition of a military burial. As I sat there thinking of my father at the funeral, I looked up to see him standing next to the casket. He pointed to the flag and told me telepathically to give it to my youngest son Connor.

Interestingly I later found out that both my mother and my son had also sensed my father's presence in the exact spot I had seen him to the right of the casket.

Many months later I was in my room putting together one of those ski exercise machines when I quickly got a strong whiff of my father's scent. I would know him anywhere as he always wore Polo Sport cologne and had an unmistakable smell about him. As I said, I'd know that smell anywhere.

At that moment I acknowledged my father's presence, and the odor was gone. I suppose he was just stopping by to say a quick hello.

Being a professional medium definitely has its advantages. For instance, both my father's death and viewing his body in the casket were not upsetting to me. I know his body was just a garment he wore while on this earth. It's no longer him. In fact he is more alive now than he ever was.

About Glenn Dove
When he was just seven-years-old after the death of his grandfather, Glenn had the first of numerous encounters with him. Despite his extraordinary psychic abilities, he pursued a career in the music business and even released a couple of albums.

After a close friend was killed in a tragic accident, he visited a medium who told him that he would work in the same vocation.

Soon after, people began to seek him out for spiritual advice and readings, and he has never looked back. Over the past twenty years, Glenn has performed thousands of readings and has helped people across the globe. For more information, please visit www.glenndove.com.

White Tulips

Santina
New Jersey

I have always believed in the afterlife and the idea that the deceased can contact us from beyond. Yet when my friend's deceased mother contacted me in a dream with a message for her daughter, I hesitated. I didn't want to upset my friend and much worse, have her think I had lost my mind.

The dream was so incredibly clear. I was in my house when I heard a knock at my front door. When I opened the door, I saw standing before me my friend's mother seemingly very happy, holding a beautiful bunch of white tulips.

I looked at her baffled as she handed me the tulips and said, "Give these flowers to Kathy, and let her know that I am okay." With that, she was instantly gone, and I woke up wondering why her mother had chosen to come to me and not her daughter.

A few months went by, and I still hadn't mustered enough nerve to approach my friend. One day, however, I saw her at a school function and figured it was now or never.

I nervously approached her and asked her what had been her mother's favorite flower. Kathy looked at me surprised, unsure why I would ask such a question but answered, "She loved white tulips." I knew at that moment that I had to give her the message and proceeded to tell her what had happened.

She was a bit staggered and kept repeating, "Oh, my God, Oh, my God." But in the end, she thanked me for my honesty, and I knew that I had done the right thing. Her mother had trusted me with a message for her daughter, and I feel honored to have been her messenger.

They Will Find My Body

---•◦∞◦•---

Judy C.
Colorado

On January 28, 1986, millions watched the space shuttle Challenger as it blew up just seventy-three short seconds after taking off from Cape Canaveral, Florida. That same night I was visited by the spirit of Christa McAuliffe, one of the seven crew members, who was to be America's first teacher in space. She came to me in a dream that was all too real.

We were standing in her house, and then we sort of glided down a hallway as she took me to each of her children's rooms as well as to her husband's room. She told me she had one son and one daughter. When I say that she "told" me, I mean telepathically. There were no spoken words. Yet, I could literally feel her communicating with me.

She went on to communicate that she died for this mission and that everything was okay. Everything was meant to happen the way that it did. She wanted me to say goodbye to her family for her and to let them know that she had incredibly strong love for them.

It's difficult to explain, but at the time, I was so sure of what I was experiencing. I could feel myself moving down the hall. I could feel the incontestable deep, profound love that Christa had for her children. Yet, the next morning I did nothing. Gone was my assurance from the night before as doubt crept in.

I was just sixteen-years-old and didn't know what to make of what happened. At the time I was in denial and told myself that it couldn't have been true. I did not even know if Christa had children and at that time was too young to care or to even give it a second thought.

A short time later I was reading an article about Christa and read that she did, indeed, have two children. She had one son Scott and one daughter Caroline. I was stunned as I remembered my "visit" with Christa. I wanted to try to contact her family, but fear took over me as I tried to put the experience out of my mind.

One year later my brother Charly joined the army. I missed him terribly and used to lie on the floor in his room for hours, holding his dog tags and crying. For some reason, I knew with my entire being that he would not be on this earth for very long.

He actually survived the army, but one day four years later he was missing. Charly was serving in the Army Reserves. One day he left for work and never returned.

When my father called to tell me the news, I didn't have the heart to tell him that I already knew my brother was dead. I was overcome with fear thinking that I would not survive the loss of my brother if they didn't find his body. So I prayed and prayed that they would find his remains. Having his body would at least give me the closure I needed.

Later that night my brother came to me in an incredibly vivid dream. I was, again, so sure of what I was experiencing. It was, again, so real. Only this time there was no denial.

He told me that I was right; he was dead. But he went on to say, "It will be okay. They will find my body." In the dream I could clearly see his dead body lying next to a bush in a grassy clearing surrounded by trees.

His body was found ten days later in brushy area known as Thousands Acres. Charly was brutally murdered. He had been stabbed and beaten to death. It is still one of Portland's unsolved cold-blooded murder cases.

The Wild Bunny

Karen Lasso
Connecticut
Jets6216@yahoo.com

My mother passed away after a quick bout with cancer. She needed twenty-four-hour-a-day care so we had to put her in a rehabilitation center. I promised I was going to take her out but never got the chance. She was in the home for only three days before she died.

It was a Thursday night, and I went over after work to visit her. When I got there, she hadn't eaten and looked a mess so I told her we were going to get her fixed up. I picked out a very soft white night gown for her to wear. I washed her up and brushed her hair, thinking how beautiful it looked and what a shame it would be to lose her hair as a result of the treatment. She was very sleepy from her medication, but I wanted her to get some fresh air. So I opened the window to her room and sat her up in a chair.

At that moment, there was a wild bunny sitting right outside facing her window. I told her to look at the beautiful bunny. She just smiled.

I then tucked her into bed, gave her a kiss, and told her how much I loved her. She said, "Thanks for everything you have done for me." To which I replied, "You don't have to thank me. Call me if you need me."

Shockingly she passed away that night. The next morning I ran to her room, and it was obvious that they had tried to resuscitate her because things were thrown about the room. I happened to look out the window, and the wild bunny was still there, only this time it was facing the opposite direction. I sensed that this was a sign from my mother, and it was. In fact, it was the start of many "visits" involving bunnies.

One Mother's Day I was feeling extremely down and missed my mother terribly. I told my children not to mention Mother's Day and that I did not want to celebrate it in anyway because it was too hard not having my mother around.

My husband was outside mowing the lawn when he told my son to run in and get me. I walked outside in a somber mood to find him pointing to something in the grass for me to see. I looked down and to my amazement there was a little hole filled with about six baby bunnies huddled together. I looked up at the sky and said, "Thank you, Mom, and Happy Mother's Day!"

My once somber mood did an about-face, and I told my children cheerfully that we were going out for dinner. I still get the chills when I think about it; I have no doubt these bunnies were a sign from my mother.

Bunnies are not the only signs I have received. On the day of my mother's funeral, I was hysterical and hyperventilating thinking of what had just taken place. I was a mess, and my husband couldn't console me. Between my sobs I suddenly heard a tapping noise on the floor and asked, "What the heck is that?"

My husband walked over to the closet and noticed that my mother's robe was on the floor. My sister had insisted I take it as a keepsake. The fan was on, and apparently the robe had fallen off the hanger with the snaps hitting the floor.

At that moment I calmed down and an incredible peace came over me. Again I spoke to my mother saying, "I'm sorry, Mom; I'll stop. Thank you." My mother always finds a way to communicate with me at the most opportune times. For that I will forever be grateful.

Carol's Story

Should we not offer up a prayer first of all to the local deities?
                                                                    Socrates

Prayer is a way of communicating with a higher power, and ancient texts verify that the existence of prayer dates back many thousands of years. All the world's major religions have various forms of this devotional act. Prayer acts as a dialogue between the Divine realms and earthly existence. The power of prayer can bring about transformation and healing.

Annamaria Hemingway
www.practicingconsciouslivinganddying.com
Reprinted with permission from *Practicing Conscious Living and Dying: Stories of the Eternal Continuum of Consciousness*, O Books.
www.o-books.net

There is a story about a woman who had a near–death experience following a horrific car crash. As the badly–injured woman left her body, she could hear the thoughts of all of the people who were stuck in a traffic jam that resulted from her auto accident. At one point, she noticed some twinkling "lights" coming towards her. They entered her body, and she felt nourished and loved. She wondered where the lights had come from. Suddenly, she was transported to the fifth car that was caught up in the jam. She saw and heard the driver, who was inside the vehicle, praying for whoever was in the accident. Before returning to her body, she got the license plate of the car. Following her recovery, she managed to track down this person's address, and personally delivered a dozen red roses. She explained that she was the person the driver had been praying for.

* * * * *

CAROL

On my wedding day, which should have been the happiest day of my life, three of my friends came up to me and said, "Do you know who your mother-in-law reminds us of? They went on to ask me if I had ever seen the film *101 Dalmations*, and remembered the character of Cruella de Ville!

Sadly, this unfortunate caricature very accurately depicted my husband's mother, Jean, in appearance, tone, and actions. She picked and started a fight when my husband and I returned from our honeymoon, and the constant friction and rows soon doomed our marriage. The divorce negotiations ended up taking twice as long as our marriage had survived; Jean paid for my husband's attorney, and they were hell-bent on suing me for alimony. During this difficult and painful period, I took solace in my charity work, which had trained me as a volunteer in hospice, to ensure that no one need die alone.

One day, while I was at work, I found out that Jean was on hospice care; the doctors did not expect her to live for more than a few days, and my ex-husband Alan had no support in caring for her. As soon as I heard this news, I closed the door to my office and prayed in silence that God would surround her with love and light, and make her transition an easy one. Later that day, I called and left Alan a message, saying that if he would like me to sit with Jean for a night so that he could get some sleep, I would be happy to do so.

I didn't hear anything back, so I went to my regular spiritually-orientated study group meeting. I added Jean's name to the list of people in transition from this world that we wanted to pray for. At the end of our group meditation, in addition to having her name read out loud, there was a special moment of silence when my colleagues were praying to amplify whatever prayer I was offering. I prayed once more for Jean to be surrounded with love and light, and that God would make her transition a peaceful one.

After the meeting ended, I checked again for messages from my ex-husband. There were none, so I went home. I felt quite exhausted, and crawled into bed and turned out the light. Within moments, I felt as if someone were in the room. I switched the light back on, and discovered that directly in front of me was a pearlescent figure. It was solid in appearance, because I couldn't see the wall behind it. I was startled by this manifestation, and screamed. Immediately, the figure collapsed, as if withdrawing from the veil it had pushed through to visit me. I never took my eyes off it until long after the silhouette of its shadow had started to fade, and once again, I was looking through where it had been and could see the wall across the room. I knew this apparition had been Jean.

Oddly, my first thought was, "Well, I'm glad that doesn't happen to me very often!" I thought I would call a mutual friend of mine and my ex–husband's, to see if Jean had made her transition. So when I woke up in the morning, it was the first call I made. The friend confirmed that Jean had indeed passed the night before. I then enquired as to the exact time of death, and discovered it was during the period that we had been praying for her.

It's a strange and fascinating thought, that the person with whom I had by far the most difficult relationship in my life ended up giving me the greatest gift that I had ever received. For I knew this was confirmation that we do survive the death of the physical body. It also provided me with the knowledge that I had grown enough to be able to feel compassion, and sincerely pray for someone who had caused me such a lot of grief.

Later, I was to discover that Jean had also changed a lot during the final stages of her life. She had come to realize that many of the ideas and concepts that she had spent a lifetime valuing were irrelevant, and that loving her children was the only thing that really mattered.

* * * * *

Carol discovered the amazing healing power of prayer when her former mother–in–law was in the dying process. She had always believed that each of us has a soul that survives physical death, but her experience with Jean was the first time that she had ever received such concrete evidence. For this profound insight, she will always be grateful.

About Annamaria Hemingway

Annamaria is a writer, spiritual counselor, and member of the International Association for Near-Death Studies. A sought-after speaker, she is the author of *Practicing Conscious Living and Dying: Stories of the Eternal Continuum of Consciousness*. She has also appeared on numerous radio programs. For more information, please visit www.practicingconsciouslivinganddying.com.

My Beloved
Aunt Janet

———··◄◘►··———

Ellen Reid
Ohio

My great–aunt Janet, then eighty–eight–years–old, and I were extremely close. On December 24, 2008, she was rushed to the hospital with chest pains. This had been going on for some time as she opted not to have open–heart surgery to repair a malfunctioning valve.

Her breathing capacity was severely impaired, and the doctors of–fered her a less invasive option. There were, of course, no guarantees, but she chose to try the procedure. On Christmas Day, I drove two hours to see my aunt before the surgery which was scheduled for the next day.

We had plans to go to North Carolina to visit with my husband's family on the day of the surgery, and we did not cancel the trip, think–ing that my aunt would be fine. That morning, we called the hospital and were told that she was doing well and that the surgery had gone smoothly.

Grateful for the good news, we began loading our car to leave for

North Carolina when we realized our kitten was missing. My kids (ages six and two) were devastated, and we put our trip on hold as we searched madly for Sox.

As the day turned into night, we searched endlessly with no luck. Then, when we returned home, we got word that my aunt had suffered internal bleeding in her sleep and had passed away. I was shocked by the news but made one last final appeal aloud to my beloved Aunt Janet. "I guess it was your time to leave us after all. I have one last favor to ask of you—please stop here in Ohio and help us find Molly's cat before you move on to the Happy Place." I went on to tell her that if Sox turned up within the next forty-eight hours, she'd get full credit.

That night Sox showed up at the front door of the most friendly, faithful family in our neighborhood. They called us at 1:30 a.m. Our cat was just fine.

Later that same night, I lay on my bed, still wide awake and quietly gave thanks to my aunt. "Thank you, Aunt Janet." Then, without warning, she was there in the room with me. It's hard to find the words to describe what this was like. She was not there in bodily form, but yet I could sense her presence in the form of energy.

Her presence was unmistakable; I had no doubt whatsoever that she was there and was not alone. With my aunt were her two older sisters, Jennie who had passed in 1989 and Helen (my grandmother) who had passed in 2002. Again, I could not see their bodies. I could only sense their presence and feel them laughing joyfully and happy to be reunited. They had always been such a "tightknit" trio, so it was fitting that they would all come through together.

Aunt Janet told me in a sort of mind-to-mind communication that I was very welcome for her help in finding the kitten. My grandmother went on to comment on how beautiful my kids were, and then they were all gone.

The experience lasted not more than a minute, yet somehow they were so happy, content, ageless, and timeless. Looking back, I realize I had received a special gift. I figure every once in a while God throws us a bone—it's our choice to either cherish the experience or rationalize it and walk away.

A Phone Call from Michael

Cindy Bigham
South Carolina
csutton16@charter.net

Since my son Michael's untimely death, I have received many signs and "visits from heaven." He even told me in a dream that he wanted me to tell everyone about my "visits," no matter how skeptical people might be. He said I would help others by sharing his story. So I know he is happy about the book you now hold in your hand.

I even had a reading with a medium who confirmed that I was meant to share his story. She told me not to concentrate on how he died physically but to emphasize that he is now alive in spirit and that life continues. My son is certainly good at providing proof.

One of the most cherished and remarkable signs that I received from him was an EVP (Electronic Voice Phenomenon). It was Easter Sunday several years ago, and I returned home to find that I had a few messages on my answering machine.

I pressed play and listened to all the messages. Then the machine noted, "You have no more messages" as it typically did when it reached the last recorded message. But I soon found out, however, that there was another message on the tape.

After hearing "You have no more messages," I heard a dial tone followed by this strange static noise. I listened wondering if there was something wrong with my answering machine. Then suddenly, my heart raced as I heard the voice of my son's paternal grandfather who was also deceased. His grandfather, who was from New Jersey and had a very distinct voice, said, "They're not home." Then to my continued amazement I heard Michael's voice, clear as day say, "Hey." Then the phone went dead.

I know that there are a lot of people who may find this hard to believe. But I also want to point out there was no number registered on my caller ID for this particular call. Also, when I called the phone company hoping for some logical explanation, they had no record of a call being made on that day at that time! Also, whenever my son would call and I would answer, he would always announce himself by saying, "Hey." This was his signature greeting.

Like his grandfather, he had a very distinct voice. In fact, I let family and friends listen to the message without saying anything to them at first. Everyone who listened to the recording agreed that it was Michael's voice. I even compared it to a tape his best friend had of his actual voice when he was on this earth. You can tell without a doubt that the voice is one and the same.

My sister also heard him call her name right after the funeral. She was standing on her back porch, and she lives out in the sticks so no one else was around. She heard my son say, "Snook." This was his affectionate nickname for his aunt.

Also, my daughter Hannah was just five-years-old when her brother died. She later told me that at his visitation, she saw my son's spirit. Although no one else could feel or see him, she told me that her brother was going around hugging everyone. She also said that he was glowing and told her that he could see everyone's auras in the room. According to Hannah, after his funeral he came up to me, kissed me, and said, "I love you, Mama. But I have to go." He then went into a beam of light with his grandfather and some angels.

I am so blessed that my son is able to communicate with me so plainly, and I do believe it is because I'm so receptive to it. We can all communicate with our loved ones; we need only open our minds.

Music Was His Life

Barbara Yule
Texas
www.jerryyule.com

My husband Jerry Yule was a well-known concert pianist who performed around the world, mingling with such well-known personalities as President Kennedy, Johnny Cash, Rodney Dangerfield, and General Douglas MacArthur. Music was always his life.

In his later years, a failing heart kept him from playing the piano professionally. After several heart attacks and many trips to the hospital, I knew his days of playing beautiful classical music were numbered. His heart was shutting down, and there was nothing anyone could do about it.

He had been home from the hospital for just three days. There was nothing very unusual about this particular evening. He was lying on the couch, and I told him to make sure he ate his soup. I remember saying, "Eat your soup because you need to keep your strength" as I made my way to bed.

I woke up at 2:00 a.m., and something told me to go check on Jerry. I walked into the living room watching him, anxiously waiting for him to take a breath. He never did take that breath, instead his defibrillator went off. His whole body shook, and I knew it had just attempted to restart his heart. But I also knew that it had not worked; I knew that my husband was gone.

I have no idea how long I stood watching him, but I had a strong sense of peace. I had a sense that I was being told to go back to bed. It was such an overpowering feeling that I did as I was told and made my way back to bed. As I lay down, I heard a voice say, "the bed is so comfortable . . . so comfortable." I fell into a deep sleep and didn't wake up until 5:00 a.m. When I did, I could not remember how I had gone to sleep, but I did know my husband was dead.

Then I cried for the first time since his death. Anyone, who knows me, can attest to the fact that I am a strong person, but I don't know how I was able to go back to sleep knowing that Jerry had just passed. How is that possible? The only thing I can say is that he didn't want me to deal with his death at 2:00 a.m. He wanted me to get my rest and deal with it in the morning. I had always been afraid to be by myself at night, and my husband knew this.

After his death, I had a hard time listening to his music or tuning into his favorite station FM 101, which is a classical station here in Dallas, Texas. Just listening to the music he loved so much would bring me to tears. Instead I would listen to an AM oldies station and would frequently leave the radio playing for my pets when I left for work.

Jerry made sure I knew that he still preferred his beloved classical music. Twice when I came home from work, the radio was playing classical music. The radio was set to FM 101 and not to the oldies station I had left it on when I went to work. But how could this be? I thought I was imagining things until it happened again.

I came home a second time to find FM 101 once again playing on the radio. I was certain that I had not put it on this station. Doing so would require pressing a button to select FM and then pushing another button to tune into the classical station. I was convinced at this point that it was my husband telling me that he was still around and still listening to music.

Another interesting thing is that I have been at peace since his death. I was always scared before, but now I don't feel the need to be afraid. I know he is still with me. And I know he continues to make beautiful music.

Asking for a
Sign or Message

*What we call life is a journey to death. What we call death
is the gateway to life.*   Anonymous

·◦◦◦◦

Louis LaGrand, PhD
louislagrand@msn.com
www.extraordinarygriefexperiences.com

History is replete with examples of humanity seeking help and comfort
from a power greater than the self. Significantly, many millions have
reported success in their search. In fact, there is considerable scientific
evidence suggesting the powerful impact on mental and physical health
in those who believe in and establish a relationship with a Higher Power.

In earlier centuries the expectation of receiving some sort of contact
with deceased loved ones or reassurance from a divine being was commonly accepted; it was not particularly extraordinary. The technologi-

cal revolution changed all of that. Notably, the scientific method disposed of contacts with those in the afterlife as wishful thinking or at best simply hallucinations or illusions.

However, this did not stop the flood of communication and community that still persisted between the bereaved and their deceased loved ones. The only significant difference was that the reporting of these experiences went underground. Specifically, "visits from heaven" or what I refer to as the Extraordinary Experiences (EEs) of the bereaved were shared much more carefully by mourners. The fear, of course, was centered on the ethic that those who had reassuring contacts were in need of counseling and/or considered delusional. There are still many today who are very careful whom they talk to about the subject.

Nonetheless, the fact that these experiences continue to take place and are sought out by the bereaved is clear. All you have to do is ask if anyone has ever heard of someone who is grieving and reported a sign or message. Not surprisingly the stories of what they have heard about others come pouring out. (Every time I go to a professional conference or to a doctor's appointment I often inadvertently ask "Have you ever heard of . . . ?" and sure enough someone will tell of a patient or relative who was convinced he has had a contact.) Millions of people have had an Extraordinary Experience. The issue to be solidly addressed and contemplated is not whether these experiences are real—but the fact that people do have them and for what purpose. I submit that the purpose is to provide comfort and the realization that love and the relationship will never die.

Does this mean you dial one up any time you feel like it? No, it doesn't. While many people have the experience, many others do not. No one knows exactly why some do not receive the gift. It is commonly speculated that some do not need them, are too distraught and dismiss the sign as "the craziness of grief," do not believe contact is possible, or give up asking (praying) because they have not received an immediate response. In my own work with the bereaved, at some point in my meetings with them, I emphasize the following:

* It's okay to talk to your deceased loved one. It is healthy and normal to do so.

* It's okay to pray for a sign.
* It's important to establish a new relationship with your deceased loved one.
* You can move forward and reinvest in life and learn to love in separation.

Relationships with our deceased never end. They, too, want the relationship to continue and know it strengthens the spiritual dimensions of our lives. One of the tasks of grief is to build that new relationship, and often the contact experience is a major thrust in the right direction. You can reinvest in your new life and strive to grow in love. One way to do this is to ask for a sign and be open to the expanded awareness that these signs tend to generate. One soon learns there are many invisible connections. Some call them miracles.

Talking to the deceased is not only healthy, but it is also a form of loving in separation. It is not to be looked at as pathological. There is absolutely nothing wrong when you feel you are at your wits' end or feeling dejected to call out to your loved one or a divine being for comfort, insight, or strength to deal with a particular problem. Here are some ways to request a contact experience.

Praying for a sign or message is a frequent approach for seeking a spontaneous communication. There is no particular type of prayer to be suggested. Whatever you feel comfortable with is appropriate. Talk from your heart. Then stay alert for signs that may come in nonverbal or symbolic forms as well as through a vision or a dream. As the great psychiatrist Carl Jung said, "Only the symbolic life can express the need of the soul the daily need of the soul, mind you." Consider the following preparation:

1. Find a quiet place in your home, shut off all of the noise–making equipment. Set aside time each day to meditate and petition. If it is right for you, light a candle or play soothing music. Write down and then present your appeal for a sign of love. The American industrialist Lee Iacocca said, "The discipline of writing something down is the first step toward making it hap-

pen." Be specific in your request and single-minded in your focus to find an item, have a vision, or see a particular object. Then, stay alert to what happens in your environment.

2. It may be more meaningful to you to pray in your house of worship. For others, finding a place in nature by the seashore or in a beautiful botanical garden is appropriate.

3. If you believe in the doctrine of The Communion of Saints (which includes asking the deceased to intercede for you to God and is part of the beliefs of several Christian denominations), ask your loved ones to pray for you or ask them to pray to God to allow them to give you a sign.

4. Look for symbols in nature associated with your loved ones as an answer to your prayer. Consider people who come unexpectedly into your life on any given day and help you through a crisis.

Here are examples of the many ways mourners have received signs: sensing the presence of the loved one, feeling a touch, hearing the voice, unusual behavior of birds or animals, telepathic thoughts, a scent associated with the beloved, the movement of an object, a sign given to a child for the adult, a vision, synchronistic events (some call them Godincidences, not coincidences), finding coins or other objects in unusual places, electrical manipulations including lights, computers, and television sets that automatically come on or turn off, butterflies that light on or stay close to you, and rainbows which unexpectedly appear after your request. There are many others. Tune into examining closely what happens for the better in your journey to adjust to your great loss.

5. Stay alert and focus on the positive things that happen to you in the midst of your grieving. Expect your petition to be heard and something good to happen. Be aware of the important thoughts that pop into your consciousness at just the right time. Where do they come from? Meditate on that. Always review your day for unexpected events that uplift or help give

comfort. Give thanks when you receive a sign. They often come when you need them most.

Asking for a visitation dream from the deceased is another frequent approach used by many mourners. For motivation, consider what dream analysis expert and prolific writer Gayle Delaney said "that dreams are a call to reality and to living life courageously." Counselors who are open to EE phenomena often suggest to the mourner to pray for an encouraging sign that the loved one is okay and emphasize that dreams are a common route of communication. Try the following:

1. Each evening before you retire, ask God or your Higher Power to allow you to have a comforting dream visit from your loved one.

2. Place a pen and writing pad on the night table by your bed to record your dream when it occurs. Put it on paper before you get out of bed. A true visitation dream is never forgotten, but it will be useful to write down immediately all the small details of the dream for later use and to enhance recall.

3. Try to relax and facilitate sleep by thinking of some loving memories when the beloved was alive. Take some deep breaths and focus on the comforting images you have created. Go over the scene in detail: the time of day, place, weather, what was said, who else was there, and the conversation. After a few minutes, repeat the word peace or sleep each time you exhale, and try to go off to sleep.

4. Be patient and have faith in God or your Higher Power to hear your petition. Also, many spiritual counselors suggest asking, as you would in whatever is your faith tradition, for protection from any unwanted dreams or evil forces.

5. Remember that most people, who are mourning, will dream of their loved one but not all dreams are "visits from heaven." A visitation dream possesses a very special sense of clarity, meaning, and reality. It will be an extremely positive experience, and you will know you have been given a gift of comfort.

6. When you receive your dream, give thanks, and be sure that you write it up so you can use it as a resource for dealing with unwanted

thoughts at a later time. It is also a record to pass on to your children or relatives and becomes a part of family history.

The Swiss psychiatrist Carl Jung, the founder of analytical psychology, has long suggested that many of our psychological battles are won with spiritual solutions. After the death of his mother, he had an Extraordinary Experience when riding on the train home to go to her funeral. People from all walks of life have reported them. So don't be afraid of looking for dream help through your spiritual beliefs. Trust in the unseen. The results will be meaningful, and you will make it through this difficult time.

Be open to asking others with similar beliefs to pray for you to receive your dream or other contact. Persist. Although we are conditioned by the culture to expect immediate results when we want something, be willing to present your petition each evening. Take time to meditate and pray each day for your request.

LET PEACE BE YOUR GUIDE

When something unusual or unexpected occurs and you are not quite sure how to interpret the experience, let peace be your guide. Has the event brought you some measure of inner peace? Do you feel more assured? Is your anxiety lessened? Is this the kind of thing your loved one or Higher Power would do to help you along the road of transition? Peace is an inherent part of the results of these contacts. You will know it and feel it deep inside.

Don't let the unbelief and negative forces, generated by a secular society and the media, rob you of the natural wisdom that is part of the mystery of life. Remember this quote by the respected science writer Dr. Chet Raymo, "Knowledge is an island in a sea of inexhaustible mystery." Mystery is an important and healthy part of life to be embraced and enjoyed; it will always be with us.

Your openness and expectancy will bring you in touch with the peace and comfort that comes with the answer to your petition. You can walk in the realm of the spiritual side of life and receive gifts that are available to whoever asks for them. You will find the impossible possible if you commit yourself to the discipline of fully giving your petition to your Higher Power.

. . . .
About Louis LaGrand, PhD

Louis LaGrand is a grief counselor and the author of eight books, the most recent, *Love Lives On: Learning from the Extraordinary Encounters of the Bereaved.* He is known worldwide for his research on the Extraordinary Experiences of the bereaved (after-death communication phenomena) and is one of the founders of Hospice of the St. Lawrence Valley, Inc.

He has appeared on numerous radio programs and TV shows including *Unsolved Mysteries, Art Bell Coast to Coast,* and *Strange Universe.* With over twenty-five years of counseling the bereaved, he is an international speaker who gives workshops and lectures on death-related topics. His monthly Ezine-free Web site is www.extraordinarygriefexperiences.com.

What Death Is

The day which we fear as our last is but the birthday of
eternity   Seneca, Roman philosopher, 1st century AD

P.M.H. Atwater, LHD
www.pmhatwater.com

The following materials (*What Death Is* and *What It Feels Like to Die*) were
excerpted from two of P.M.H. Atwater's books—*Beyond the Light: The Mysteries and Revelations of Near-Death Experiences* (Avon Books, New York City,
1994), and *We Live Forever: The Real Truth about Death* (A.R.E. Press, Virginia
Beach, VA, 2004). It is based on first–person commentaries from over
3,000 adult experiencers of near–death states.

Both selections are reprinted with permission from their publishers:
Avon Books and A.R.E. Press.

There is a step–up of energy at the moment of death, an increase in speed as if you are suddenly vibrating faster than before.

Using radio as an analogy, this speed–up is comparable to having lived all your life at a certain radio frequency when all of a sudden someone or something comes along and flips the dial. That flip shifts you to another, higher wavelength. The original frequency where you once existed is still there. It did not change. Everything is still just the same as it was. Only you changed, only you speeded up to allow entry into the next radio frequency on the dial.

As is true with all radios and radio stations, there can be bleedovers or distortions of transmission signals due to interference patterns. These can allow or force frequencies to coexist or commingle for indefinite periods of time. Normally, most shifts up the dial are fast and efficient; but, occasionally, one can run into interference, perhaps from a strong emotion, a sense of duty, or a need to fulfill a vow, or keep a promise. This interference could allow coexistence of frequencies for a few seconds, days, or even years (perhaps explaining hauntings); but, sooner or later, eventually, every given vibrational frequency will seek out or be nudged to where it belongs.

You fit your particular spot on the dial by your speed of vibration. You cannot coexist forever where you do not belong.

Who can say how many spots there are on the dial or how many frequencies there are to inhabit. No one knows.

You shift frequencies in dying. You switch over to life on another wavelength. You are still a spot on the dial but you move up or down a notch or two.

You don't die when you die. You shift your consciousness and speed of vibration.

That's all death is . . . a shift.

What It Feels Like to Die

Any pain to be suffered comes first. Instinctively you fight to live.

That is automatic.

It is inconceivable to the conscious mind that any other reality could possibly exist beside the earth–world of matter bounded by time and space. We are used to it. We have been trained since birth to live and thrive in it. We know ourselves to be ourselves by the external stimuli we receive. Life tells us who we are and we accept its telling. That, too, is automatic and to be expected.

Your body goes limp. Your heart stops. No more air flows in or out.

You lose sight, feeling, and movement—although the ability to hear goes last. Identity ceases. The "you" that you once were becomes only a memory.

There is no pain at the moment of death.

Only peaceful silence . . . calm . . . quiet.

But you still exist.

It is easy not to breathe. In fact, it is easier, more comfortable, and infinitely more natural not to breathe than to breathe. The biggest surprise for most people in dying is to realize that dying does not end life. Whether darkness or light comes next, or some kind of event, be it positive or negative, or somewhere in between, expected or unexpected, the biggest surprise of all is to realize you are still you. You can still think, you can still remember, you can still see, hear, move, reason, wonder, feel, question, and tell jokes—if you wish.

You are still alive, very much alive. Actually, you're more alive after death than at any time since you were last born. Only the way of all this is different; different because you no longer wear a dense body to filter and amplify the various sensations you had once regarded as the only valid indicators of what constitutes life. You had always been taught one has to wear a body to live.

If you expect to die when you die you will be disappointed.

The only thing dying does is help you release, slough off, and discard the "jacket" you once wore (more commonly referred to as a body).

When you die you lose your body.

That's all there is to it.

Nothing else is lost.

You are not your body. It is just something you wear for a while, because living in the earthplane is infinitely more meaningful and more involved if you are encased in its trappings and subject to its rules.

. . . .
About P.M.H. Atwater, LHD
An international authority on near-death studies, P.M.H. Atwater is the author of 10 books including *Coming Back to Life*, *Beyond the Light*, *We Live Forever,* and *The Big Book of Near-Death Experiences*. Her writings have also appeared in numerous magazines and newspapers.

P.M.H. has lectured twice at the United Nations and been a guest on TV and radio talk shows such as *Sally Jessy Raphael*, *Larry King Live*, *Entertainment Tonight*, *Regis and Kathie Lee*, *Geraldo*, and others. She was awarded the "Lifetime Achievement Award" from the National Association of Transpersonal Hypnotherapists and the "Outstanding Service Award" from IANDS (International Association for Near-Death Studies, Inc.). To learn more about the near-death research of P.M.H. Atwater, LHD, PhD (Hon.) access www.pmhatwater.com.

What We Can Learn from Children who Have Almost Died

We are not human beings having a spiritual experience.
We are spiritual beings having a human experience.

Dr. Wayne W. Dyer

Melvin L. Morse, MD, FAAP
www.melvinmorse.com
www.spiritualscientific.com

The most remarkable lesson that we can learn from children who have nearly died is that they are astonished that they are still alive! That is alive during the time when not only did they expect to be dead, but the doctors resuscitating them also thought they were dead. And not just alive, but bathed in a loving light, a light that "has a lot of good things in it," a light that "told me who I was and where I was to go."

And not just a light, but a light that these children, without the cynicism and cultural baggage that often shields us adults from the truth, clearly identify as "God." Well, not always "God," one three-year-old boy told me it was "the sun, the sun, I saw the sun, and it had a happy face for me." The fact of being alive, completely contrary to their expectations, is often disorienting and frightening. Fortunately, they typically describe some sort of companion who explains and reassures them throughout the experience. This companion presents itself in the form of a pet, a stuffed animal, a dead relative, or some other person or comfort object that has meaning to the child.

My favorite description of a comfort person was from a twelve-year-old girl who nearly died in a bathtub when her radio accidentally fell into the water. She accurately described her lengthy and complex resuscitation and told me it would have been frightening except for the nurse who held her hand throughout the procedure. She wanted me to find the nurse and to thank her for her kindness. She was visibly disappointed when I told her that, in fact, our hospital does not provide a nurse to hold patients hands during resuscitation. It is too confusing already, and there is not enough room to have a nurse dedicated to sitting next to her and tenderly holding her hand, as she described. Perhaps a more religious child would have described this person as an angel.

My years as a critical care physician specializing in the resuscitation of critically ill children has made me aware of two very important things: (1) I am so honored and fortunate that I happened to hear dozens and dozens of critically ill children tell me what it was like to die, and (2) I feel an obligation to share this wisdom from children with others, especially grieving parents or really anyone struggling to understand the loss of someone they love. Most of these children who told me of "being sucked back into my body," and "I saw you stick a tube in my nose" while they thought they were floating out of their bodies were my own patients whom I personally resuscitated or knew the physician who did resuscitate them. They are real life flatliners, returned from clinical death to teach us not just what it is like to die, but how to live, as well.

The fact that these were either my own patients or patients resuscitated at my hospital, Seattle Children's Hospital, is so important, as it resolves instantly for me the issues that trouble other scientists about near-death experiences. For example:

(1) Are near–death experiences just dreams? Absolutely not. Dreams happen to healthy people while they sleep with characteristic brain wave functions, not to my patients who were profoundly comatose while they had their experiences.

(2) Are they making it up to reassure themselves and their families that they were not really close to dying at all and that a heaven and a God exist? Perhaps they are unconsciously conforming to the expectations that others have that they see something dramatic to account for why they survived.

I actually used to believe this myself, until patient after patient told me detailed descriptions of what actually happened to them in the emergency or operating room. They would recount incidental conversations, saying things like "then the nurse whose cat had just died came in," or "I saw my mother and grandfather hugging each other in the lobby of the hospital," events that they should not have been able to remember or have seen.

(3) Don't drugs or a lack of oxygen to the brain cause this experience? Again, no! Emphatically, NO! I also used to believe this, as a Johns Hopkins–trained physician steeped in conventional medical science. The gods of science that I worship, Plum and Possner (who wrote a textbook about coma) state that "coma wipes clean the slate of consciousness." I always assumed these patients, therefore, were not really in coma but suffering hallucinations from drugs or brain dysfunction. We did our own study of this issue at Seattle Children's Hospital in 1990–2000 which showed, to our surprise, that drugs, a lack of oxygen to the brain, and the psychological stresses of nearly dying do not cause this experience. My research partners included the heads of the departments of Child Neurology, Neuropsychiatric, and the Intensive Care Unit at the University of Washington. Our research design was so excellent that we published our findings in the American Medical Associations Pediatric journals.

(4) Do you have to nearly die to have the experience, or can it occur at other times in one's life? Our research team concluded that we all have an area in our brains, our right temporal lobe, which facilitates and interprets the experience for us. This very same area of

the brain is responsible for similar experiences during meditation, child birth, times of severe pain or psychological stress such as being tortured, or as happened to one patient of mine, simply spontaneously occurring while he was in typing class.

So what exactly have I learned from over twenty years of studying the experiences of dying children?

First and foremost, I learned that it is not scary to die. As one child put it, while she condescendingly patted me on the hand, "You'll see, Dr. Morse; heaven is fun." This fact is of enormous comfort both to me and parents who have been through the agonizing and brutal experience of seeing their child die with the assistance of modern medical technology.

I am proud of my skills as a critical care physician. If it was not for modern medical technology, almost all of these children would have died. Yet only a small percentage of patients survive clinical death (the loss of a heart beat and spontaneous breathing) with the aid of modern medicine. For every child who survives to tell me of angels and tunnels to golden fields where they can run and "double jump with God," there are hundreds who suffer all of the trauma and invasive techniques of the modern intensive care unit. Their parents, by simply witnessing these events, suffer horribly, as well.

Based on the testimony of the children, it is clear that during the times I am starting IVs in their arms and putting tubes into their lungs, they think they are floating above us. Often they want to reassure us. One child told me her parents were so sad that she knew she had to return to life just to tell them that she had been OK throughout the entire experience of resuscitation.

Children who die suddenly, such as victims of car accidents, murder, or suicide, still have this same experience of dying painlessly and peacefully. Even if someone doesn't buy into the more profound spiritual implications of my research, it is enormously comforting to know that the process of dying protects us from the pain and invasive medical procedures associated with dying. For example, children who fell from great heights and amazingly survived similarly describe the experience as "pleasant" and "peaceful." For example, they typically do not describe feeling pain on hitting the ground but rather being "taken out of my body and being safe with God all the time I was falling."

As stated above, typically children are accompanied throughout the dying process by a guardian angel, dead relative, beloved pet, or some comforting image from their own life. Many children do not know a loved relative who has died, so they will often describe, as one boy did, the family dog "who nagged at me to go somewhere with him." One little girl told me that her "Lammie," a stuffed animal she had since infancy, was in the tunnel with her. This comforting presence can even take the form of living teachers or friends. My favorite example is that of a four-year-old boy who told me that a bumblebee accompanied him as he traveled in a "huge noodle that had a rainbow in it" to the "human heaven." He stated that he knew the bumblebee liked him as it "gave me some bread to eat."

All of my scientific research has clearly documented that we die conscious, awake, aware of spiritual realities such as angels or a "God" (whatever God is and frankly I personally do not know) and that we learn lessons of love when we die. Patients will have this experience whether they appear to be completely unconscious or in coma or they have died in their sleep. When I am at the bedside of a dying unconscious child, I encourage the family and medical staff to talk to the child as if he or she can hear everything as my research documents that they usually do.

Our results have now been replicated in adult studies in both Europe and the United States and published in the world's most prestigious medical journals. Even studies from the United States National Warfare Institute validated our findings. There is no longer any doubt; the near-death experience is, in fact, the dying experience. It documents that we do not have to have a functioning brain in order to be conscious and aware.

I will never forget the first child I ever resuscitated who told me of her near-death experience. I had never heard of these experiences before as this was back in 1983 before they were commonly written about.

"Can this child be saved?" I thought to myself, when Krystal, age seven was rushed to the emergency after nearly drowning in a community swimming pool. The medics told me that she had no heartbeat for at least nineteen minutes. I gritted my teeth and thought to myself that

I had to start to prepare myself to tell yet another set of disbelieving and horrified parents that not only would their child die but that their lives would never be the same again.

I quickly and efficiently started the many varied lifesaving procedures that I knew had to be done. I was proud of my team; even in a case like this where there was no chance of survival, they were thorough professionals and gave the same excellent care they always did. Satisfied that all that could be done was either done or initiated, I spent a few moments in the hallway with the parents. It is not my job or my nature to shield others from the medical situation as I know it. Furthermore, these parents might soon have to make difficult decisions about organ donation, how aggressively to pursue end–of–life care, and preparations for funeral services. I told them to prepare for her "immediate demise," as I unfortunately put it.

Yet Katy did not die. She lived to tell her parents several weeks later that she was mad at me for putting a tube in her nose and that one of the reasons she wanted to stay in "heaven" was that she could look down on her body and see all the painful and terrifying things we were doing to her. "I told my guardian angel that I didn't want to go back to my body as it looked all messed up, but she said I had to go back to help my mother, as my baby brother would soon be born with a heart problem." Her mother knew she was pregnant, but the child was not yet born. He did, in fact, have a heart problem diagnosed after birth. And everything Katy described about her own resuscitation, including trivial conversations with nurses or that I went to the phone and called my superiors to ask them what to do next as she was surely dying, was accurate.

As I heard her story in total disbelief, Katy patted my hand condescendingly and said, "You'll see Dr. Morse, heaven is fun." She looked me in the eye and laughingly told me, "When you thought I was dead, I thought I would be dead, too! But I wasn't! I was alive! When you are dead, you're still alive, isn't that weird?"

These children grew up to be adults who were not afraid to die. As one young woman told me, "I am not afraid to die, because I feel I know a little bit more about it (Death). I am not in a hurry to die; my near-death experience taught me that life is for living and the Light is for later." Another boy dispassionately told me that not only was he no longer afraid to die, but that I had to "tell all the old people not to be afraid."

After twenty years of hearing these experiences, I can confidently state that I am not afraid to die. I know this because I was recently on an airplane flight when we unexpectedly hit severe turbulence. As the plane was bumping up and down around the sky, my instinctive very first thought was, "This isn't too bad. Now I will see for myself what the children have been telling me," and I had absolutely no fear whatsoever of dying.

So much of our lives are dominated by our fear of death and concern that all of who we are will end someday. This fear of death is so prevalent that the American Medical Association has estimated that much of the wasteful and invasive medical care we inflict on the dying is directly because of our fear of death. Conservative estimates indicate that as a society we spend over six-billion dollars a year on medical care that does not prolong life one minute. All who have investigated this situation agree that the reason for this expense is that our fear of death paralyzes our ability to make rational choices about end-of-life care. As one commentator stated, "End-of-life care, unfortunately, is all about what we can do in terms of aggressive medical care, but not what we should do."

Studies have shown that doctors feel they have to over treat and -medicate the dying because patients expect it. Ironically, interviews with patients document that they often do not want this invasive care but feel the doctors want it. Even worse, studies of dying children show that children often know they are going to die, and yet they won't tell their parents or talk about it as they don't want to upset the adults.

Children who have had near-death experiences often feel passionate about this problem and take it upon themselves to educate the dying. One girl I know nearly died of a severe brain infection. She told me that to her great surprise, she floated out of her body and met "Jesus," a nice man who wore a red hat and was sitting on a rock. She saw a rainbow that was "the light that told me who I was and where I was to go."

As a teenager, she started visiting Children's Hospitals and talking to children with life threatening diseases. She told them what to expect about dying and what happened to her. Just these informal contacts with hospitalized children resulted in enormous benefit to the children and their families.

It is my experience that when we educate people about the "facts of death," they will, on their own, have powerful understandings and insights that can help with the dying process and the horrific grief that can follow the death of a child. One mother told me with tears in her eyes that now she understood why her son abruptly woke up out of a coma and smilingly said to her "Mom, the moon, the moon, I am taking a rocket ship to the moon. They are taking good care of me, Mom, so you don't have to cry. I am okay, Mom." He then lapsed into coma again and died within twenty-four hours. Prior to hearing about our near-death research, she had assumed that this was some sort of hallucination caused by drugs or the high fever he had at the time.

One reason we, as medical professionals, are afraid to tell patients about the spiritual aspects of the dying process is that we fear we will be criticized for bringing religion or excessive spirituality into the medical environment. We are trained not to intrude on a patient's religious or spiritual beliefs or complete lack of such beliefs. We are afraid we will seem unprofessional or even pandering to the patient's grief and fear of death if we bring spirituality and/or religion to the bedside. This is so true that a recent study of nurses on a cancer ward showed that they rarely discussed death and dying, religion, or spirituality during their working hours with patients. Yet those same nurses would often return and simply spend time with parents and patients discussing those very same issues, which they felt they could discuss more comfortably person-to-person rather than nurse-to-patient.

There, perhaps, was once a reason for this strict separation of spirituality and science; however, it clearly no longer exists. Teaching patients about what to expect about the psychology of dying is just as important as telling them what to expect about side effects of medications, their treatment courses, and what their treatment plan is. We have an obligation to give patients informed consent about all aspects of their care and this includes a discussion of the spiritual aspects of dying.

Specifically, proper informed consent of the treatment of critical patients includes: (1) a recognition of the fact that dying patients are frequently alert and aware of what is going on around them, even if they seem profoundly comatose, and (2) dying patients, as well as their medical caretakers, family, and other loved ones will typically experience a wide variety of visions before death, shared dying experiences, after death visions, and spiritual dreams. (3) The process of dying is typically joyous and spiritual and often involves the facilitation of "spiritual helpers" who care for and assist the dying patient.

One huge problem is that we don't have a shared vocabulary to discuss these experiences. Often just the words alone that we use offend or alienate the very people we are trying to educate and help. I once gave a lecture in which I just blandly stated that dying children often see something they describe as "God" as part of the experience. I received a firestorm of angry questions and comments along the lines of "what do you define as God," "when you say God, do you mean the Judeo–Christian male authoritarian figure that is rejected by so many people," and fairly commonly "I don't believe in a God, but I believe in a Higher Power, and I wish you would have said that instead." I once had the head of a Department of Pediatrics at a major Children's Hospital congratulate me on my lecture and then shake his head and say, "If only you wouldn't use the word 'spiritual,' your lecture would have been far better received."

I don't know any other way to describe the fact that dying comatose patients think they are awake, aware, are outside their body, see a "God," and are often comforted by "angels," "doctors who were fourteen feet tall and had light bulbs in their bodies," or their family pets who had died!

The main lesson I have learned from these children is quite frankly the first lesson I learned in medical school. Good patient care is not about me and my beliefs; it is about the patient and what he believes. When I counsel a parent who has a fussy infant with severe colic, my goal is to listen attentively and try to help the parent understand what a fussy infant means to them! For example, one mother might not really be concerned about the infant's crying but is worried that others might think she is a neglectful mother. Another parent might only be concerned to be assured that there is nothing physically wrong such as an ear infection that can be treated. A third parent might benefit from learning the natural history of colic, that it seems to be a precursor of language at times, and will spontaneously resolve. I don't have to review with the parent all the controversies over the "objective reality" of colic; I simply have to understand what colic means to them.

So it is true with spiritual experiences. I find that parents are fascinated to learn that the experiences are normal, natural, and even have a large area of the brain dedicated to allowing the experience to occur. One dad commented to me that learning that our brain has a "spiritual insight area" just like the language area and the "move-your-leg area" made his experiences more real for him, as obviously these are not the result of hallucinations or brain dysfunction. This allowed him to believe his own experiences and trust what they mean to him and not to worry if "science" or "doctors" believe him.

Frank Oski, Professor Emeritus of Pediatrics at John Hopkins University, where I trained, taught us to trust our own intuition as the most important thing that dying patients can teach us. What an astonishing statement! As a medical student I didn't think the two had anything to do with each other. Furthermore, I was so overwhelmed with just learning the hard science of medicine and remembering all the drug doses and side effects that I didn't want to hear about intuition.

All of that changed one night when we resuscitated a critically ill infant who went on to die. I was devastated. We worked so hard for so many hours, and the baby died before he even had a life. As physicians, we were exhausted and angry and tearful after the experience and even started to blame each other for not doing everything perfectly. To our great shame, the parents overheard our conversation as they sat in an isolated room silently grieving over their dead child, holding him in their arms one more time. They came out to the main area and took our hands and thanked us for all we had done. They told us that our fears and anxieties were the same as theirs, "Had they done enough? What could they have done differently or better?"

Dr. Oski then told us about a similar experience he had when a patient of his died at an early age. He told us he had a dream that night in which an angel in white appeared to him at his bedside and told him that children who die at an early age know secrets of living that cannot be learned in any other way. He told us that it stretches our humanity and makes us better doctors and human beings to care for children who are less than perfect.

He concluded by telling us, "Don't believe me when I tell you what happened to me. I was a medical student once, and I know that I would never have believed someone who told me such a dream. I ask only that you be attentive to the ordinary miracles of your everyday life."

I never understood what Dr. Oski meant by that until I studied near-death experiences in children. I had such respect and awe of Dr. Oski, who was otherwise an intimidating person because of his medical knowledge and experience, that I always remembered his comment. However, I could not get past the fact that he did not have an ordinary miracle in his everyday life; he had an angel in white appear at the foot of his bed.

The children have taught me differently. They learned from encountering this Light at the end of life that life is about love and finding pieces of the Light in our everyday lives. One girl told me that she learned from her near-death experience that she didn't mind waiting in line at the supermarket anymore, as the "Light is there, too, you know." Another girl told me she brought the Light back with her, and she sees pieces of it everywhere, "even when my mom is mad at me and in mean people, too." Another boy told me he was told to go back to life as "I had a job to do." I asked him what he thought his job was, and he was astonished. "I just told you. I just got a job working construction; I am making good money $18 an hour. I bet I can put myself through junior college next year and help out my parents (by paying for his own schooling)."

The message from the children is clear. Death is not to be feared, and life is for living. They tell me the hardest lesson for them to learn is that they have to accept the love that awaits us all at the end of life. One said it best, "I learned that we must bring this Light into our ordinary lives and to anchor the Light in this world to learn to love in this life."

About Melvin L. Morse, MD, FAAP

Dr. Melvin Morse, voted one of America's top pediatricians, has researched near-death experiences (NDEs) in children and adults since 1980. According to Dr. Morse, by studying the neuroscience of the NDE, we learn that human beings have an underused area of the brain which is responsible for spiritual intuitions, paranormal abilities such as telepathy and remote viewing, and the power to heal not only the soul but the body, as well.

His interest in NDE research evolved from his experiences working in Critical Care Medicine at Seattle Children's Hospital. He published the first description of a child's near-death experience in the medical literature and was funded by the National Cancer Institute to complete the first case control prospective study in near-death experiences. He is the author of such groundbreaking books as *Where God Lives, Closer to the Light* and *Transformed by the Light*. For more information, please visit his Web sites at www.melvinmorse.com or www.spiritualscientific.com.

Awakening to Our Inherent True Nature

The things which are seen are temporal; but the things which are not seen are eternal.   The Apostle Paul

---

Nancy Clark, CT
Ohio
healeygarden@msn.com
www.freewebs.com/nancy-clark

What does it mean to be awakened to our inherent true nature? Why is it important to learn who we really are? For most of us, we think we already know who we are. For instance, we define ourselves by the jobs we have: I'm a chemist; I'm a real estate broker; I'm a mother. Or I have blond hair and blue eyes and I just graduated from college, or I'm homeless and I'm a cancer survivor.

We are more than our ego's characterization of ourselves. We have a powerful identity which is the very essence of life inhabiting the physical body. It is the soul, the manifestation of the Divine Presence within us. This is our true identity! Our ego nature is our false self. I would like to tell you how I know this for a fact.

In the early sixties I had a near–death experience during childbirth. I had a toxemic pregnancy, characterized by extreme edema and high blood pressure resulting in convulsions and death. I woke up in the morgue. Years later, in 1979, I had a deeper and very profound near-death–like experience while delivering a eulogy for a dear friend. Once again the Light that I experienced in the early sixties during my near-death experience was calling me "home" to experience communion with the Divine and to open my consciousness to wisdom, truth, power, and love. I was not close to death or suffering from illness or physical trauma at the time I was delivering the eulogy in 1979; however, I experienced the identical features of a classic near–death experience, proving there are many triggers for this type of transcendent experience with the Light and that coming close to death is only one of them.

I experienced the following features of that sacred event: tremendous peace that can best be described as the "peace that passeth all understanding;" my spirit–self lifted out of my physical body; I encountered and merged into oneness with the Light of God whose unconditional love is ineffable; I traveled through the dark universe at a tremendous rate of speed; I witnessed at least eleven dimensions; I experienced timelessness, telepathic communication, a life review, and a life preview; I was given total knowledge; twelve guides were with me; I wanted to stay but was told I had to return to share what my Great Teacher revealed to me so that I could help humanity raise its consciousness to Light–consciousness, and then I experienced a rapid reentry into the physical body. I was forever transformed from that moment on.

What I saw and what I learned from my Great Teacher during those fifteen minutes that "Nancy" was delivering the eulogy will forever be cherished as the most supreme and sacred event in my entire life. The all–encompassing Presence and my ego–self "I" disappeared into the radiance of the eternal realm. Its sudden onset by the grace of the Divine Presence instantly transformed my life, clearing from my mind old beliefs and ushering in an awareness of my authentic true self. I wrote about this experience in great detail in my first book, *Hear His Voice: The True Story of a Modern Day Mystical Encounter With God*, PublishAmerica 2005.

Because I promised the Light of God that I would help others as I was helped, I was sent back from the loving arms of the Creator to begin sharing the knowledge my Great Teacher revealed to me. Ever since my own awakening, I have been actively pursuing this teaching that was placed in my heart to help others ascend toward Light or Divine consciousness. There is no greater joy than to spread the Light's message of love and the knowledge that we are each expressing the One Divine Power through our humanness.

I am well aware that for some people it may sound bizarre, if not downright crazy, to hear me admitting that my spirit–self was taken up into God's Presence while delivering a eulogy. It may be easy to surmise that I may be a lunatic. Typically if we don't understand something of a supernatural nature, we have a tendency to label it, and once we do that, we don't have to deal with it anymore. We think we have all the answers, but we don't. We must remember that our Creator is greater than our little finite minds, no matter how many PhDs we may have or how many awards we have been given for our brilliant works. If the Divine Presence seeks us out for a purpose and we are open to receive it, then there is nothing we can do but follow the passion in our heart to serve the Light and our fellow man. This has been my promise to God ever since my experience. So my advice to you is this: Draw whatever insight from my message that touches your heart. Allow the Spirit that is within the depth of your soul to speak its own truth to you. For it is in the union of Divine Spirit and your own soul that God can move you to the next level of a deeper and more intimate experience of the Sacred within.

I learned from my Great Teacher during my transcendent experience that man's true destiny is to realize the truth of the Divinity of one's self that is ever present within the self.

The reality of the Presence is so all–encompassing and magnificent that it defies any possible imagined idea of ecstasy. Trying to describe the Divine Presence is like trying to describe color to a blind person. Many have attempted such explanations, but all have failed because the Divine is beyond our finite minds and the language humanity has created.

How, then, do I attempt to explain the all-encompassing rainbow colors of the Divine Presence within so that people will begin to create a vision of the Ultimate Reality? I can't. No one can. The best I can do with our current language is to inspire people to awaken to the knowledge that is placed directly within every single person so he can discover for himself the existence of this truth that I personally awakened to. This discovery must be personally experienced; there is no other way. No amount of factual knowledge will convince anyone of its truth unless he inwardly perceives that it is true.

My Great Teacher gave me the seeds of Light to scatter, but I realize that some seeds will fall on fertile soil, while others on rocky soil. Many teachers strive to instruct others in this quest for understanding the innermost mystery, but we must remember that each person is unique. Just as there are no two fingerprints that are exactly alike, so too are all individuals set apart in their uniqueness. Each person can perceive only what he is capable of perceiving at whatever level of growth he happens to be at the time. I will describe some of the teachings my Great Teacher infused into my heart during my transcendent experience so that you may begin to take responsibility for your own life transformation should you choose to embark upon this magnificent Light-filled task.

Following my transcendent experience, my life became a beautiful expression of genuinely satisfying happiness and inner peace. Although I have experienced many crisis events in my life since that transcendent experience in 1979 which include our house burning to the ground, the loss of all of our material possessions, my husband becoming disabled with very serious health issues, my becoming a caregiver to assist him in however long he remains on this earth, the loss of our medical insurance, and many other events, I never experienced painful states of anxiety. Inner peace prevailed. How is this possible?

The answer to that question is the reason I agreed to write this chapter for this book so that you, too, can find the inner peace which is beyond intellectual understanding. A rich and purposeful life is to be found within oneself, no matter what the exterior world throws our way. Make no mistake, when the veils are removed and we finally "see the Light," (pardon the pun), then this glorious Light within sings its song of overflowing love, joy, and everlasting peace. A new world will be revealed to us, and we will dwell within it. The outer world will then have no power over us to cause our struggle, suffering, and fears.

I am convinced that within every heart there is a longing for something above and beyond our observable reality. I believe that in every heart there is a yearning for freedom from the darkness of heartaches, frustrations, and guilt which this harsh world seems to inflict upon us. We believe there must be something better than all this. But what? It is the LIGHT, the indwelling Divinity that we are part of—our true nature, our authentic real self!

Prior to my transcendent experience, I knew nothing about ego, spirituality, and our true nature. I was an average married woman who raised a family and had a thirty-year career as a cytologist engaged in cancer research at a major university. I was vigorously trained in the scientific method to accept as fact only that which is verifiable by science and objective reality. However, my transcendent experience with the Light of God was subjective "proof" that a far greater reality beyond our sense world exists. From the deepest source of Divine Love, I was illumined with the knowledge of man's true nature for the purpose of helping others become aware of something they simply forgot.

Before I discuss the Light and our relationship to the Divine, we must first understand our ego's role in the way we relate to life, our thoughts, and feelings, and how our ego causes separation from our awareness of our true identity, the LIGHT within. The ego is highly motivated to dominate our lives by using fear to condition our minds to claim authorship of all our subjective experiences. Ego reinforces our need to be "right" at any cost and voraciously clings to its cherished beliefs. We invested a lifetime of living from an egoist perspective because everyone is attached to the hopes and expectations, failings, gains and losses, and human suffering. The "I" self identifies with roles, titles, and behavior, but this creates the illusion of an independent, separate self. Probably the most tragic consequence of our ego's need for dominance is the fear that "I" will one day be faced with the prospect of death. This makes the ego very fearful. We haven't been taught that the ego is our false self, the illusion we have about ourselves.

During my transcendent life-transforming experience with the Light of God, I learned there is only one true, authentic Self; it is our higher Self, the Divinity that we came from, belong to, and return to. I was shown how we must peel away the layers of illusion we have about our false self, like the layers of an onion, until we reach down to the core of our true being. There, at the core of our being, the manifestation of perfection shines forth. We have come "home" to the indwelling Divine love, power, healing, and knowing. From this perfection of our true identity comes self-acceptance, self-expression, and our justification for being, all expressed as the Divine Presence through our true Self on the human level.

How do we peel away the layers of illusion of our false self so we can begin to live a life we were created to live? Remember this: Our ego will resist change. The ego wants to be in charge at all times; that's its nature. It is simply a collection of thoughts, feelings, memories, data, and beliefs, but ego also tries to convince us that this is who we are. Ego motivates us to become insistent, desiring, yearning, greedy, spiteful, fearful, challenging, resentful, angry, contriving, and all the other negative and destructive traits that dwell in the illusion of our false self.

I don't mean to imply that ego is a bad thing to have or that we need to get rid of it. Certainly, ego has a purpose to fulfill in our daily lives if we are to live in this world of information and knowledge. Our minds need to experiment with ideas—then, probe, listen, and absorb. The ego only becomes a problem when it convinces us by the various negative thoughts and feelings we become attached to that the world we live in is threatening and chaotic. We have been taught from an early age that we are separate individuals who need to protect, defend, or advance ourselves in some way. We try to impose our agenda on life to satisfy our ego needs at all costs, but in doing that, we experience suffering.

I was shown during my transcendent experience with the Holy One that it is our birthright to become detached from the sorrows of our outer life experiences by living with the awareness of the Kingdom of Heaven within. This so-called "Heaven" is our true self—the Divinity that is the Light of the world. Every loving thought, word, and deed arising from our true self unites our two worlds together—the physical with the spiritual. Our lives become a manifestation of God's love, healing, harmony, wisdom, and power in the midst of all activity on the earth. No matter what our exterior life experiences will be, our interior world embodies all the qualities of the living Light of the Divine. In reality, we are each Divine, not separate, but united as one. This was such an astounding "light–bulb" moment of truth for me during my experience when I understood that our awareness of this truth was essential to a deeper and more profound experience of the Divinity of existence.

Knowing our oneness with the Divine and with all transforms our egoist life into a life of peace and wisdom. Our inner being has become fearless, aware, and, oh, so loving. It is as natural as the sunrise revealing itself in the early morning, shining light onto the shadows of darkness that existed only moments earlier.

Intellectual understanding of our oneness with the Divine and with all will not result in the consciousness necessary to dwell in this glorious state of awareness. The mind or our ego is not the soul. Only the soul must experience this sacred truth for itself. We cannot force ourselves to believe this. We cannot use willpower to try to destroy the ego's hold over us. The ego is very cunning and clever. It will discourage us every step of the way to pull us away from experiencing the Divine Presence within.

What is needed is simply to understand that the ego holds mistaken beliefs about who we really are. So give the ego a break. Forgive the ego for what it doesn't know. Then all we need to do is to learn how to heal the ego's grip over our lives. We do that through our willingness to go deeper within the mystery of our self to surrender our self to the One who calls us "home." I do not believe we can do this by intent or our trying to achieve these results on our own because this only reinforces perception through the ego. Rather, the awareness of the reality of our true nature is facilitated by humility, faith, trust, and the realization that God's grace will bring the result we seek through the various processes necessary for one's spiritual development.

When we invite the Beloved to work with us in shedding the illusion of our false self, we can be assured the Eternal Power which created us can lead us into wholeness by healing us in every nook and cranny of our being. The sweet gentleness of Spirit within will express the intrinsic qualities of the Divine through all the pathways of our life as we walk lovingly forward with a new life—a life of joy, a life of peace, and a life of grace.

This is not idle talk. This is truth as revealed to me during the miracle of my transcendent experience. It can be your personal truth, as well, if you accept it. A musician composes exquisite music to be shared with others—not to harbor it all for oneself in the silence of a soundproof room. The musician must share the gift received; otherwise it would not be heard, never enriching our lives in such a beautiful melodic way. So hear your own music! Know your music! Be your music! You will, then, know the revelation of what it means to be yourself—your spiritual identity.

We have each been given the connection to the Divine to compose the rest of our lives from the symphony of Holy Love, the portal to the unification of Heaven and earth. This is our ultimate fate even if we are presently unaware of this. We are each channels for Light to lift the consciousness of all people. Every word, thought, or deed carries the potential for bringing Light into the world with hearts being opened to a strong infiltration of Divine Glory.

Let us each begin the process of self-discovery to expand our capacity to recognize the power of the Divine Presence within—the life that will bring new life to the old life. Let us each open our hearts to find our own love center, the greatest love we have ever known. Begin by claiming the truth that the Divine is individualized in every soul-being and that this is given to us by grace. When we can consciously realize this Presence as our true nature, we will no longer condemn any part of our being or anyone else for that matter. The miracle that exists within us is a powerful source of pure, unconditional love. Accept it and grow with it. Your selfhood is Divine. Know it and honor it. Let nothing separate you from this truth!

Every day take the time to reflect upon your Divinity and your true worth, and be grateful to the One who created you to be who you truly are. When the ego sneaks in through the back door of your mind, trying to deceive you through false judgments, work to rid yourself of your preconceived ideas of how life ought to be. Forgive the ego for trying to separate you from the truth of your being and allow Spirit's voice within to speak to your heart to heal you of that mistaken notion.

Just as automobiles sometimes need front–end alignment, our thoughts also need alignment to clear our mind of old beliefs and to release us from past experiences. When we begin to align our life with the Presence within and to heal our ego's need for control, we will begin to experience the promise given to us by the One who loves us beyond our imagination, as He said, "I am with you always, even unto the end of the age."

Go with love, knowing that within you are the wisdom and the guid–ance to help you begin a new way of living. Love is the answer. Love is the key. God IS Love.

About Nancy Clark

As a result of having both a near-death (NDE) and near-death-like experience (NDLE), Nancy's passion is to help others while serving a higher purpose. A former cancer researcher and cytologist (a biologist who studies the structure and function of cells), her scientific background enabled her to analyze her own mystical experiences objectively before arriving at the ultimate conclusion that parallel realities do indeed exist.

Now retired, she is passionately devoting her life to the spiritual work that is so important to her by inspiring others toward the transcendent nature of life and into the mysterious union with the Light of God. She is the founder and coordinator of the Columbus, Ohio International Association of Near-Death Studies, (IANDS), a member of the Academy of Spirituality and Paranormal Studies, Inc., a member of the National League of American Pen Women, and the International Writer's Association. She is the author of a nationally award-winning book, *Hear His Voice, The True Story of a Modern Day Mystical Encounter with God* and *My Beloved: Messages from God's Heart to Your Heart*. For more information about Nancy Clark, her books, and her work, please visit her Web site: www.freewebs.com/nancy-clark.

Bridging the Gap Between Science and Metaphysics

Science without religion is lame. Religion without science is blind.
Albert Einstein

———··❦··———

Marie D. Jones and Josie Varga
info@mariedjones.com
www.mariedjones.com
www.josievarga.com

It was once said that science disproved the metaphysical. Nowadays, however, scientists are realizing more and more just how much the two are intertwined. But before we discuss the similarities, you must first understand the differences.

Many mistakenly think that religion and spirituality are one and the same. But the truth is they couldn't be more different. Spirituality refers to looking within for answers while religion looks outward. The same can be said about science and metaphysics.

In the early twentieth century great scientists, like Albert Einstein, Max Planck, Niels Bohr, and Werner Heisenberg, realized that the world may not be about what can be seen. In fact, they proved instead that the physical universe is essentially nonphysical. Through their collective efforts into the study of matter and energy, the field of quantum physics was born.

For example, Einstein established in 1905 that light consists of tiny particles called photons. Although this discovery would later become one of the foundations of quantum physics, it is important to note that, ironically, Einstein strongly rejected some of the claims of quantum mechanics. He felt that a more conclusive theory, one which would get rid of the probabilities of quantum mechanics, was needed.

Having said this, quantum physics has little to do with Sir Isaac Newton and the famous falling apple, which was believed to have inspired his gravitational theory. Instead, quantum physics studies reality not as it appears to us but as the possibilities which exist to explain the unexplained. It is a branch of science that seeks to tell us the fundamental nature of reality or existence—just as metaphysics seeks to explain the nature of who we really are. It studies, for example, parallel levels of reality, near-death experiences, "visits from heaven," remote viewing, ESP, and others.

As more of these "quantum" studies were conducted along with advances in technology which allowed them to measure with more precision, the more paranormal or "above-normal" phenomena were observed.

Ultimately, even Einstein did not believe that all the findings of quantum physics could be explained by science alone. In a more recent experiment, for example, it was found that one particle could be in several places at the same time. These subatomic particles seem to instantly travel over space and time. Albert Einstein described these types of findings as "spooky action at a distance" or beyond our physical world.

Quantum physics also theorizes that there may be many, if not infinite, parallel universes while metaphysics explores the possibility of "mirror universes" where other versions of us may actually exist. This is extremely important to understand because it may mean that anyone who ever lived is still alive in some form on some level.

This leads me to the question which I have presented in this book: if everything that ever lived is still alive and if there is no death, is it then possible for the deceased to communicate with the living? And further, is there a God or some Supreme Being or Force responsible for this life? If so, can this be proven?

Famous psychologist and philosopher William James tried to find evidence of life after death and as part of his research focused on mediums. After years of studying a medium named Leonora Piper, he remarked, "If you wish to upset the law that crows are black, you must not seek to show that no crows are: it is enough to prove one single crow to be white. My white crow is Leonora Piper."

This has come to be known as The White Crow Formula. Simply put it is possible to prove the probability of something just by proving the authenticity of one such case. So if you believe that just one of the "visits from heaven" presented in this book is possible, then it must be proof that there is an afterlife. Likewise, if you believe in the validity of just one case out of the millions of reported ghost or near-death experience (NDE) accounts, then you must conclude they are possible. I'll admit that I am a bit biased or subjective here. But having experienced my own "visit from heaven," I am a firm believer. And, to me, even though scientists and skeptics are quick to point out that there is no definitive proof, I believe the accounts in this book do prove the existence of life after death.

Take, for instance, the case of hospital worker Teresita Basa, who was found brutally murdered and burned in her Chicago apartment on February 21, 1977. Police were baffled by the case as they found no clues and no witnesses.

A woman named Mrs. Chua worked at the same hospital as Teresita but barely knew her. One evening Mrs. Chua suddenly went into some type of trance and announced in a totally different voice, "I am Teresita Basa." She then went on to say that Allen Showery had murdered her, stolen her jewelry, and given her pearl cocktail ring to his wife.

When the incident was reported to police, detectives were highly skeptical but investigated since they had no other leads. When they searched Showery's apartment, they not only found Teresita's jewelry, but his wife did indeed have the pearl cocktail ring!

When Mr. Showery was confronted by police, he confessed to the murder. At the trial, however, his attorney moved to dismiss the case on the grounds that the evidence was provided by a ghost.

Luckily, the judge did not agree, and Allen Showery was sent to prison.

Going by The White Crow Formula, this case alone, in my subjective opinion, is enough to prove life after death and the ability of those on the Other Side to communicate with the living. As for my other question—is there a God or a Supreme Being responsible for this life—I believe we need only look at the what is known as the anthropic principle which attempts to explain the fact that things must be just right in order to allow life to exist. It goes on to say that the outwardly unrelated constants in physics have one thing in common—they are exactly the right amounts needed to produce life. Any slight deviation would make life impossible.

For example, had the nuclear weak force been a slim bit weaker, there would be no hydrogen, as we know it, making water impossible. And speaking of water, ice is lighter than water. If water in its solid state was not lighter, the oceans would freeze from the bottom up. The essential constants in the universe had to be just right in order for us to be here. The likelihood of all of this being due to a series of random events is believed by many to be nil.

And if the creation of the universe was not a random act, then there must have been a beginning or a Beginner, if you will. Einstein himself came to the conclusion that there must have been a Superior Power bringing everything into being. While working on his theory of relativity, he reasoned, if the universe started with The Big Bang, then something must have existed beforehand.

But what did exist beforehand? To help answer this and many other questions, I had the privilege of interviewing Marie D. Jones, a highly acclaimed author who has been working for most of her life to bridge the gap between science and the metaphysical or paranormal.

1. How did you first begin to research the paranormal?

I have been interested in the paranormal since early childhood. I have always had an incredibly overactive imagination and was really into ghosts and UFOs since I was, maybe, four. I swear I saw Bigfoot in the woods behind my house, only my mom said she thought it was our hairy Italian neighbor. When I was five, I wrote a book about life on Mars! I bound it in cardboard. I still have that thing. The paranormal and all things scientific have just always been a part of my life. As a teenager, I began seriously exploring the occult, esoteric matters, and UFOs, and I never looked back. I became an active field investigator for two MUFON* groups and spent fifteen years doing that, as well as studying and writing about paranormal and metaphysical subject matter for magazines. I was also really into science fiction—what a nerd! I was editor–in–chief of both my high school and college newspapers and was always assigning myself stories to look into the paranormal. I interviewed witches, alleged vampires, psychics and all kinds of people who had unusual experiences, that is when I wasn't backstage at concerts interviewing rock stars! Being editor–in–chief had its privileges!

I was raised by a very creative, spiritual mom and a scientist dad so I got to walk between two worlds and always knew that science and the spirit worlds were linked. It was something I just knew but could not find proof of. Although I don't need proof to know what I know, I still seek proof because I want to understand the hows and whys behind paranormal and unknown phenomena, including what happens to us after we leave this level of reality.

2. How does quantum physics explain or prove the existence of an afterlife or life after death? How does science prove the existence of an afterlife?

Quantum physics opens the doors to the possibility of explaining life after death but does not yet do so definitively. Neither does science. But some of the most fundamental laws of physics tell us that energy does not cease to exist—it simply changes form (Law of Conservation of Energy*) and that particles which come in contact with one another remain so over vast distances of space/time (nonlocality) and that there may be a field of virtual potentiality in which past, present, and future all exist at once, as well as every bit of matter and form and energy that ever existed (Zero Point Field*).

We do know that energy does not die. Therefore, on some level we, as bodies of energy, do not die. We change form. We take a new shape. The body may turn back to dust, but the energy that is us, our essence, does not end. It goes somewhere, and that is what we are focused on: Where does it go? How does it get there?

We can also look to the theories of parallel universes and alternate dimensions to suggest that we, or another version of us, exist on many different levels and not just on this one that we are aware of right here, right now. This is a bizarre thought that we are alive and well on an infinite number of levels, yet we can only be consciously aware of one level at a time. The theory of wormholes, or shortcuts in the space/time continuum, might explain how we get from one level to another and how ghosts and UFOs and spirits move between worlds.

3. **Do you believe that life after death can be proven? If so, what is the single most compelling piece of evidence?**

I do believe it can be proven, but we are nowhere near close to doing so yet. We may be getting closer with more researchers and investigations using the scientific method to look for patterns and commonalities in the experiences of NDErs [near–death experiencers]. There is no single compelling piece of evidence. One person may have seen a ghost of his dead mother, and that would be his single piece of compelling evidence. Someone else might point to EVP* of a dead child that can be traced to a certain location and call that the single piece of compelling evidence. But neither is provable on an objective level quite yet.

I am not sure that we will ever have a collective single piece of compelling evidence. I suspect (and I know readers won't want to hear this) that each of us will have our proof when we die—at that moment when we slip from this life into the great beyond. That will be our proof, and for those of us chasing that proof in the here and now, it is quite frustrating to think that might be the case.

Still, we search . . .

4. **Have you researched afterlife communication? If so, what have you concluded?**

I have done some research, especially when writing my book *PSIence: How New Discoveries in Quantum Physics and New Science May Explain the Existence of Paranormal Phenomena*, and I have seen an awful lot of subjective and experiential data that does indeed point to the continuation of the soul, or spirit, after death. Whether we are talking about apparitions and ghosts or EVP, it does appear that millions of people are experiencing glimpses of the "Other Side." These experiences have been going on since the beginning of recorded history, too. So this is nothing new.

But, there is no definitive proof. Perhaps there never will be. Maybe we are meant to take all of this on faith and believe the experiences of others and often those we have ourselves that cannot be duplicated in a lab or reproduced according to the scientific method. The sheer volume of experiential data, though, begs to be paid attention to. Are there patterns we can discern from that data? Do certainties emerge from the variety of experiences reported? What environmental anomalies are always present?

The one constancy is energy. We are talking about energy and the fact that we know energy does not cease to exist. I do believe in life after death and that energy from those other levels of reality can engage in crosstalk with our own. How they do that is the sixty-four thousand dollar question!

5. **Is it the spirit or the soul that has energy? Can this be proven? If so, can this energy really maintain personality and bonds with loved ones as so many "visits from heaven" seem to indicate?**

Those are difficult questions to answer, because, again, we have no proof of anything involving the paranormal or what happens beyond death. But if we look at the laws that govern us in life, we do see that all is energy either in one form or another and that energy does not cease to exist.

Can emotion and love and thought have energy? I believe so, and it seems this is what all of the current studies into intention are showing—that strong thought and emotion have a "frequency" that affects their surroundings. Those, who have died, have simply changed form, in essence, and perhaps we are on the verge of discovering that emotion, especially extreme emotions of fear, love, and despair, do have an energy of their own which would explain a lot about ghosts and associated hauntings. Extreme emotion may be like trapped energy that is not freed or released upon death.

Ghosts may also maintain the personality they were associated with before their deaths because of the observer or the person who is consciously experiencing the ghostly sighting may be affecting the outcome of the perception, as we see in quantum physics. There are so many possibilities that it is fascination, but again it all seems to point to the transfer of energy, whether physical, emotional, or even spiritual. Prayer has power as we have seen in many experiments involving collective and long distance healing prayers. Thus, any emotion with force behind it can be thought to have power, and that, of course, suggests there is energy moving behind the thought.

6. What is the message you hope to give your readers?

If I had to boil it down to one simple concept, it would be that there is more to life than meets the eye. There is another life we lead, albeit mostly unconsciously, and we get glimpses into that other life every now and then in the form of experiences that we describe as paranormal. Life does not end at death. It just changes into a different kind of life or a different kind of reality. I think we all know this on a deep, intuitive level, which explains the utter fascination people have for death and for what might happen afterwards.

I also would like readers to know that science is not the enemy. In fact, science can indeed find the answers if those who call themselves scientists dare to be more open-minded. This also applies to those researching the unknown. They must embrace science more openly. That is why I've partnered with Larry Flaxman, Founder and Senior Researcher of ARPAST.* We have formed a venture called ParaExplorers, and we will devote our time and energy to researching and writing about unknown mysteries from a very scientific perspective. ARPAST is the premier paranormal research group in the country, using strict scientific methodology in its work, and that is what will help us one day understand the mechanisms by which this phenomena manifests in our lives.

7. **Based on your research and experience, do you believe in God? Some describe God as a supreme source or all-knowing energy. How would you describe God?**

I do believe in a creative force behind, in, and through all things. But I liken it more to The Force from "Star Wars" in that it is not an entity with humanlike characteristics. I don't think God is like anything but is like all things. It is more of a power than a *persona* to me, and when we align with it, life is joyful. When we resist it, we suffer. I also believe we are individualizations of that supreme power like pieces of a hologram, separate on one level, yet containing the whole within us.

I like the idea that the Zero Point Field* of quantum and theoretical physics may have Godlike qualities in that it is self-regenerating and it is the ground state of all matter and energy and form.

8. **What advice would you give to skeptics?**

Healthy skepticism is a must. I am not a total believer in anything. My motto is "I believe you; now prove it to me." I think skeptics must keep an open mind, though, and be willing to think outside the box and to stretch out of their comfort zone. That's where the answers to life's greatest mysteries are always found.

I think total diehard believers are just as negative as total diehard skeptics in that neither party brings anything to the table of understanding the unknown. Their rigidity keeps them from seeing different perspectives that may be necessary to theorize, then to go out, and to find proof of ideas that are not traditional or accepted by the status quo.

9. Why is the belief that death is not the end so important for people to understand ?

We are terrified of death and of our own mortality, yet isn't it funny how we cannot remember what was going on before our birth? Either we will snuff out into nothingness with no awareness whatsoever or we will continue on in another form. Either way there will be no pain or suffering unless that is the destiny we choose for the next go-around! I think people desperately want to know that they will go on and that their short time on this planet was not for naught—that they mean something and their lives mean something more than just being a mere parenthesis in time.

I also think people want to know that they will be around those they love deeply for the rest of time. Love, we are told, is eternal, and people long to know that this is true, even if the body itself turns to dust. On some level, we all want to go on forever, preferably surrounded by those we walked through life with before.

10. You have studied UFOs, quantum physics, the paranormal, etc. In your opinion, who are we really?

I truly believe we are individual personifications of the

creative force behind all things. We are made of stardust, yet also quite earthly. We are all-knowing, yet incredibly naïve, having forgotten what we know. I think we are all divine beings trying to remember our divinity, caught in human form and limitation. Those who break beyond that form and limitation are the ones we call sages, wise ones. But we are all wise ones. We just don't remember.

I think back to the one time in my life when I could honestly say I was truly happy. I was a small child, caught up in nature and the world around me. I knew exactly who I was then. I was all-powerful, all-knowing, one with my surroundings. It was a profound realization that has driven my studies and research all my life. I hope to one day get back to that amazing state of grace!

11. Do you believe in the Big Bang Theory? If so, what existed before? If not, why not and which theory do you more closely believe?

I do believe in the Big Bang Theory (BBT), but with a caveat. I believe that our universe was one of many, perhaps an infinite number, and the BBT was simply the formation point of OUR universe. M-Theory* speaks to this point, saying that there are membranes or "branes" upon which universes exist, and when "branes" collide, it can create Big Bangs and new universes.

What was there before? Space, other universes, endless time . . . How could there possibly have been nothing? The point of singularity that turned into the moment of birth of our universe was no doubt repeated numerous times throughout the entirety of existence and continues to this day. There could be Big Bangs going on right now with new universes forming, but we have no awareness of them because they exist on a parallel level of reality, perhaps in another dimension.

I also tend to lean towards the Information Theory—

the idea of the Universe as a giant quantum computer that is programming itself into existence and programming all of reality as it evolves. It makes sense, as information drives matter and form and energy.

It's an exciting time to live in, when science is coming up with these amazing theories that include elements that can only be described as "paranormal." Finally, it seems that we are seeing the bridge between these two worlds emerge from the fog and take form.

. . . .

About Marie D. Jones

Marie D. Jones is the author of *2013: End of Days or a New Beginning- Envisioning the World after the Events Of 2012*. She also wrote *Psience—How New Discoveries in Quantum Physics and New Science May Explain the Existence of Paranormal Phenomena, Supervolcano: The Catastrophic Event That Changed the Course of Human History* written with her father, geophysicist Dr. John M. Savino, and *Looking for God in All the Wrong Places*.

She has an extensive background in metaphysics, spiritual studies, and the paranormal. She has appeared on hundreds of radio stations all over the world and has been interviewed for dozens of magazines, newspapers, and Web sites. Marie recently formed a professional partnership with Larry Flaxman, President and Senior Researcher of ARPAST, for a venture called ParaExplorers. Their books include *11:11—The Time Prompt Phenomenon* and *The Resonance Key: Exploring the Links between Vibration, Consciousness And the Zero Point Grid*. For more information, visit www.mariedjones.com or contact her at info@mariedjones.com.

*Explanations:

ARPAST: The Arkansas Paranormal and Anomalous Studies Team

EVP: Electronic Voice Phenomena which occurs when unexpected voices are recorded

Law of Conservation of Energy: This law states that energy remains constant; therefore, it cannot be created or destroyed. It can only take on various forms (e.g. kinetic energy can become thermal energy).

MUFON: Mutual UFO Network

M-Theory: This theory is the Mother or Master of all string theories which search for the smallest form of matter and show how all the particles in the universe can be made up of one-dimensional slices or strings of two-dimensional membranes. These strings vibrate in multiple dimensions to create every form of matter or energy. M-Theory brings all other String Theories together.

Zero-Point Field: The Zero Point Field is filled with a sea of energy (Zero Point Energy) and light contained in a huge quantum vacuum. This massive energy is in its lowest state which makes it is invisible to our eyes but is located everywhere. This is significant because if this ZPF exist everywhere then everything that exists must be connected.

The World Hereafter—
Life in the Garden
of Souls

Heaven is a city without a cemetery.
Anonymous

------••⟨∞⟩••------

George Anderson
www.georgeanderson.com

After nearly a half-century of hearing from the souls, there is one statement the souls make that is the most important, by far, of all their
communication—they do exist, and thus there is another world beyond
this lifetime. That statement alone is enough to strike awe in some and
abject fear in others, but there is a small part of every human being that
hopes the statement is true. Hearing the words from the most reliable of
sources—the souls—and to hear their incredible accounts of their existence in that place, help those of us on the earth who struggle with their
uncertainty to be able to believe. There is a world hereafter, and there is

life beyond the one we know.

In truth, it should surprise no one that there actually is a place where the souls return after having struggled on the earth through a journey of lessons—all designed to help us grow and learn in our spirituality. Since the dawn of organized religion, we have been taught that at the end of our lives here, when the body ceases to function and dies, we are elevated to a place of rest near the Supreme Being of our particular religion to whittle away the rest of eternity. To many people it is a vague and slightly disconcerting concept. As those of us who grew up Roman Catholic know, we are taught that when we pass over, we sit at the right hand of God in joy for eternity. To me growing up, that statement struck fear in me—at my best moments I can't sit for a half hour, let alone an eternity.

The problem with proclamations about a world hereafter by those who have not seen it is that they are uncomfortably vague and rather poorly thought out. It seems to me that this kind of story ends at the very beginning, and it is nearly impossible to grasp. I understand that not many people are able to see souls or hear communication from those who have passed on, but those who can and do have a responsibility to share the unique and ever-changing story that is the world of the souls. When the souls tell the story, it does not end at the beginning. The souls know that in their new life in the hereafter it has only just begun.

THE ROAD TO THE HEREAFTER

I think it's important, when discussing where we go, to understand where we have been and how we actually get from one place to another. The souls talk constantly about our lifetime being a journey of specific circumstances, both good and bad, that each of us must face while we are here. We face them, we deal with them, we learn from them, and we move on, sometimes in spite of them. The lessons are very specific here and designed to allow us to grow spiritually on the earth. Some lessons we face will teach us humility, some will teach us patience, some will teach us how to love in spite of pain, and others will teach us acceptance of things we cannot change. We are given the circumstances, and we are allowed to accept the challenge or lay it down and walk away. We can shine in having become better people as a result of our life lessons, or we can lose our way and avoid the very hard work of becoming a more spiritual soul as a result of our time here.

It is all up to us, but the souls tell us that in order to learn, we must take the journey before us. What we learn and accomplish here, no matter how long or short the time, is a reward we build for ourselves when our time is done. The more we accomplish on the earth, the better the reward for us in the hereafter. The message of the souls is very clear with regard to what exactly our life here is about—they have told us that our work here is to create Heaven on the earth, in whatever way we can. Their hope is to bring our two worlds closer together, and they have told us that it can be done. Each of us holds the power to make this world more like the next—a life that includes joy, generosity, peace, kindness, and caring. At best we have had limited success. But even having tried to be more like the souls in how we have been able to impact the world around us while going through many challenges on the earth is what will be our crowning achievement, when it is our time to pass from the earth to the beauty and joy of the hereafter.

THE PORTAL

There comes a time in the life of every living creature that the journey on the earth will come to an end. Because we do not understand it, the concept of death brings such fear and loathing to people that it has taken on epic and unnatural importance in our lives. Our innate beliefs and hopes seem to fail us at the very time we need them the most, and we fear what will be the most important transition in our lifetime, even more important than our birth. Our physical death is to be the marker by which we know we have come to the end of the struggles we endured on the earth and to receive the benefit of our hard work, our pain, our tears, and our relationships with those whose lives we touched. We are like the young birds that begin by shaking their wings, then walking with wings outspread, then hovering and falling, then jumping and falling again. At some point, the struggle will end, the lessons will be learned, and the fruit of all their work will be found—they will look toward the sky, leave the ground that held them, and do what was previously thought by them to be impossible—they will fly.

The transition between this world and the next has historically been cast in a terrible light because it is perceived to bring with it all the things we fear the most—pain, suffering, and loss. Finding ourselves at the end of our physical life or having those we love making the transition brings us to the most vulnerable point we will ever have to face. It is a last, final lesson that the earth will hand us before we see the face of Light on the Other Side. For some, it is a moment of complete clarity about life and the journey they were on, and for others it is a fear that they had not done enough to make a dent in this lifetime and truly affect the world around them. No matter what the circumstance, we will all find ourselves at the moment in which the Portal opens, and the souls signal that it is time to shake off our physical connection with the earth and to follow them to a new world. On the clock of our lifetime, just as there was a specific day and hour we were born, so is there a specific day and hour when our journey comes to an end.

As much as it is a big transition from one world to the next, I have found in talking to the souls that once they have entered the world hereafter, the transition was not quite the monumental experience they had thought. Many have described how easy the actual transition was— they report that it was as easy to pass into the hereafter as it would be for us to walk from one room to the next. Many souls have reported being accompanied by the souls of loved ones who had passed previously, and still others tell how, at the moment of death, the Light that they saw ahead of them was lovely and irresistible. As surprising as it may sound, the souls say universally that they left the earth of their own free will. Given the opportunity to see and feel the beginning of their new world made them want to walk toward it, and having friends, loved ones and pets greeting them made it a comfortable and beautiful experience.

In a session for his bereaved parents, there once came through the soul of a young man who very clearly recounted the thrill, beauty, and peace of his transition in order to help his grieving parents understand that no matter how horrible the circumstance of passing seems to appear to us, it is a wonderful experience to the souls.

The young man recounted how, after begging his parents to use the family van to go out one evening with his friends, lost control of it on a hill and crashed into a tree. He immediately got out of the car and realized the heavy amount of damage, and his first thought was "my folks are going to KILL me." But he stepped back and noticed the calm—there was no sound, there was no movement and he felt a peace that he had never felt before. He decided to walk from the car up the road that he had been traveling, and he marveled at how as he moved, he felt lighter and more peaceful, and the ground beneath his feet felt softer, and the sky became lighter and lighter until he was bathed in the sunlight of dawn across a beautiful field.

It started to occur to him that he may not be on the earth any longer, as grandparents could be seen waving and smiling up ahead, and the pets from his childhood gathered near him as he walked forward. Although his parents were grateful to hear that his transition was not anything like the grisly scene the paramedics encountered when they found his body, I was more gratified to hear the souls speak so clearly about the moments they move from this world to the next, and how everything is designed to make the transition a peaceful and happy one.

Another time in a session, I had the benefit of hearing how compassionate the Infinite Light is when it comes to protecting the beauty of our souls, even at the most difficult transitions.

The very distraught parents of an eight-year-old girl came to see me in a session after their daughter was murdered behind a train station in broad daylight. She was lured there by a man on her way home from school. She described in her session that he pulled her to an area that was hidden from the street and began choking her, but she screamed in fear and tried to break away. Sensing that he might be caught, the man found a brick nearby and intended to smash her head. The scene police found when they discovered her was horrific, and the parents were suffering greatly thinking how frightened she must have been—her hair had gone completely white in the struggle and the parents were despondent thinking that her innocent young life had to witness so much horror before she died.

This little girl spoke with such remarkable clarity during her session about the events that unfolded that it surprised even me. At the moment she was to be struck with the brick, and while she was still actually alive in the physical sense, she told us in the session, "A beautiful lady came and made time stop. She lifted me up and said it was time to go, and we walked to Heaven." It was stunning to hear that even before she had actually passed on, in an effort to spare her the fear and pain of her eventual death, her soul left her body before it was actually dead. If there was any small consolation to be had in the loss of a child, the parents were so relieved to hear her state emphatically that she never felt any pain.

The transition to the hereafter seems universally to be an experience that the souls find surprisingly easy and peaceful, regardless of what it may have appeared to us. There seems to be a design in place that will suit whatever need we may have in finding the most appropriate means of transition in order to make the experience a pleasant one, and at the same time, a life lesson for those of us left on the earth who will struggle to find some way to understand and cope with the loss. Some souls have recounted falling into a sleep state in order to ease the transition, so that when they open their eyes again, they are in a world of light, peace, and joy. It helps us to understand that our fear of the moment of death is, at the very least, unfounded, and at the very most, completely off-base, as the souls freely attest. The circumstance of passing, whether it is due to illness, accident, or violence, is only the final circumstance of our physical life, and the vehicle which propels us to the next life.

What has always intrigued me about the souls and their recounting of their passing is that to them, now that the transition was made and they are happy in their new world, the actual moment of their passing does not hold much real interest to them. It was something they did, and aside from a few remarkable changes, it was done. It seems so matter-of-fact to the souls that it makes one wonder about how easy it must have been, and how beautiful their world must be that the actual leaving of the earth somehow doesn't matter anymore. It is a lesson to us all to understand the souls' unique perspective so that we can look upon our own transition with wonder and awe, and not fear. The souls truly do see their own deaths as not an ending, but as an invitation to the most beautiful place they have ever seen.

THE GARDEN OF SOULS

The more we hear from the souls about their world, the more we understand. And the more we understand about their world, the more we can appreciate why they have graduated from the earth and the more confident we can be that with the story of any struggle or loss comes a very happy ending.

I have learned very much over the years in my communication with the souls and their messages to loved ones still on the earth. The souls do the best they can to help us understand that the world they find themselves in after having struggled on the earth is by every account a reward for having lived here. In recent years, the souls have been helping me to understand the concept of life hereafter as a Garden of Souls, because things that are planted in our lifetime bloom for us later in a world of joy. Their analogy of the hereafter being like a garden is not just a pretty picture to fill our heads with—it is the closest thing on the earth that they can use as a reference to how the Other Side works and how a garden is a good example about living beauty, order, and purpose. After hearing so many stories about life on the Other Side, I think the example of a garden couldn't hope to compare with the beauty of life there, but it is the only reference we will be able, at this point in our very limited education, to understand.

Life in the world hereafter, in the Garden of Souls, is a perfect day, forever. What strikes the souls as both funny and poignant is that the hereafter is a mirror image of the earth, or rather, what the earth could be. It is a world as recognizable as the one they just left, only better—it is filled with joy, with beauty, and with an ongoing current of light that makes everything shine.

Once the souls are on the Other Side, they understand that their world is not bound by the conventions of ours—they are not encumbered by a physical body, but they are recognizable to themselves and others. There is no physical conception of time and space, so they can be where they want when they want, and the joy of being with other happy people brings with it a sense of peace and love.

The souls, entering this world, still bring the biases of the physical world with them, and part of their understanding in their new world is how little they actually need or want the things that they prized so much on the earth. The hereafter seems to build to suit whatever the souls feel they need or want, until they realize that it is no longer what they need or even want any more. Many of the souls who struggled on the earth in poverty now find themselves in the hereafter surrounded by everything they ever wanted on the earth in abundance. Those who were sick or injured find perfect health, the old suddenly find themselves young and vital, and the lonely find themselves surrounded by those who truly love them.

They move about in a community, not unlike the earth, and find friends and relatives to reunite with, and they revel in the sheer beauty of a life filled with joy. As the souls grow in spiritual maturity, they realize that the things they thought would make their lives on the earth complete are only trivialities and that knowledge and understanding are more important than objects. But the souls choose when and what pace they come to these understandings—for some souls it may take longer than others. Everything happens in its own time there, and because the hereafter is not bound by time, there is no hurry to growing spiritually in understanding until they are ready. Until then, their world is theirs to enjoy in whatever means will bring them personal happiness.

Many of the souls have reported in sessions that they understand the earth for the first time in their lives. This is especially true with those who struggled through turmoil, anger, or bitterness on the earth. Part of growing in the hereafter is understanding the earth in a way that the souls could not even grasp was possible—they get to understand the motivations of people they knew on the earth by looking into their hearts or learning that their own way of thinking was not actually what they thought. With the perspective of the new world they live in, the souls finally understand why so many things happened on the earth, and how much value each circumstance had in teaching a valuable lesson that they have now benefited from. The understanding of why things happen is perhaps the most important discovery the souls report to their loved ones here about their new life. They are proud to have completed their lives on the earth and understand it in a way they never could while they were here. As hard as it was, looking back and understanding exactly why things were the way they were is something that brings the souls a profound sense of accomplishment.

I had a cousin Alice whose life on the earth seemed to be a crazy quilt of impossibly bad luck and difficult circumstances. Her brief marriage ended, she was in a vehicle accident that left her in pain for the rest of her days on the earth, and the medications she took on a daily basis wreaked havoc on her mental state. In spite of being very lonely on the earth, she was always so upbeat about making the best of her bad luck, knowing that the next world would be better. She had such great devotion to the Blessed Mother that it got her through many tough times on the earth. She passed suddenly one day from a heart attack, and in a flash, her bumpy journey here had ended.

I actually heard from Alice within a day of her passing. What made it all the more complicated was that I knew my relatives, especially my aunt, Alice's mother, were hoping that there would be some sign from Alice that she was alright. Well, it did come, but it was not at all what I expected—she told me that she was in the hereafter, but she honestly was too busy to really communicate at that point. This left me very uneasy since I know that if her mother asked, I would have to tell her the truth about what I heard.

At Alice's wake, her mother asked me if I had heard from Alice yet. I told her I did, but I tried to preface it by making the excuse that it was a very quick message and I'm sure Alice would communicate more once she was there for a while. My aunt looked perplexed and said, "Why? What did she say?" I had to be honest and tell her the real truth of it, but as soon as the words left my mouth, I saw a look of relief in my aunt's face. "Thank God," she said. "Alice and I spent many, many years together, and I was so hoping she would be too busy right now because she is making friends and having fun. It's the only thing I ever wanted for her." I felt so relieved at her response, although I should have trusted that the souls know exactly what they are doing all the time.

The second time I heard from Alice in the hereafter was as much a lesson for me as it was for anybody else. Alice came though one afternoon in a bit of a surprise appearance, but she was excited like a little girl who has big news. So I listened to her story—she was so excited because she finally got to meet her hero—she met the Blessed Mother. To Alice, this was better than anything she could have ever hoped for: meeting the Lady who brought peace to her dark world on the earth, and the one person who gave her a reason to continue. Alice tried to give me just a small sample of the joy that was in her heart by transferring it to my heart. I was so overwhelmed with the joy and beauty of that feeling that it made me burst into tears. It was almost too much to bear when you have to live and struggle in this world, but it was a wonderful lesson to me that in the hereafter, anything and everything is possible. According to Alice, "All dreams come true."

BUILDING THE GARDEN OF LIFE

In telling people about the hereafter and the remarkable peace, joy, and beauty in abundance there, I often worry that I make it sound too much like a theme park—that all there is, is an endless stream of joy and fun. Depending on the soul, it may very well be an endless stream of personal joy and happiness. Dreams do come true there, but dreams also mature into a real sense of purpose in the hereafter. The souls know that their spiritual work is not finished, and one of the things that brings the souls the most enduring happiness is the ability to give back to others, both in the hereafter and on the earth. They choose a mission which will be their spiritual work in order to bring the joy they learned to others in some small way.

I had a session where the family of a young woman came to hear from their daughter. She was murdered two years previously by a jealous boyfriend, who also took his own life at the same time. She was an aspiring model with the prospects of a big career in front of her—she was to fly to New York after being discovered by a well-known modeling agency. But she had fallen in love with a boy who had a troubled past, in whom she had tried to instill confidence and a sense of self worth to limited success. He came from a broken home, had trouble with addictions, and had run afoul with the law many times. As much as she tried to be a force of good in his life, differences in their dreams had started to separate them, and they decided to part as friends. Unfortunately, faced with the prospect of losing the one person in his life who truly believed in him, he killed her and then himself.

The session ran no differently than others. She spoke about her passing, about the circumstances leading up to it, and how she made the transition to the Other Side, where she found happiness and joy. She told her family she was in a wonderful safe place and understood why things went the way they went. And then the session turned to a male who came forward, sheepishly and vaguely, but by name. I looked up to see the mother's face had gone ashen. The father simply responded, "I don't think we want to hear from him." But their daughter pressed forward on his behalf, telling them that he wanted to say he was sorry and that he never meant to bring them pain. She explained that he was finding himself in the hereafter and that he realizes he has a lot of spiritual work to do in order to earn the joy and happiness he received there in a caring and nonjudgmental environment.

To the complete and utter frustration of the family, she continued on and told them that his chosen spiritual job in the hereafter is to be a type of "guardian angel" to her surviving brother, who himself was having his own troubles on the earth, not unlike her boyfriend. She asked her family to pray for him and told them that he was helping in ways they could not even imagine. Needless to say, at the end of the session the family was very unhappy at hearing what they heard, but more than one year later, I received a letter from the mother, who told me that, although it was a bitter pill for them to swallow, she did her best to try and think about this boy in a better light. They knew it was necessary to their own spiritual journey not to waste the rest of their lives in bitterness and hatred, so they tried the best they could to remember the boy they knew and not the boy who killed their daughter.

Soon after, she did find it necessary to ask for this boy's help because her own son was going down the same road of drugs and trouble, and she held her daughter's boyfriend responsible to help in any way that he could. She wrote that within weeks her son turned his life around, went into rehabilitation, and enrolled in college. She ended her letter by saying what a big life lesson it was to learn humility and that she marveled at her own resolve in order to be able to credit the boy who ended her daughter's life for saving her son's life.

Once souls have become acclimated to the hereafter and understand a little better how this world works, they want to give something back to the Infinite Light as a means of growing spiritually when they are in the hereafter. The souls acknowledge that our existence on the earth is a short but difficult spiritual learning process, but in the hereafter, amid the peace and joy, souls want to continue to move even closer to the Light by continuing their spiritual lessons in a much easier way than on the earth. So many souls will set about the business of finding their heart's desire for using what they have learned in the hereafter to help make life here a little more bearable for us.

When people think of "guardian angels" and "spirit guides," they are under the assumption that they are somehow separate entities from those who love and care for us. Many people fail to realize that it is the souls themselves who are our guides and angels—they continue to be part of our life here in order to help us when the struggle threatens to be too much to bear, and they continue to work with us until we have finished our journey here. They understand from their perspective how vitally important it is to keep to our purpose here, and part of their spiritual journey in the hereafter is to help us on our journey and to keep us to our purpose. There is also a generosity of their life spirit to want to help those in need, both on the earth and in the hereafter. The souls are willing and able to help us as often as we are needed, and helping to ensure our spiritual lessons here is the reason for their joy in helping us.

Life in the hereafter is very much like life as we know it here—people do things, they have friendships and associations, they learn about others and about themselves in the process of discovery that is its own spiritual journey. It is just a far better circumstance that they learn in. Many of the souls have told me in sessions that they have specific duties in the hereafter that bring them joy—in one session a woman who loved being a grandmother on the earth is now a kind of "surrogate" grandmother to children who pass at a very young age, who may not know those in their family who have gone before them. Her character of "grandmother" is very recognizable to children, who gravitate to her once they pass, so they feel safe and nurtured. Others have stated that they work as councilors to other souls who have passed in turmoil or through their own hand—souls that need extra comfort and compassion due to a tortured existence on earth. The souls find it a joy to be able to share their peace and understanding to help the newer souls to feel safe and happy.

So where is this world of the hereafter? This is something the souls cannot completely answer for us, since we don't have the ability yet to understand the concept of a life free of physical restrictions. They have mentioned many times that it is a dimension that runs parallel to our own and that there is a type of "veil" of electromagnetic energy which separates the two dimensions. They are so far, but so close. Because we are bound to the logic of what we know on the earth, there are parts of the hereafter we cannot hope to understand until we find ourselves there.

There have been many people who have reported seeing glimpses "behind the veil" either through visitations of their loved ones in spontaneous apparitions or through near-death experiences. People who have been lucky enough to catch a glimpse of the hereafter have been treated to a life-altering gift—for them, life here will never be the same after having been touched by the beauty of that world. For those who have seen the Garden of Souls firsthand, it is both an honor and a responsibility to share that knowledge with others on the earth.

I was lucky enough to have a "visit" from St. Anthony who took me to the Garden of Souls in order to understand why it was so important for the souls to use me to communicate to their loved ones. In this "visit" I remembered seeing grass that was so full of energy it was alive and water that seemed to be made up of the energy of millions of diamond-like lights and colors so unusual there was nothing that could be used to describe them. I, like many of the people who have had a brief visitation to the Other Side, have come away with the same feelings—at first being dazzled at what was witnessed, then awestruck at a perfect existence beyond anything we could comprehend.

Then, there is also the feeling of sadness that we live in a world so hopeless in its imperfection that we long to go back to that beautiful place. But the story is the same, and the advice from the souls is also the same—no one can be there until he is ready. Those, who have been sent back to the earth after a near-death experience because it wasn't their time, keep the feeling of the hereafter in their hearts for the rest of their lives. The experience was too vivid to be a dream, and the lifelong effects of having experienced it cannot be passed off as hallucination. It is too powerful to ignore, and it changes the way people think about death forever.

My father was injured on the job when he worked for the railroad as a young man. His injuries were so severe that they did not believe he would live through the surgery. During the surgery, he found himself running through a beautiful field, where the sun shone like diamonds among the flowers and tall grasses. But he quickly came upon three men dressed in white, who called him by name, and told him he had to go back—that it was simply not his time. At first he resisted, because he wanted to stay, but they filled his heart with peace and told him it would all be his in due time.

My father never forgot that feeling for another fifty years of life. When he thought about it, he always choked up at the feeling of pure love he felt—it never left him through all those years. At the end of his life, on his deathbed, he made us laugh by telling us, "Well now they HAVE to take me!" It was a poignant reminder that we receive the greatest gift at the end of our life, and for many who were lucky enough to experience even a brief second of it, it is a chance at long last to come home.

The world of the hereafter will continue to be a mystery to us, but the understanding that there is a hereafter should be no mystery at all. Our faith, our hope, and our understanding all tell us it is real, and that at the moment of our death, we go on to the world that this one should have been, to go on to become the people we could have been but for struggle and hardship on the earth. The souls already know that our lifetime has a happy ending. The Garden of Souls is waiting for us in an ever-changing, moveable world that holds all the things we held dear to us that somehow got hopelessly scattered on the earth. There, in a place of beauty and life, all that we lost, the hopes and dreams, the joy and peace, will be returned to us in a garden of light.

About George Anderson

For more than forty years, George Anderson has been able to bridge the gap between the hereafter and the earth. George has received worldwide recognition and acclaim for his extraordinary ability to help reunite the souls with their grieving families here. He remains the only medium in history to have his ability featured on a national network prime-time television special, "ABC-TV's Contact-Talking to the Dead."

The author of the New York Times Bestseller, *Lessons from the Light, Walking in the Garden of Souls*, and the subject of the National Bestseller, *We Don't Die, We Are Not Forgotten*, and *Our Children Forever*, George has dedicated his life to helping the bereaved understand that all is not lost to physical death. For more information, please visit his Web site at www.georgeanderson.com.

Final Thoughts

In writing this book, I gained much more than the absolute certainty that death is not the end. I gained much more than the privilege of having no fear of dying. You see, I found out I have a son. How could I, as a mother, not know I had a son? Let me explain.

My research for this book led me to the Web site of a well-known medium named Joyce Keller. Joyce offered to help me, and we proceeded to e-mail each other a couple of times back and forth. When Joyce found out we both lived in New Jersey, she suggested that we meet for dinner.

At this time, I e-mailed her back telling her that I had two young daughters and would need to find a babysitter but would love to meet her and her husband for dinner. Joyce jokingly wrote back asking me if I was going to try for a boy next to which I replied that I had always wanted a boy but unfortunately could not have any more children.

Her response shook me to the very core. In fact, no words can accurately describe the myriad of emotions I felt at that time. She wrote back saying, "Josie, I have a boy spirit here. He says he's your son. I'm getting the name Michael John. He is very handsome and tall just like his father."

I was speechless. How could this woman who barely knew me and my family know that I had a miscarriage and it was a boy? How could she have known my husband John and I were going to name the baby Michael John? No one knew the baby was going to be named Michael John except for my husband and me.

I read the e-mail again and again as tears flooded down my face. I hugged myself trying to stop myself from shivering as the memories of losing the baby came back to me. It had been a difficult time in our lives. But I never thought of myself as a bereaved mom. The thought that my son's spirit was actually alive and well on the Other Side had never even entered my mind.

In my shock, I didn't know what to think and e-mailed Joyce back asking her to tell me how old my son was then. To my continued amazement, Joyce replied that he was about ten-years-old. I miscarried in 1998, and it was 2008. So she was once again correct. He would have been ten-years-old!

How could a practical stranger know something so personal about my life? How could she have known the name of a child I never had?

Throughout the writing of this book, I received many validations from the Other Side, but this one, of course, means the most to me. I now know I have a son watching over me, and for that, I am extremely grateful. I am also deeply indebted to Joyce for her precious gift.

I am reminded of a quote by a wise scientist named David Searls who said, "Seeing death as the end of life is like seeing the horizon as the end of the ocean." The horizon may seem like the end because this is what we can see with our naked eye. But the essence of the ocean is actually much more and continues far beyond the horizon.

The idea that our consciousness survives death and lives on into eternity is difficult for most to grasp. Just because you cannot see something, doesn't mean it doesn't exist.

Consider the analogy to water. When temperatures drop, water begins to solidify and becomes ice. When the temperature rises, this ice will melt and become water once again. Further, if the water is left there long enough, it will eventually evaporate into thin air. What was once a highly visible chunk of ice has now turned back into its invisible, gaseous form. However, the underlying molecular structure, (H_2O), remains.

In other words, the essence of the ice, though now invisible, still very much exists. Just as when we die, our essence is very much still there, for eternity.

In death, we transform back to our original energy form much the same as the ice changes back into its gaseous appearance. The First Law of Thermodynamics refers to the conservation of energy and basically states that energy cannot be created or destroyed. The amount of energy in the universe remains conserved and constant and can only change from one form to another.

We are all energy beings and can never be destroyed or cease to exist. Life forever lives on, love forever lives on, and so do we.

Dr. Werner von Braun was a renowned rocket developer and pioneer of the U.S. space program between the 1930s and '70s who claimed he had "scientific" reasons for believing in life after death. "Science has found that nothing can disappear without a trace," he explained. "Nature does not know extinction. All it knows is transformation. If God applies the fundamental principle to the most minute and insignificant parts of the universe, doesn't it make sense to assume that He applies it to the masterpiece of His creation—the human soul? I think it does."

I've often been asked, "How do I know if I received a "visit from heaven" if no validations occur? My answer is simply trust your intuition.

According to Carolyn Coleridge, intuitive healer, trust is an important part of the experience of connecting to the Other Side. "Your heart and mind are the indicators that you are tuning into your loved one from the Other Side. Trust your senses. Just like in the earth plane, when someone familiar approaches you, from behind, you sense his energy."

As we reach the end of this book, I ask again, "Is there life after death? And if so, is it possible for those who have crossed over to communicate with us?" I can say with absolute certainty that there is no death. My answer to both of these questions is a resounding "YES."

Your response is entirely up to you. But you need only look within to find the answer.

Appendix:
Forming a Psychic
Development Circle

A man is not completely born until he is dead.
Benjamin Franklin

Cheryl Booth
cheryl@cherylbooth.com
www.cherylbooth.com

When I first began opening up to my psychic gifts, the main thing that kept me from thinking I was crazy was the psychic development circle that I sat in one night a week for close to three years. My mentor, a wonderful British medium named Brian Hurst, suggested I join a circle he knew was just forming. Another member of that group was James Van Praagh. James sat with us for a short while before he moved on and began his own group. The validation that we all received from dedicating our time and energy to this circle was invaluable. Whether you

341

wish to ever do readings professionally or simply to hone your intuitive gifts for yourself, your family, and friends, I cannot recommend anything more highly than creating such a development group.

Ours was fairly "old school," conducted in much the same manner of traditional spiritualist churches. I have modified the guidelines slightly in ways that I feel enhance the experience. I wish you the very best and encourage you to begin even with three people, if that's all you have at first. It's well worthwhile.

First of all, it's best to be assured the people you invite to join your meditation/development circle are committed to being there on a regular basis—the same way you would any class that was important to you. Members must all be of like mind. They should be there because it's their desire is to improve/enhance their own psychic ability, and each one needs to be willing to share what he experiences in the circle, as well as any noteworthy occurrences that take place from one week to the next. It is not uncommon, for example, for those sitting in a development circle to suddenly find that their dreams take on a much richer, deeper quality or that they begin to feel/hear/see/smell spirit contact much more frequently, even when away from the group.

Generally, an effective circle can be made with as few as three people or as many as twelve; yours may consist of fewer members or perhaps a few more. An intimate group of five to seven seems to generate excellent energy. Each of you should have a notebook and a pen or pencil to jot down your impressions at the end of the meditation, before you verbally compare your experiences.

GUIDELINES

1) Commit to meet once a week on the same day of the week at the same time of day or evening. Weekly groups create the optimum results, for "repetition is the mother of skill" — consistent, regular practice will jump–start your efforts much more rewardingly. Routine helps build the energy, and like anything else, practice makes perfect! Since there are so few constants in doing this type of work, having a set time frame is one variable you CAN and should control.

This lets those in other dimensions who are working with you all know that you are seriously committed, just as to any other activity or class you take part in. Plan on sitting in circle for at least three months—longer is better; my original circle met for about twenty-two months.

2) It's a good idea to light a white candle at the beginning of each meeting—white represents purity of intent and spiritual enlightenment. It's also great to have some water nearby—water in a wooden or glass bowl is fine—this is helpful, because water helps conduct spirit energy. If you wish to have a small fountain running, that works nicely, too.

3) Everyone should have a notebook and pen/pencil with him each time to take notes on what he tunes into at the end of the sitting (more on this later).

Appoint someone as your "regulator" or moderator—or you may choose to take turns from week to week or month to month. Either way is fine. Here are the moderator's duties:

A. Once all members have arrived, dim the lights (in fact, we used to sit in total darkness except for the candlelight), light the candle, set a timer, if you wish (it's good to start by sitting for thirty minutes, then increase it to forty-five minutes, then an hour and hold it at an hour or ninety minutes once you've reached the point where everyone is comfortable with that length of time.)

B. Next, the moderator will say an opening prayer or invocation. My group was moderated by an older, very traditional English

woman who always played either a singing or
spoken rendition of The Lord's Prayer, then
followed that up with her own brief invocation. Whatever the group feels comfortable
with is fine. JUST BE SURE you do some sort
of invocation of protection! Here's an example:

*"Father/Mother God, we meet this evening to benefit the Highest Good of each
one present and to uplift every creature on Mother Earth. We declare this to be
a protected sitting, therefore only energies/entities which emanate from the
Source of the One True Light are welcome to send us messages, visions, and
clarity. We thank you and bless you in advance, Friends, for your willingness
to work with us in this way. So be it."*

At this point, each member should begin focusing on his breathing—
breathing in POSITIVE energy with each inhalation and releasing any
negative energy, i.e., anxiety, stress, worries, etc., with each exhalation.
Remember to "be here now"—give yourself permission to let go totally
of anything that happened previously and just commit to sitting silently in an attitude of receiving. Often, placing your hands palms up-
ward on your lap helps. From this point forward, NO TALKING with the
exception of a channeled message which may periodically come
through someone. (Often, people develop an ability to channel sitting
with one of these groups after awhile. As long as it's not disruptive, let
it happen. If possible, it's best to save this type of activity for the end.)

Sit in the darkness and silence in the posture of receiving. Clear your
mind, don't try to force anything to happen, just relax, notice how your
body feels supported in the chair—release all worries or need to think
about anything—BE PRESENT IN THE MOMENT AND ALLOW! If it
helps, imagine being connected to Mother Earth with "roots of light"
flowing out of the soles of your feet into the core of the earth. Through
these roots, you may draw support and feel grounded. This can also
help remind you that you are sitting for the good of Mother Earth and
all of her inhabitants, and you are blessing her as you allow more Light
to flow through you and into her.

Once the timer goes off or you all stir and it's apparent the energy has broken, then the moderator should slowly turn up the lights. Once you're sure you're back in your body, you each should grab your notebooks and pens and then take a few minutes to write down any feelings, visions, odors, sounds, words, etc., that you experienced. You do this so that you don't influence each other by sharing too quickly. Once everyone is done writing, one by one, you go around the circle and share aloud your experiences. You will begin to discover more and more similarities between the members, which will simply add more validation to what you're receiving.

This group activity is great for increasing your trust and belief in the messages you are receiving! It's not uncommon for a group that's been sitting together for awhile to see/hear and even smell the same types of things. Those in another dimension can send us what can be called "Spirit Flowers" —and it's lovely! Sometimes it may be the smell of something Aunt Mary used to bake or the pipe tobacco Grandpa Henry smoked.

Auditory contact is fairly common, too. One group that I helped launch heard a squadron of World War II fighter planes that used to fly over their meeting place regularly. It would last for only a couple of minutes but was an unmistakable sound. The second time it happened, several group members couldn't help themselves and ran outside to gaze skyward—there were no visible airplanes! Two of the members had fathers who had served in the Air Force in WWII, so they figured it was a message their dads were lending their support to the group. This happened nearly every time that group met, and they learned to just smile and silently say "hello" to the invisible flyboys.

Another common occurrence is for members to periodically get specific messages for each other during the group's meditation time. These messages can be shared in the group or privately—just use your discretion.

If you develop a real rapport with someone in the group, perhaps you can do some partnering and practice some "transmitting/receiving" exercises on your own during the week. This could be along the lines of setting a specific time where one is designated the receiver, the other the transmitter. The transmitter focuses on one clear thought or image at a time visually and also may silently attach the identifying word. If you're doing it from your separate homes at a coordinated time, the transmitter can certainly speak the word(s) aloud. The receiver writes down whatever she/he perceives, and then you compare notes a bit later, or the next time group meets.

Don't forget to HAVE FUN while you're doing this! Working with your intuition is a right brain activity, and if you approach it as a game, you'll most likely have better success than if you stress and strain about doing it right. Try to keep an open mind and heart, and be a clear channel/receiver to the best of your ability. Do your very best to accept your first impression, even if it doesn't seem to make a lot of sense. If you allow your left brain to get in there and analyze everything, you'll undoubtedly cheat yourself (and/or the group) out of some valuable messages. Remember, you are the "telephone" or messenger between the dimensions. The messages usually aren't supposed to make absolute sense to you but hopefully will be helpful to the person(s) with whom you share them.

Group energy is awesome—it's a great way to advance your abilities and receive a validation from your loved ones. Think of it like psychic boot camp—intense as well as skill expanding. And again—remember to have fun!

About Cheryl Booth

Cheryl Booth is a psychic medium, hypnotherapist, spiritual life coach, and author who lives in northern California. A metaphysician for more than twenty years, she shares much of her background in her book, *Johnny Angel Is My Brother, A Psychic Medium's Journey*. Cheryl's brother John was born with severe cerebral palsy, and she considers him the biggest blessing she has ever had in her life. For more information, visit www.cherylbooth.com or contact her at cheryl@cherylbooth.com.

About the Author

Josie Varga is the author of *Footprints in the Sand: A Disabled Woman's Inspiring Journey to Happiness* (PublishAmerica) and a former communications consultant. She has also served as the director and editor for an automotive trade association. A motivational speaker, she encourages others to focus on the positive by choosing to be happy.

Josie writes treatments for reality television and has many projects in the works including a documentary film and three new literary projects, one of which is the sequel to this book. A creative thinker, Josie is the holder of two patents. Married with two daughters, she lives in Westfield, New Jersey. For more information, visit her Web site at www.josievarga.com.

EDGAR CAYCE'S A.R.E.

What Is A.R.E.?

The Association for Research and Enlightenment, Inc., (A.R.E.®) was founded in 1931 to research and make available information on psychic development, dreams, holistic health, meditation, and life after death. As an open-membership research organization, the A.R.E. continues to study and publish such information, to initiate research, and to promote conferences, distance learning, and regional events. Edgar Cayce, the most documented psychic of our time, was the moving force in the establishment of A.R.E.

Who Was Edgar Cayce?

Edgar Cayce (1877–1945) was born on a farm near Hopkinsville, Ky. He was an average individual in most respects. Yet, throughout his life, he manifested one of the most remarkable psychic talents of all time. As a young man, he found that he was able to enter into a self-induced trance state, which enabled him to place his mind in contact with an unlimited source of information. While asleep, he could answer questions or give accurate discourses on any topic. These discourses, more than 14,000 in number, were transcribed as he spoke and are called "readings."

Given the name and location of an individual anywhere in the world, he could correctly describe a person's condition and outline a regimen of treatment. The consistent accuracy of his diagnoses and the effectiveness of the treatments he prescribed made him a medical phenomenon, and he came to be called the "father of holistic medicine."

Eventually, the scope of Cayce's readings expanded to include such subjects as world religions, philosophy, psychology, parapsychology, dreams, history, the missing years of Jesus, ancient civilizations, soul growth, psychic development, prophecy, and reincarnation.

A.R.E. Membership

People from all walks of life have discovered meaningful and life-transforming insights through membership in A.R.E. To learn more about Edgar Cayce's A.R.E. and how membership in the A.R.E. can enhance your life, visit our Web site at EdgarCayce.org, or call us toll-free at 800-333-4499.

Edgar Cayce's A.R.E.
215 67th Street
Virginia Beach, VA 23451–2061

EDGARCAYCE.ORG